THE BODY OF MEMORIES:

A COLLECTION OF MEMOIRS & PERSONAL ESSAYS

Edited & Compiled by Lopamudra Banerjee

Setu Publications
PITTSBURGH, USA

The Body of Memories: A Collection of Memoirs & Personal Essays

Edited and compiled by
Lopamudra Banerjee

Setu Publications
* Pittsburgh, PA (USA) *

© 2021 Lopamudra Banerjee

ISBN-13 (paperback): 978-1-947403-21-5
Cover Art: Meenakshi Mohan
Distributed to the book trade worldwide by Setu Publications, Pittsburgh (USA)

We would be pleased to receive email correspondence regarding this publication or related topics at setuedit@gmail.com.

Although every precaution has been taken in the preparation of this work, neither the author nor the publisher shall have any liability to any person or entity with respect to any loss or damage caused or alleged to be caused directly or indirectly by the information contained in this work.

Setu Literary Publications, Pittsburgh, USA

THE BODY OF MEMORIES: A COLLECTION OF MEMOIRS & PERSONAL ESSAYS

Table of Contents

"The memory of our lives could be called its own bit of creative nonfiction."

Years back, when I had delved into memoirs and personal essays at the University of Nebraska, USA as part of my literature studies, I had been deeply intrigued by this short, succinct description of memoir writing. It was during those days when I discovered a gem of a book/anthology of memoirs/essays, 'Tell It Slant', edited by Brenda Miller and Suzanne Paola, two modernist/contemporary American essayists, which I still refer to, where they elucidate in great details how and why memoirs and narrative nonfiction have great resonance as a deeply reflective, meditative genre of literature. They also illustrate how the act of writing about one's own life experiences in terms of one's family and immediate surroundings have the profound beauty, power and aura that it has been characterized with, for years now.

While the adult self assimilates into the external world with disparate individuals, cultures and experiences, the immediate family still remains at the core of his/her values/impulses, they still remain "the first objects of love, anger and loyalty". Hence, it becomes a complex, nuanced journey, with the marriage of memory and imagination, with the amalgamation of the familial world, the microcosm and the greater universe, the macrocosm.

I forayed into this genre of memoir/narrative nonfiction, also being a poet and fiction writer striving to unravel the mysteries of human psyche in my own small way. Along the way, this quest of finding myself in close connection to the private, personal as well as the universal assumed newer shades and nuances, while my book 'Thwarted Escape: An Immigrant's Wayward Journey' was born and read by many readers. Meanwhile, in all these years, I have asked myself these pertinent questions, which, to me, sums up the essence of memoir and personal essays.

'How can one seek meaning and resonance in his/her memories while crafting them into compelling stories that bring structure, coherence?

How can we narrate the details of our experiences cogently, powerfully, while writing about our life stories, and the physical world around us?

How can we write personal stories as a cathartic act as well as a piece of art?'

When Dr. Sunil Sharma, editor of Setu mag asked me to guest-edit a special edition of the journal focusing on memoir writing, these questions knocked my door yet again, and it was my quest to find answers to these which was at the heart of the submission call that I shared with my writing circle friends. The seed of this beautifully intimate anthology of memoirs and essays was sown with some of the pieces published online, and later, in the months that followed, my quest gained more momentum as more writers willingly submitted their personal narratives written with passion and honest ingenuity, and I was introduced to their respective worlds through this portal of storytelling, filled with empathy and understanding.

Writing and publishing memoirs and narrative nonfiction, I have known or heard, is a relatively secondary genre in literature, compared to fiction, drama and poetry, in terms of their mass popularity. However, the huge outpouring of submissions of personal essays, memoir, travel stories and exquisitely personal narratives which form the body and being of this collection not only overwhelms me, but also stokes my curiosity as I think I have found some answers to my afore-mentioned questions while reading each individual essay/memoir and internalizing its significance in a postmodern world ravaged by COVID-19 and numerous existential questions of humanity.

These are the diverse voices of writers, poets, artists, sojourners, educators dispersed all over the globe, individuals who are exemplary social innovators, and explorers of life's myriad secrets and experiences, evoking universal emotions, impulses and a collective consciousness of being, of belonging. Some memoirs intersperse poetry within the framework of the narrative, and it flows seamlessly, like rivers and brooks melting into the mammoth ocean of creative, intimate expressions.

Candice Louisa Daquin, in her finely nuanced essay 'The Grass Grew High and Seeded Her with Doubt' documents how her grandmother found a new lease of life and picked up her splinters and shards to not only live amid the wilderness on the top of a mountain, but also to leave behind a legacy for her granddaughter. The essay of Kelli J Gavin, born and raised in Minnesota traces a topography of her fine, nuanced mind absorbing the potency of her parents' words and their legacy with her unique artistic vision. Joyce Yarrow, in her fine, crisp prose documents her formative years in Southeast Bronx, New York, the insights and wisdom, the myriad mysteries of life that unraveled in her psyche during that phase, almost like a visual drama of 'bildungsroman'. The essential truths of rediscovering childhood, the queer equations of love in the family and the complex web of memories are brilliantly documented in the memoirs of Santosh Bakaya, Amita Ray, Chaitali Sengupta, Anindita Bose, Moinak Dutta and Rhiti Chatterjee Bose. In a touching memoir about her deceased husband, a scientist in USA, Meenakshi Mohan looks back and celebrates his life, his poetry and the memories unbound that keep him alive in her heart. In a delightful assemblage of food memories, Nishi Pulugurtha and Nabanita Sengupta's essays bring to the readers the lively, multi-hued tastes, smells and touches of regional cuisines and the essence of life triggered by these food memories.

Some essays like 'Poetry in the Times of Coronavirus' by Megha Sood and 'Stolen Threads, Stolen Memories' by

Jharna Choudhury reflect on the poetic and artistic life of the authors and how the existential truths of their inward journeys become studies in self-exploration. Antara Banerjee in her exquisite style, weaves an unforgettable tapestry of the creation of human life.

People and places also feature as backbones of poignant personal narratives like 'It's Not Your Fault' by Niharika Chibber Joe, 'My Father, My Father, the Chariots of Heaven by Dr. AV Koshy, 'Finding Bibhabati Debi' by Gopa Bhattacharjee, 'Of Homes and Winter Heartlands' by Sonia Dogra, while travel narratives like 'A Sojourn to Remember' by Ipsita Ganguly, 'Memories of a Pilgrim' by Satbir Chadha and 'Lost in Time: Somewhere Near Prague' by Piku Chowdhury celebrate the organic relationship of the human psyche with the expansive, ever-evolving physical world, the quest of exploring the greater universe, the macrocosm and situating oneself within that universe.

All good memoirs and nonfiction work begin with the writer's impulse to tell a true story with honesty, passion and urgency. And yes, this comes from the depth of life itself, life as a metaphor for exploring memories, life as a metaphor for revealing truths beyond the literal. The personal narrative pieces in this issue come in various avatars, covering multiple themes, ranging from travel essays to lockdown stories, from haunting family truths to humorous tales of cooking and discovering books, childhood and the mystic truths of our daily paraphernalia. In some of these pieces, the thin line between fact and fiction dissolve as the authors frame their personal experiences with specificity and detail, the hallmarks of fiction writing, thereby exploring emotional truths and pertinent realizations in the form of fictional memoirs. 'The Lovesong' by Nandita De, 'Finally, She Showered' by Anita Nahal and 'Alternate Masculinity' by Nandini Sahu are fine examples of such writing.

The anthology also features excerpts from book-length memoirs and autobiographical novels, in which the authors present little universes of their tryst with their childhood memories, familial life while also playing with their language of memory, as they depict emotionally impactful details, which we have known as 'the moments of being' in Creative Nonfiction writing. 'The Banana Lane' by Kavita Ezekeil Mendonca, 'Till the Rivers Run Dry' by Bhaswati Ghosh are fine examples. All the more special to me is a daughter Anita Nahal's lovingly written review of her academician father Chaman Nahal's memoir which was published years back, in which she also meanders through the various vicissitudes of his life, his accomplishments.

I hope the diverse, refreshing voices of these writers unfolding their personal journeys and their 'body of memories' will resonate with readers. I believe their narrative voices, in all their spontaneity, have reinterpreted truths, perspectives, at once personal and universal, sincere and redeeming.

Lopamudra Banerjee

Author, Poet, Editor

Winner of International Reuel Prize for Poetry (2017) and International Reuel Prize for Translation of Tagore's novella 'Nastaneer' into 'The Broken Home' (2016)

Recipient of Journey Awards (Narrative Nonfiction, 2015) for her memoir 'Thwarted Escape: An Immigrant's Wayward Journey', hosted by Chanticleer Reviews and Media, USA

MEMOIR / ESSAYS

The Body of Memories

Twins and Twain

Amita Ray

Childhood remembrances shimmer in memory to be revived when one trips over a coincidental experience narrated by others. I had always been a voracious reader. It was while going through Orhan Pamuk's 'Istanbul: Memoirs of a City' that I was pleasantly bewildered by little Pamuk's preoccupation with his "ghostly other" self, residing somewhere in Istanbul, his birthplace. Pamuk's allusion thus unleashed a spurt of recollections of my early childhood, an exuberance of fancy nestled in nostalgia.

Instinctively, I went back to my childhood days. Like Pamuk, I had been obsessed with a fantasy. I would revel in the thought that someone exactly like me was somewhere around. I even fantasized meeting her someday. No, for me the notion of the 'other' ME was not just a vagary or a fitful fancy in the mutating landscape of imagination. Rather, it was one of those convictions the like of which many a child nurtures in the deepest recess of the heart in some form or other. I have no idea about the origin of such a belief. Maybe childhood beliefs weave around collective fragments of fairy tales or bedtime stories heard from our parents or grandparents. The imagination of children was fed with such stories in those times when the modern modes of entertainments emerging from technological advancements were unheard of. One of my childhood friends firmly believed that she would someday meet *Chand Mama* who would descend from the moon to parade on earth!

Playing Dark Room was one of my favorite games as a child especially when my aunt together with her kids would come down to our house for vacationing. All the little ones then would gather in a room, shut the doors and windows and play our favorite game. The game was supposed to be played in silence so as not to betray our hiding place. But kids as we were, giggling and whispering went on without restrain. It was at this time when I would cherish the furtive desire to bump into the 'other' ME in a room engulfed in darkness where the kids herded in a game of hide and seek. The much-anticipated encounter with my identical 'self' remained elusive as I groped in expectant playfulness.

Revisits of this longing would occur at other times too. My father would often drop me to school on his way to office. On those days, I would reach school early enough when no student was in sight. It was when entering the empty classroom that this delightful feeling descended on me - What if I come across the little 'ME' ensconced in my little chair! Eerie though it may seem now, it was then one of the most cherished desires of my heart.

Or on one of those days while playing with friends and straying away on the meandering lanes on a winter's balmy eve, it would strike me, "What if I meet the 'Other' ME at the crossroads or in the hideout of some forlorn lane?"

Thus I fancied a brush with my lookalike, of a never-to-happen confrontation, a willing submission to fitful feelings. I did not know the cause of such a feeling nestling in me and kept the secret wish lounging within me. I was then too young; I had not even come across any twins which could probably give rise to such a thought in my consciousness. Then one day I asked my father, "Papa, do I have someone who looks like me?"

Bemused, my father asked, "Why dear, what makes you think so?"

I do not remember the answer I gave to this question, but I still remember that my father lovingly told me that God had created each one differently. There might be similarities between two people, but only identical twins looked alike. That was the first time I heard the word "twins".

"Where is my twin, Papa?" I flung an innocent question.

It was then that Papa introduced me to the biological concept of twin in its most rudimentary form. Though I was sadly convinced that there was no chance of bumping against the other ME, I didn't abandon hope altogether. It took another incident to get over this puerile conviction for good.

One winter afternoon my father took me to the nearby park. Children in colourful woolens played around. I was amazed to find among them two children playing who were identical, it was very hard to differentiate one from the other. The dying sunshine of the cold winter afternoon shone on the duo looking like two fluffy woolen balls. They pranced about; their cheeks suffused with a pink blush.

Holding my hand, my father took me to those children. They too had come with their fathers. I could hardly hold my surprise when my father told me that those two girls were "Twins". I was introduced to them, their names rhyming in similarity. It was a great moment in my life grappling with the fact what 'Twins' were for the first time. Within the periphery of my innocent realization, I could figure out twins as same looking sisters living in the same house and having same parents. How I wished I too had a twin sister! Though disappointed for having to forgo my fantasy, my expectation of meeting my look alike someday, I was exalted at being face to face with two children looking exactly the same. I played with them, smeared with the warmth of the residual sunshine of the dying day while our fathers chatted leisurely.

That night I dreamt of my twin sister. Both of us dressed in pink frilled frock were walking hand in hand in a beautiful valley of flowers. Suddenly she left my hand and ran away to catch a butterfly flitting about on the flowers. She kept on running, as if driven by a force to flee from me. Then she looked back, waved me good bye and vanished into thin air.

I woke up whimpering, but that dream marked the end to my tryst with the fantasy for good. Later when my sister was born, I was pretty delighted to hear from others that she resembled me a lot. Though not twins, the twain were happy in each other's company and still are; an everlasting bond binding us in the sinuous journey of life.

Bio:

A former associate professor in English, Amita Ray is based in Kolkata. An academic of varied interests, she is a published translator, short story writer and poet. She has two books of translations to her credit. Her short stories have been published in The Sunday Statesman, Cafe Dissensus, Setu and other online magazines. Her new collection of short stories 'Trail of Love & Longings' has been recently published by Authorpress, Delhi. Her poems have been widely published and featured in anthologies.

Coming to America

Amitav Sanyal

I remember the 1950s as the 'good old days'. I had just graduated with a degree in Mechanical and Electrical Engineering from BITS Pilani in the latter half of the decade. I got an opportunity to pursue higher studies at Carnegie Institute of Technology at Pittsburgh in USA. My scholarship was funded by the Ford Foundation. I was ready to embark on an exciting new journey. I boarded an Air India (the National Carrier of India) plane called the 'Bengal Princess' from Bombay and landed on the shores of America.

The year was 1958. New adventures began and slowly I settled in at my institute in Pittsburgh. The house where I was living was the founder of Carnegie Institute, Andrew Carnegie's daughter Margaret Carnegie Miller's house. After six months of attending lectures with Prof. Mcbright, Prof. Bain and Prof. Mehl, as the spring semester was about to end, wanderlust gripped me and a couple of my friends. We decided to travel to the Grand Canyon. Five intrepid travellers started on a road trip in a recently bought second hand Chevrolet. It was a long journey and we took turns driving the car. I was the map reader of the group and was the designated navigator of the trip. Our journey started in Pennsylvania and we drove through the states of Ohio, Indiana, Illinois, Missouri, Kansas, Colorado and New Mexico. It was the wet season and so we were constantly following the weather forecast from the meteorological office and were amazed at the accuracy of their forecasts. The journey was as magical as the destination. As we drove through the different states and cities, we marvelled and soaked in everything we saw with awe, be it the tail fin cars, newly made highways or the friendly people. We stopped at roadside diners and restaurants in small towns and cities for brunch and dinner, and mostly ate burgers and sandwiches at the Mom-and-pop businesses. Fast-food restaurants had

The Body of Memories

taken-off in the 1950s as people were getting busier and needed something quick to pick up and also wanted something they could eat while watching their brand-new television sets.

Finally, our journey took us to New Mexico, the penultimate state we would cross before we entered Arizona to realize our dream of seeing the Grand Canyon. We were driving down the mythic and 'Historic Route 66'. During World War II, military vehicles traversed this route, but now, this route has become a popular route for road trips in a prosperous economy as America's love affair with big cars gained momentum. Now, it was my friend Joseph's turn to drive. Joseph seemed to be enjoying his new-found freedom behind the wheel and the wide, empty highway. He upped his game and was driving at 80-85 mph while all the passing signboards we crossed so far in the different states screamed at us, letting us know that the highest speed limit was never more than 60-70 mph. I was no longer the intrepid traveller I had started out as, I was feeling quite chicken-hearted by now. I repeatedly asked the speeding 'Jo' to slow down but to no avail. 'Jo' was having too much fun. Alas, the excitement and enjoyment of racing soon came to a rude and abrupt end. While negotiating a sharp turn, our speeding car turned turtle. The doors of the car flung open and three of us were thrown out of the car. I landed on a mound of sand unable to move and my clothes were completely torn.

The 80-85 mph speeding car must have alerted the cops. Soon, a few policemen showed up and started asking questions. Our tan skin colour and the fact that all of us had expensive Rolleicord and Rolleiflex cameras convinced the policemen that we were smugglers who had crossed over from Mexico. No amount of convincing on our part could make the police think otherwise. In the end we showed them our student identity cards and the police called up our contact person Mr. Blickenstaff at Carnegie Institute. As soon as the phone call ended and our identity and our available medical insurance were confirmed, the policemen became very friendly and started arrangements to transfer us to a nearby hospital.

In the meantime, a truck load of native Indians (called Native Americans today) who lived in nearby villages showed up. They asked the police if they could help but were told by the police to 'get going'. The native Indians still hung around and eventually found out that we were from India. Now their curiosity piqued and they wanted to talk to us; but by then the ambulances arrived and we were transported to the only native Indian hospital in the Albuquerque area known as the Bernalillo County Indian Hospital (known as the University of Mexico Hospital since 1979) which was established in October 1954. We were laid down in trolley cars outside the hospital waiting to be wheeled into the hospital once the paperwork was done. Suddenly, truckloads of native Indian men, women and children of all ages gathered in front of the hospital, word had gone round in the nearby towns and villages and they all had 'come to see the men from India'. Christopher Columbus had erroneously thought that he had reached the Indian Ocean and referred to the residents as 'Indian'. So, Columbus' curious indigenous Indians in America came to meet the 'real Indians'. They were very friendly and came and spoke to us and asked us where we came from and what brought us to America. And then suddenly they got very excited and started shouting 'They speak British English'. A couple of them even touched and felt us to make sure we were real. We were quite amused by their innocent queries and gestures. We were then taken inside the hospital and the crestfallen onlookers left as they were not allowed inside the hospital.

Dr. Justin Wolfson examined us for broken bones and injuries. We were kept under observation in the Indian hospital at Albuquerque for two days and then transferred to a orphanage for a couple of days. However, the atmosphere, conditions and the food at the orphanage was abominable. The uncomfortable bunk beds, and the dry bread and donuts offered at the orphanage left much to be desired. The kind

The Body of Memories

lady who took our X-rays at the hospital came to our rescue and hosted all five of us at her house. Each of us were given our own room and a television set in the huge house which was not surprising as Mrs Jayme O' Malin and her husband Davis were shareholders of the Metro-Goldwyn-Mayer Studios Inc. in Hollywood. Our hosts also took us to a nearby Indian restaurant, but interestingly the food in the Indian restaurant back then was anything but Indian food. We got to eat boiled corn and some soup with peppers in it and the cuisine was actually Mexican. Mrs. O' Malin also had a racing car and racing cars was her hobby. Since, we did not manage to 'race' so well in our car, we also got a lesson in racing cars and navigating treacherous turns at 80 mph. One day she took us in her racing car up a hill at 80 mph and showed us the strategy of safely navigating a car at that high speed.

We were at the generous Mrs. O'Malin's place for six days, recuperating. She and her husband were extremely influential and offered that they could arrange for an American Air Force plane to take us back to Pittsburgh. But we were very jittery after the accident and could not think of boarding a flight. Our hosts also offered $1000 to each of us as we were students, when we declined to take the money, they insisted that we should take at least $500 so that we could return to Pittsburgh. We thanked them for their generosity but told them that each of us had $250 with us and that would be enough to fund our return trip to Pittsburgh. We decided the safest option was to take a train run by the famed Santa Fe Railways to return to Pittsburgh. We boarded the 'Super Chief' which was the flagship passenger train of the Atchinson, Topeka and Santa Fe Railway at Albuquerque in New Mexico. The train was a luxury passenger train replete with a dining car, an observation lounge, a baggage-buffet lounge, and to top it all, the continental food served on the train was exquisite. We travelled overnight and crossed New Mexico, Colorado, Kansas, Missouri, Iowa and Illinois. We got off at Dearbon station in Chicago. We spent five days with some friends in Chicago and then caught a train back to Pittsburgh. And thus, ended our tryst with the Grand Canyon. I have still kept some precious stamps that Mrs. O' Malin had given me as souvenirs as I was an avid stamp collector back then. But even though we did not make it to the final destination, I recall the events with nostalgia and am reminded of the quote that 'it's about the journey not the destination'.

Bio:
Amitav Sanyal was born in Lucknow and was brought up in Lucknow, Allahabad, Kanpur, Etawah and Bareilly. He studied Mechanical and Electrical Engineering at Birla Institute of Technology and Science, Pilani in India and Carnegie Institute of Technology at Pittsburgh in USA. He worked at Weirton Steel in West Virginia in USA, Damodar Valley Corporation, Martin & Burn Co and then in Steel Authority of India Limited until his retirement. After his retirement he worked as a consultant to the Government of West Bengal at Calcutta Gas Corporation in Kolkata. He lives in Kolkata now.

The Body of Memories

Personal Memoirs of Early Childhood
Amrita Valan

The year was 1975.

I was just a mite, a skinny three-year-old with a big bulbous head, so comical to look at, that I instantly became a mascot at the company daddy worked in at the time.

I am a child born in the seventies, who did her growing up in the eighties. A product of simpler times, of a pre-internet, pre-Wi-Fi pre cellular phone age.

We watched the transition from black and white to colour televisions, and we knew owning a refrigerator was not a given for every middle-class family, and yes, we listened to our music from 33 ½ R.P.M and 45 RPM records and later cassettes.

Spiritually, I identify not just with the seventies, but with the earlier hippy flower-powered sixties generation, preceding the decade I was born in. But this is a vignette of a time before I had developed a definitive identity. I am relating a tale of early innocence when the world was a fuzzy, happy-go-lucky blur of happy families and sunny climes. When cloud gazing on the terrace and discovering ogres and demons and fairy princesses in their shape-shifting landscape was heaven itself!

Tales of my childhood crowd my lens and so I must narrow the focus down further, share just a few tales. And the not-so-hidden child in me has decided to stick to some funny moments to make you smile.

As a precocious three-year-old, I loved wearing my long, flowing maxi dress to every occasion. I still remember the reddish pink hued, (called Rani colour or Queen colour in

India), a floral print on a white background, which flounced to my ankles, making me feel like a demi-queen.

That little girl was Eveready (purposely spelling it the way her daddy's company spelt their products, Eveready torches), with a shy toothy grin and a smart lisping mouth! Many a times she wisely doled out marital advice to her young parents. Once my parents got into an argument and to their hilarity, I broke the tension between them by observing like a wise owlet, 'Since you have married each other, you have to adjust."

I don't mean to imply that my parents always fought, though they frequently did, with a comic vigour. Ma stamped her dainty foot in hauteur and dad deflated like a massive balloon. Normally they were sweet on each other and Ma was the easiest person to get along with. If anything, she was the soul of grace, armed with an impish good humour, an arch observer of the vagaries and eccentricities of many whimsical relatives while remaining extremely cordial and graceful to everyone.

To this day I am equally keen to please people and I think perhaps this is because of my mother's early lessons in cordiality and amity.

I had, however, very little of her graceful, demure ways. Imbibing dad's 'lead from the front candour', I was quite the brazen monkey. I recall clambering upon the dining table whenever my two favorite uncles (dad's younger brothers) came for dinner, insisting upon being the one to serve them. High- handedly, of course!

Ma trusted me only with ladling out the plentiful *dal* (lentils) and so I served up copious amounts of watery pulses till my uncles hollered for protection from their eager niece!
I was lifted, kicking and screaming from the snow white formica dining table forcibly and sent off to bed.

However, my shenanigans with my uncles continued unabated! Especially my adventures with yet another uncle, daddy's youngest brother reached epic proportions and acquired legendary status in the family tales.

When *Dadu*, dad's father passed away, his youngest son was still a college student.

So he boarded with us, and thus began our early education in rock and roll, The Beatles and Rolling Stones and also Indian disco music, especially the peerless duo, Zoheb and Nazia Hassan.

My big brother and I dared not join in his twisting and cavorting in the drawing room to his huge collection of records. Ma frowned heavily upon anything other than classical dance and Rabindra sangeet.

We regarded him with awe mixed with envy, and I suspect my uncle, recently deprived of his father, also resented us a wee bit for the sheltering love and support we were being brought up in.

He had lost both parents then. The brilliant engineer he went on to become, at that vulnerable age, he had to find his moorings fast.

Hence, later when he was well placed in life, he showed us tremendous fondness; but at that early age he played with us like we were his cat's paw, cubs in the zoo and he, our trainer.

The horrendous training I received at age five was learning to cat call casual passers-by on the street, with obnoxious names. Yep! Believe it or not. He would point out a bearded hirsute fellow and teach me to call him a roadside chimp! I was his pet, a smitten kitten, completely obedient, as otherwise he would threaten me jovially, 'I will throttle you by the skin of your throat, Kit Kat!' That's about the only adequate translation of his exact Bengali words that I can attempt.

Ma was blissfully unaware of these behind-the-scenes events, as he was very respectful and courteous in front of his *Boro Boudi* (elder sister-in-law).

But the stage was set for discovery the day I visited a tall, hairy and yes, bearded *Pishomoshai*. (Father's sister's spouse). He was extremely hirsute, with myopic eyes, covered with heavy-rimmed glasses. Not very child-friendly, I guess. To add to my discomfort, he pinched my cheek (a practice I abhorred) and asked me fondly, 'Tell me who I am?'

I pitted eyeballs with him and muttered through clenched teeth, "A roadside chimpanzee!'

I can still visualise his eyes bulging like moons over his glasses!

Ma was summoned immediately to explain and of course she protested her daughter's innocence. It seemed I wouldn't be capable of such rudeness!

Just then, I glared at him and threatened maliciously, "I will throttle you by the skin of your throat, Kit Kat!".

Ma's stunned dismay was offset by the half-smile my uncle desperately tried to hide.

I can't help it. I still giggle to this day at my uncle's awestruck, almost admiring expression and my mother's frozen composure.

Under subsequent interrogation, I unravelled swiftly and revealed the identity of my admirable Guru, the Lennonloving, Beatles worshipping Bumblebee uncle. Yes, that was his nickname, but I am running ahead of myself.

Oh boy! Was he in for it that day when we returned home? Even dad had a few choice words to say about it. After that, youngest uncle was extremely careful to address us children with a modicum of adult formality.

But we still hero-worshipped our cool hip-swinging, disco loving, jiving uncle.

And many years later, once he was professionally established, he visited us, annually bearing beautiful gifts of bouffant flouncy frocks for me each Durga Puja.

Ma finally conceded, '*Bolta* has a big heart.'

Yes, that was his rather curious nickname, *Bolta* or Bumblebee.

Somehow, recalling those days makes me want to sing out from one of his favourite records, "Sing Muhammad! Muhammad Ali! Who floats like a butterfly, stings like a bee! Sing Muhammad. The black Superman. who calls to the other guys A-ali ! Catch me if you can!

Indeed, *Bolta* kaka, (uncle) was our dusky, handsome superhero and childhood role model.

Those were idyllic, Edenic days, hallmarked by an utter lack of inhibition, total innocence and one hundred percent spontaneous expression.

Bio:
Amrita Valan is a writer from India and a mother of two boys. She has been published in several anthologies and online journals.

Memoir of my Dream

Antara Banerjee

The sun-kissed sand of gold shimmers with a mellow sheen, lusty honeybees flutter around fragrant blooms, seeking nectar... the coral reefs reflect vibrant hues across crystal waters...soft splashes of frothing waves, lull me into a rosy reverie....

A dream descends upon my slumbering eyes like feathery fluffs of luminous clouds that fill the ambient sky; neither is it day, nor night... pages of the memoir of a time, long forgotten, come floating upon tranquil blue waters of the hypnotic senses. They remain hidden amidst shadows of the blooming lotuses of consciousness; holding an ancient dream within the magic words that fade slowly from their worn faces. For only a dream can recount a tale so long past that time itself wonders wherefrom the visions appear.

The story laden leaves dance gently upon the lilting ripples, speaking in soft tones, of a moment that preceded creation, when there prevailed nothing but a deep, dense gloom. Shrouded in the nothingness of the primordial dark, God lay twisting on a vast bed of painful melancholy. Languishing in the desolate vacuum through aeons, He suffered an unending solitude that came with His primal existence. Or could the lonely gloom have preceded the Almighty ever so silently and crept upon the Primal being as the First-born Himself did arrive?

Ages of tormented desolation weighed upon His lone heart, until in a pang of divine anguish, a gush of creative ardor burst forth at last. A great spasm of seminal ache escaped His wrenched soul and from its pregnant seed bloomed the infant universe. An overwhelming mirth shone with awesome brilliance in His loving eyes.

The Body of Memories

Renounced lay His dark, age-old shroud as the lord wrapped His new-born creation in the affectionate embrace of a doting father. No more could waves of melancholy touch the shores of His blissful contentment for His imagination had birthed a plaything that was alive with cheer and hope.

Having lost favour of the lord as His novel creation engaged him in its infant charms, the dark countenance of the sultry gloom darkened still. Brooding over the Lord's rejection of its devoted company, darkness shuffled its shrinking black mantle and lamented as it sought leave from the Almighty.

The precious moment of time that transformed the primal singular into universal Father held the Divine loner in ecstatic rapture. His stunning gaze wrapped the entire creation in a dazzling radiance that became the first light of the world. Bursting forth from the vigorous sparks, the sun, the moon and the planets shot into orbits of their ethereal paths. Galaxies of countless stars and luminous celestial dwellers filled the gloomy primordial void and the bleak darkness turned into a vast stretch of bewitching blue. The blessed lights twinkled in delight against the deep azure sky, setting the infinite heavenly expanse alight.

Breaking the silence of long ages past, the rhythmic pounding of His excited heart echoed within the soul of creation. The unison of those harmonious throbs vibrated in the ears of cosmos as the first sound that was ever heard. Drops of sweat that fell to earth from the exertions of His delightful toil made the salty brine of the very first sea. It was His marvelous art that laid grains of golden sand along foaming white waves of the mighty oceans and covered the naked brown earth with a robe of lush verdant foliage. Snow-clad mountains rose heavenwards to rival the lofty clouds while fathomless gorges tumbled into the depths to explore mysteries of the netherworld. Water froze, rivers gushed and streams whirled in their own course by his supreme craft.

By His wish did flora and fauna roam the earth while He strung them all in an enchanted cycle called 'Life'. Many were the wonders that lay abundant in His world; in life, in death and in birth. The sun and the moon hung in the sky as did riches lay hidden deep within the womb of earth. Spurred by the creative seeds sprouting in His own imagination, He wrought His entire godly strength to nurture this magnificent creation.

Time flew and aeons passed as the Master sat conjuring wondrous elements and weaving them into the fine brocade of life. Creation was ensconced into a new cosmic order, relinquishing the disarray of the primordial chaos. Night followed day as did day follow night, thunder followed bolt as did fire melt ice. Death followed life as did life follow birth. Each element of the cosmos was bound to another by a thread of intriguing association. Numerous cycles of the universe, ruled by unique rituals and litanies of their own, conjoined to create a greater order in the cosmos. Attending to the harmonious order instated by divine will, the infant cosmos attained a mature autonomy.

Though creation relieved the Lord of His lonesome tenure, it took little time for the Great one to be weary of mundane rituals of the cosmos. The joy of creation having past, little thrill remained in watching the universe go about its course in the unchanging cycle of cosmic order. The sun rose in the east each dawn and set in the westerly horizon at dusk; the stars twinkled on in the sky each night. The rising and falling tides of water, the changing crescents of the moon or even the diverse colours of the varied seasons tired Him with their wonted litany. The worn soul longed for a spectacle that would never tire Him of its capricious feats. His art struggled to conjure the device that

The Body of Memories

would undo the ennui that weighed down upon His jaded divine spirit.

In vain did His imagination labour to soothe the disquiet of His thirsted soul, but inspiration deluded the Genius for long until a deep slumber descended slowly upon the exhausted eyes of the Lord...

... slumber drew the Lord into a blissful dream, conjuring a wondrous spectacle over His somnolent senses, where neither the sun, nor the moon or the stars claimed the firmament. The idle sky remained ambient with the pearly luster of dreamy clouds. The enchanted vapours created a luminous aura all around as though the milieu had leapt out of the unrelenting grip of time and escaped the battle of fact and fantasy.

The vision carried Him into a fragrant haven of mystic flora, heavy with virgin buds on their slender shoots. Young tendrils cascaded down the taut boughs like the flimsy shoulder cloth that slides off the white bosom of an unmindful maiden by the wanton art of a mischievous breeze. Ravished by the pollen-clad bees of shameless manner, the buds bloomed into tender blossoms of many hues... the delicate petals opened under the gentle shadow of iridescent puffs of clouds, smiling at the persistent banter of the teasing bees. Honey dripped from warm bellies of the flowers, lapped away greedily by the lustful nectar-bugs.

Upon this landscape of exotic beauty descended a brook of silver water. Sparkling crystals of the splashed tides created a jewel-encrusted haze at the edges while sudden streaks of golden rushes darted amidst the chromed silver streams of the spry rivulet.

Drops of dew gathered within the shallow contours of sensuously smooth rocks, creating little pools of still water. The soft green meadow remained dotted with the little pieces of rainbow sky that mirrored from the wee pools of celestial mead. Mesmerized stood the heavenly Sire for His own divine image gazed back at Him as He peered into the tiny patches of limpid water. What tenderness did the noble gaze bear as His own sublime smile held Him entranced by its serene charm!

An impassioned inspiration stirred the Genius as the resplendent precincts of this ethereal vision invoked His divine art to a masterful creation... thus He created a youth after the image that reflected from the dewy pools... an image of His own... Crafted from the abundant beeswax, its flesh exuded a soft splendour while the taut gait of slender boughs imbued the lithe male form. Sweet golden nectar ran through its veins in the stead of briny crimson blood. Soft curls played upon its handsome forehead like tendrils that cascade daintily from fresh green sprigs. Its eyes remained closed like two delicate buds that waited in anticipation of the pleasure of bloom. Placing a piece of His own divine heart in its young chest, as a final stroke of genius, the Sire whispered the enchanted spell of life into the inert form with a gentle kiss upon its fair forehead.

Buds bloomed into beauteous blossoms as the youth opened its wonderstruck eyes into the miraculous light of life... the Sire smiled in contentment, for His art had at last begotten the ingenious creation that promised to present ever-novel delights to His jaded soul... God's own Muse....

My divine reverie is interrupted by the strident call of a visiting gull... God's own Muse... a sense of déjà vu envelopes me with a strange twinge...the sun is still showering opulence across the golden sands.... the gull is wading atop a receding wave...farewell my dream... return to me yet another time... in yet another place....

Bio:
Antara Banerjee is an award-winning author of the books, 'The Goddess in Flesh' and 'To be a Woman'. She is also a tri-lingual poet with the book, 'Pieces of a Tormented Mind' to her credit. Her poems have featured in anthologies like Peacocks in a Dream, OPA, Freedom Raga, Macabre Tales and Erothanatos. Masters from Goldsmiths College, London and graduate from Presidency College, she is the recipient of Sanmarg Aparajita Award 2019, Young Achiever-Literature and Udaan Empowering Women Awards 2017, for her contribution in women-centric literature.

Motherhood and I

Anindita Bose

"What had happened to her?"

Sometimes even when we know, the answer is lost deep inside our psyche. I was advised not to sleep in her room. Yet that night when I was sitting alone in my mother's room, contemplating that people do leave at fifty-five, I took in the strangeness of the night with the emptiness of that room. The room in which I had memories of my childhood like yesterday's reality existed in clear personification: laughter, tears, fights, loving words and her agonies of unrequited support from some members of the family. Once, I was too young to understand what agony a woman can go through, leaving her poor maternal household after marriage, if she cannot prove the worth of her existence. She may receive love, material goods, support from in-laws but she may not receive the respect of an independent individual.

I was so naive that I could never understand my mother's anguish and pain until she fell sick, due to medical blunders, until she was unable to leave the bed. Sometimes I wished to punish myself, but then I realised that I must forgive myself since forgiveness can open the portal to achieve better visions. And I did achieve that when I realised how much I loved my mother. I had finally received the justice of the universe in the form of supporting my Ma selflessly when she needed someone to stand beside her, to bid her a comfortable goodbye when she was crossing over to another world. In the process, I suffered a lot. I went through a transformation myself, I witnessed unbearable pain, I saw tragic truths about human existence. Finally, I felt that some of us are not mere humans, but entities that roam around this world to transmit messages to the others.

We are messengers. I am a messenger.

That night when I was sitting in silence meditation, my thoughts were torturing me with the last words and actions of my ailing mother. It was suffocating, but only for a while. When my tears came like a wild river, at that same moment a thunder rumbled. I felt as if someone somewhere was watching the whole episode. I opened the windows, there were two windows in my mother's room and a door that opened to the balcony. I walked barefooted to the balcony and the cool breeze touched me. The rain was wild that night, the thunder and lightning were opening portals. I had not realised at that moment itself, but when like a helpless human I came back to my bed and slept, I witnessed a life-changing incident.

A dream.

The genie came to my dream and whispered the basics of this world. He said I was not supposed to cry since I had accomplished a very important task. This was my entry into the world of entities.

I had a rough sleep, I remember. It was difficult to tread into the world of sleep, dream and waking layers at the same time. I saw my mother smiling and saying that she was fine. I saw the genie teaching me lessons, in which he said I needed to explore life and existence. I saw myself sitting under a tree and watching a flowing river. What was happening? Was I too exhausted? Perhaps yes, but if I had not believed anything at that time, my life would have been stuck - with the thoughts of mere life, birth and death.

It was not the first time that I had felt something unusual and unique about my life. Since childhood, I had witnessed certain things that I could not reveal to others. I was never close to my parents. Sometimes we are disconnected from our parents and it is not a crime. My parents always had my brother who was just a year younger to me. A joint family meant that some children could be closer to other family members, and I was an example. I loved my grandmother

(Amma), but whenever I tried to explain my thoughts to her, she smiled and told me that I would discover the truths about existence at the right time. And in 2016, she left this world on a *Rakhi Purnima,* like she had always predicted herself.

Life of a human is more than what we see; a world exists within me and it perishes with our existence. I wish to restructure the past by adding and deleting facts but I cannot stop imagining - two Muslim boys on racing bikes in an empty road near our home, and my mother about to cross...

I had left for Ooty after my Amma left the world, because my senior colleague Ms. Priya thought that I would do justice in mentoring the high school students from the Good Shepherd School for IELTS; and also I must thank her that she did realise I needed a change.

Perhaps the mountains were calling to transform me!

After two encounters with death, both being my mothers, I realized that life never continues in the same patterns. Childhood is not an alter-ego for adulthood, rather it is the ambit that remains forever within the urge of humans to outgrow the circuit of innocence and reach the shores of experience, for the latter has power to attract the curious mankind. And so finally, we all walk through different stages in life, yet the traces of a child remain in us forever. But among us, those who unknowingly hold onto the doors of the nascent images of being the self, we suffer.

I left behind a part of me amidst the serene beauty of the mountains. I had decided to give some time to my aching heart and focus on the equation of my relationship with my parents. The acknowledgment of the fact that I was far away from them till my Amma was my banyan tree made me restless. It was not that I did not care for my parents, but the connection was not as children usually have with their biological parents.

Love always finds its ways when it wishes to, and losing Amma has triggered the process of attaining closure and meaning to a blank episode in my life. That was the phase when I wrote my poetry manuscript - *I Know the Truth of a Broken Mirror*, which was published by Professor Ananda Lal through his publication the Writers Workshop, Kolkata. That was also the time when my mother came forward to protect her daughter from the dark clouds of sorrows, and she did this first time independently.

Yes, independently, I emphasize. My mother was not complaining while she was dying on the Narayana Hospital bed, rather the fighter in her was telling me to open an organization in my Amma's name; to support the people who needed true guidance in understanding the confusing truths of the medical world. She was proud of me when I could finally reach out at the right direction. Dr. Debi Shetty had sent a letter for her to the hospital CEO to treat her importantly, after many mishandlings in different hospitals.

On 30th June 2019, when I heard her words, I stood – stunned, broken. Words almost choked me and I questioned myself - *who was responsible for the rift that had always been between my mother and me?*

Amma loved me. But Ma and Amma shared a relationship of in-laws and that shattered my existence after I lost both of them...

I was drowning in grief and loneliness when Amma left the world. But when I was struggling, my mother came forward to embrace me silently; in silence because unfortunately we had never shared a deep bond before. And she left...

As I write this now, I feel the immense pain that is scratching me from within like the claws of a tiger would do to a prey. I am a prey to the circumstances that led to the story of my life, and kept me away from my mother only to bring both of us closer at that moment when she departed from this world. I feel her around me, silently whispering to me how much she had always loved her little girl but could never express…

Only if we could rewind the old times….

Selfless love is like a myth in the contemporary world, but myths are hidden truths that only brave hearts can uncover. Amma had already taught me several valuable secrets of this world. Sometimes for these kinds of knowledge I was trolled by the friends since my thoughts were not parallel to theirs. My childhood was like the fleeting clouds, quietly passing by without making a noise, for perhaps clouds believe that thunder and lightning are only dedicated to the storms. I was growing in silence, and I guess no one around me realized that I had a parallel world inside me; and a silent voice kept teaching me that perspectives matter, differences matter, solitude matters, dreams matter, being loved matters…

My mother loved to sing whenever she was happy; she wasn't a trained singer, but she enjoyed telling us a story - *'I was travelling to Gariahat on the auto, and I started singing. Do you know that the auto driver told me, 'Didi (sister) do whatever in life, do not leave singing!'* She used to laugh after relating this story to us each time. I wondered at times after she had left, what if she was a trained singer? Perhaps she would have been one of the best. Sometimes we do not get the right opportunities in life and there can be multiple reasons for that; however, there are moments when we realize that certain things are not required for us.

Yet we wish.

Her name was *Mukti*, a beautiful name but whoever had given her that name did not know that names have a strange impact on humans. I had read about this theory once but experienced the truth with my own name and my mother's.

The Body of Memories

freedom is a wish that the hearts crave
either one is alive or dead...
till the last breath one can weave
dreams of life and ways to be free...

Mukti means freedom! Throughout her life, my mother had craved for freedom—from chains of sorrows, anger, family issues, financial-dependency on her husband. Finally, we both wished freedom from the mammoth blunders of the medical boards in charge of her, both in Kolkata - Apex Institute of Medical Sciences and Irish Hospital, and Vellore CMC had committed.

She had started a home business of a *saree* boutique to become independent.

Women do try to sustain even in the face of unhappy situations. But I always failed to understand what her struggles were. It was only after that day when I picked up a burning bamboo to cremate her together with my brother that my womanhood whispered to me, *'Motherhood is not about a woman, but a human who can nurture other humans. It is a quality naturally given to women, hence they need more care and warmth from their own families...'*

My mother was gone when my inner wisdom decided to connect with me.

Nothing in this world is a coincidence. The experiences of life teach us the value of being a human; and even though I was thoughtful before, losing my mother so early in life was like a curtain removed from a dark room. From 3rd July 2019 till the month of December of that year, I had stayed awake day-and-night in her room, trying to process the relationship that I had shared with my mother. Initially everything looked blurred and meaningless, and the questions kept oscillating around me.

Why ma and I always fought if we were destined to come so close towards the end? Why did we never realize that we actually shared a strong bond beneath the social pressures? Why did fate create the rift between us, when at the end my mother had to ask me to hold her palms tightly because she had felt that only I was her strength? Why did we come so close when we had to depart so suddenly? I was in pain and there were no answers, not even the voice of my wise Amma!

I could only hear silence and sometimes I felt that my mother was telling me from the walls of her room that she was in a better place... and she was at peace.

When my mother had met with her accident in June 2017, I was not in India; and I could never see those boys who had been riding the motorbikes. In March 2020, the universal power granted my wish, disguised as an insurance officer I had visited the household of that family who still felt that those boys did nothing. *'There was an old woman who could not cross the road. It was her fault and the accident happened.'*

I heard their words and nodded in silence, and came back home. Perhaps I had attained a closure, I was yet to process it fully.

Afterlife is a story to me that I am still exploring - sometimes I keep thinking where did my grandmother and mother travel to? And I wonder when I will open a door to see the light waiting for me at the other end of the horizon, to accept my own parallel truth.

Bio:
Born and brought up in Kolkata, Anindita Bose is inspired by the zeal of her city of joy. She believes words have immense possibilities to create life out of nothing. Her poems and short stories got published in various National and International magazines and anthologies. She is an interviewer for the International Online Journal – The Enchanting Verses Literary Review. Her Solo Poetry book

is 'I Know the Truth of a Broken Mirror' [Writers Workshop, 2018].

She has worked as an IELTS Mentor and as a High School English Teacher in Blue Mountains School, Ooty, India. She is a co-founder of Rhythm Divine Poets, the six- year-old poetry group in Kolkata. Currently she is working as an independent script writer in Kolkata and has shot her first Bengali short film *Anubhobe...*, with director Prajna Dutta, which has released recently. She has directed poetry films of poet Sonnet Mondal in 2020, which got selected in Glass House Festival 2020.

Finding My Purpose

Anupama Dalmia

It was 3 PM.

As I tried to manoeuvre my way through the cramped spaces between the traffic maze, an inexplicable anxiety began to crawl on my skin. It gripped my feet, leaving me at odds with my own self. While I was trying to move swiftly as I was already running late, my bottom refused to budge. The sweltering heat metamorphosed into the rivulets of sweat trickling down my forehead. The ear-splitting honking of the vehicles propelled me soon towards the footpath next to a *Pani Puri* vendor who looked at me with expectant eyes. On some other day, I would have been that customer who would have given him his peak sales for the day. But at that moment, food was the last thing on my mind. My stomach was already feeling heavy with the burden of my decision. A decision that I had taken with the right intentions suddenly looked at me in the face and sneered, "What makes you think you can do this?"

I paused and took a deep breath. The automobile emissions made way inside my system, making me realise this was not really the spot where I could be indulging in some serious contemplation. I kept taking long strides towards my destination and before I knew it, I had reached a desolate by-lane. It suddenly went all quiet. I could hardly see people around. It was then that I decided to face my apprehension. It was my choice to resign from a lucrative and steady corporate job to pursue my creative interests professionally and work on the ground for a social cause. I volunteered to get involved with an NGO working on the rehabilitation of human trafficking survivors and in a few minutes from then, I would be in the midst of these survivors who had been rescued from an abominable world of trauma and anguish. What would I tell them? That it would all be fine? I sounded so hollow to my own ears. What was I thinking? That I could be a messiah who could change the wrongdoings of the world? But looking back was not an option anymore. I had been trained by the organization and had travelled to a different city for this event. Not turning up would do more damage to their hopes than turning up and screwing it up, I thought.

I decided to go with the flow of the brook I was in, which soon landed me in front of a shabby looking and somewhat dilapidated building. Strangely, my concern seemed to be slipping away as I began soaking in the atmosphere of the place. This was the same world where I resided. Yet, the milieu was so unfamiliar. There was a steep staircase which I had to take to reach the room from where I could hear some murmurs. From inside, the structure seemed to be well-maintained as opposed to the tattered guise outside, as if trying to put up a façade to keep the blissfully oblivious humans further at bay. The door creaked open for me and a lady in a cherry pink plain kurta and a white salwar ushered me in. I figured she was one of the key local contact points from the organization and she briefed me in a matter-of-fact way about what I was expected to do. I think she had sensed from my body language that I was a nervous wreck at that point.

"Stop thinking of yourself as their rescuer and it will become much easier to empathize and support them." She advised me, and her words have stayed with me even to this day.

I scanned the room. My eyes vigorously kept moving from one girl to another. Different age groups. Different backgrounds. Different life experiences. But their belligerent destiny had brought them together under the same roof. For a moment, I could smell the stink of my privilege. It could be me too! I was fortunate to be on the other side. And that was the moment when I was no more the same person. Something changed within me instantly, as if someone had switched on a light within my soul that was lying untouched all my life. The thought that our cocoon is an illusion struck me like a thunderbolt. I re-aligned my purpose in life. I was no more intending to contribute to the society by being here. I wanted to do this for myself. To be better. To find value in my being. To grow to be someone I can sleep with at peace.

I closed my eyes and awakened to the touch of a hand clasping my palms. My gaze was stuck at that smile. I did not notice anything else. Not even the eyes. She asked my name. I responded. She talked. I listened. She told me clearly that she had no interest in reuniting with her parents because they were the ones who had traded her for attractive moolah. Her story was horrifying and excruciating and I tried hard to hold back my tears because after all, I had to show that I was strong enough to be able to counsel and guide her. My naivety soon got the better of me when I noticed the glint of hope under those fluttering eyelashes. Hope for a better future. Hope for respect. Hope to be able to make the most of this second chance that she had got. She neither was seeking any fake assurances nor did she need a revolutionary saviour. We hugged. We cried together. I had entered the place thinking I was going to touch a life, but what transpired was actually the other way round.

Sympathy comes from a place of supremacy whereas empathy comes from a place of love and understanding. The former pities the visible imbalance whereas the latter pushes you to look within.

Bio:

Anupama Dalmia is an award-winning blogger, author, serial entrepreneur with three ventures, social influencer, creative writing mentor and choreographer. She is the recipient of Karamveer Chakra (Silver), a Global Civilian Honour presented by International Confederation of NGOs in association with the United Nations. She is a Sheroes Champion where she motivates a community of 15 million women and is also an Amazon approved Influencer. She has been featured among the top bloggers and influencers of India on multiple platforms and is the only Indian who has been nominated in the category of "Digital Transformation" by Global Digital Women, a Berlin based International network of female digital pioneers at the Digital Women Leader Awards 2020. Recently, she was conferred with the Sarojini Naidu International Award for Women 2020.

"My Father, My Father, The Chariots of Heaven!": A brief memoir on a writer's Dad

Dr. A.V. Koshy

I spent the last one day of his life with my Dad making him tell me Abdul Kalam stories. For those of you who don't know, Abdul Kalam was the President of India before he passed away, but much before that, he had been a rocket scientist and then the Director of ISRO, India's Space Research Organization, where my father had also worked. My sister and I sat on the bed and listened. She went in and out but I just sat there. My Dad being from what Keralites call Madhya Thiruvithankoor (central Travancore), was called 'Achayen' by his colleagues. This basically means a Christian from Central Travancore, probably owning a rubber estate, for those who don't get it, nothing more, nothing less or else, but though my Dad had no estate, his colleagues at his workplace VSSC called him that, affectionately and respectfully.

One day Dr Kalam asked him, "Mr Varghese, why do they all call you achayan? Shouldn't they call you by your name?" My Dad explained that it was a mark of friendliness. Then Dr Kalam - who was not yet one then, by the way, but still only just Abdul Kalam, Director of ISRO, told him, "then I too will call you the same from now on." My Dad laughed and said, "you can if you will let me call you Mr. Kalam." He meant he would not call him sir or director. Dr Kalam laughed and said, "sure, you can."

Until Dr Kalam left VSSC, and later too, they both called each other the said names, much to the chagrin and dismay and discomfort of many, seeing the easy camaraderie and amiability between them. They never stopped addressing each other as friends and equals which shows both Dr

Kalam's greatness and humility that he did not let his soon coming degrees (honorary Ph.Ds. and positions, ones greater than being the Director of VSSC) take away his simplicity. It reveals my Dad's forthright simplicity too, as I do not know anyone else who could have done that and "gotten away with it", then or later, (though there were others like Mr Nair, Kalam's secretary as President, who were treated the same way by Kalam) as Dr Kalam grew in stature.

My father passed away the next day after telling me this story. I had gone back to Bengaluru by then, but returned to attend his funeral in Thiruvananthapuram. Seeing him for the final time had been a miracle as I had come down all the way from Saudi just to see him, knowing it may be the last time, and it was as if he had kept himself going just to see me. He had been in the hospital before my coming and had almost slipped away.

There are other stories about Kalam and my Dad I want to preserve. When my only younger sister died at the age of just seven months, we were living in a house that was literally set in a hole, a small one, being not at all rich, Dr Kalam came to visit us. After sitting there quietly for a while, he got up to go. He saw a Bible on a small teapoy we had. He took it and asked if it was Dad's and on being answered in the affirmative, he said: 'This is good to have with you now, read it and you will find the answers and comfort you need at this time'.

After he left ISRO, Dr Kalam met my father, once or twice more, once in a hotel in Chennai and then somewhere else. The friendship was the same as before. When he became President, my Dad wrote only once to him, to show him a poem my daughter had written. Dr Kalam replied, via his office.

My father was a purchase officer of rare integrity, though I say so myself, as his son. One day he found himself posted to SHAR in Sriharikota. While the posting was inevitable to some extent and long delayed in his case, perhaps, as he was someone no one wanted to let go off, it was still cumbersome to leave and go, having a wife and three children and another one in a hostel. But there was no choice, he being a government servant, and he went.

My mother could never go to SHAR - she had her hands full with bringing up three children who all needed much attention. But my sister and I went for a month and came back happy to have been with him. We had a gala time with the greatest Dad on earth.

The Director of VSSC was supposedly close to my Dad, as were others in the top echelons of scientists in the organization, like Kalam.

My Dad asked the Director if there was no way to not be transferred.
He said "no."
Then he asked him if he could be brought back after a year.
"Yes, sure," said the Director. "Varghese, I'll bring you back in a year," he said.
A year went by and my Dad came back to ask the Director again to be transferred back to our home town, Thiruvananthapuram.
The Director said, "Varghese, actually, it's impossible. I can't do it, for you or anyone else. It's beyond even me."
When my Dad went out, the man who now had a lovely. flowing beard and moustache and long hair, who looked more like a sage than a scientist, another top scientist, second in command, asked him, "why do you look so downcast, Achayen?"
My Dad explained to him that he wanted to be back with his family in Thiruvananthapuram.
The scientist said, "don't worry, dear chap, I know you and you watch, I'll bring you back here."
My Dad went off, slightly reassured.

Sure enough, when he got his next very big project, the one that all know of, the top scientist, true to his word, insisted that the purchase section could be handled only by my Dad and brought him back. We were happy as a family that our Dad was back with us.

When my Dad told me this story, I felt happy about this top scientist who had helped my Dad, so I asked my Dad his name.

"Namby," he said. "His name is Namby Narayanan." This was the same Namby Narayan who later became infamous at first for being accused of spying on India in the Mariam Rasheeda case and was finally cleared and proved to be innocent only just before his death, when it was almost of no use to him. But at least before he died, he had the satisfaction of knowing that he was acquitted by the nation that had told him wrongly that he had betrayed its defense secrets.

My dad died at 89. As he was nearing 86, he used to send me messages by sms daily - all about things he does and I don't. Some of the ones I need to do:

'A gentle answer turns away wrath.'

'Hate no one.'

'Give thanks to God for everything' - love this one.

'Don't look for the bad in anyone, but look for the good and appreciate it.'

'Love is not premeditated but spontaneous.' - This one I love, believe in and try to live by.

'Behold, I have engraved you on the palm of my hands.'

'When you go through the floods, it won't make you wet and when you go through the fire, it won't singe you.'

My dad is probably the man I admire the most in my life, let me repeat, at the expense of sounding a bit proud and boring. He was my Elijah for whom I hope to be Elisha.

There are many reasons for this, but I'd like to give some here.

His dad, my granddad, was basically a rubber estate owner and farmer and did not know how to read, and write but my dad has a B.A. Hons in Economics from Ferguson College, Pune. This is like my Ph.D. for his time and place and background. My Dad knew Hamlet and Gitanjali and the Bible practically by heart and could quote from his memory long sections from it to us. He believed in plain living and high thinking, He wrote Christian books that help people live peaceful lives, and he was also a Gandhian. He started as a clerk but ended up as the Head of the Purchase Department of VSSC, dealing in things from screws to parts of nuclear warheads, to put it as hyperbole, and built the first ISRO from scratch, up the ground to what it is today, being one of its first employees along with Abdul Kalam, who was then fresh from his aeronautics engineering course, and they were all brimful of idealism and love for the country. This was shown in Kalam and him and that first batch by an exemplary devotion to their work by allowing no corruption in, ever.

While I saw many of the people my Dad's age become as rich as Croesus, something he could have done by 'fixing' just one deal with a rich Indian industrialist or someone from abroad regarding buying things for the country's space project in parts deals or for ISRO's arms programme, he never did it. This integrity led to him having then and now only enough for himself and his family and never anything more. But it also led to something else, a reputation for honestly that was worth its weight in gold. He lived till the end as he always did, in a simple manner, kind, alone, human, loved and respected by all and making his family, friends, relatives, church members, and all who met him daily, through his sensible and generous nature that looks after others' welfare and only then its own, happy. I should probably write more about him and Kalam but won't, except to say that their breed does not exist anymore in India and it was a breed that was found in nation lovers irrespective of caste, creed, class, gender and religion then, We are not worthy of our fathers who were giants.

Hats off to all our fathers who inspire us sons and daughters and grandchildren in so many ways.

My father used to get up like clockwork at six am every day. He would then switch the light on in his room. Go to the bathroom, brush his teeth, come back, put on Christian devotional music, and read the Bible. He would then write in his diary. There are whole volumes of them. While studying the Bible, he would make copious notes. They later became articles on devotion, and two books, and a quiz book, so thorough was his knowledge of it. He had read it countless times. My father did not talk much. He never used swear words. What he read from the Bible was what he lived by. He had only one bad habit which he quit finally, which was smoking. I never heard him tell a lie. I learned everything from him by watching him which was his only method of teaching. He was methodical, systematic, and respected in the neighborhood as a quiet man who lived an upright life, filled with honesty, dignity, integrity, peace, and good deeds.

Of course, he did not become all this overnight. He became all this by application and diligence. By the time he died, he had become a towering colossus in my mind of what love means, especially to his grandchildren, all eleven of them, and my two daughters who were heartbroken at his death and still are, and his extended family, and to all who came to our home. He fed us and all guests by cooking for us, being a very good cook, but never complained, and kept the house spick and span, which he had bought with his pension money. He seemed tireless, whether farming in his plot or saving money for us, his children, or planning for his future, so he gave none of us any worries or problems when he passed away. He had even bought his own tomb next to my mother's and kept all the money for his funeral expenses ready. His death was the greatest loss to my daughters as he used to talk to them every day. It has left a vacuum I have not been able to fill so far. The love he gave my son Reuel who has autism is also both unmatchable and unbelievable, laying down his life for him.

My father was very good at his job. Even after his retirement, I saw things in him which were astounding. One was the way he handled money meticulously, to make it multiply to never be in need and always have something extra to give to those in need. Though a widower, he lived a frugal, sparse life. He had no wants but sacrificed them happily for others. He saved money for others by his thrift. He was not rich but never poor and though we had nothing much, he made his best efforts to keep us happy always, so we felt we wanted nothing as his children. He succeeded, mostly. A few people may consider his life puritanical, spartan, and boring, but the truth is it was focused, concentrated, and meaningful, showing tremendous will power.

Another noteworthy habit he had on entering into any contract was to read everything in it, including the fine print. I have never seen Indians do this. He would not sign on any document unless convinced of its legal validity fully. This was what had made him powerful in his job like many other things like punctuality, hard work, dedication, neatness, cleanliness, and truthfulness, etc.
My father is my example. I have been rather unlike him but nowadays I finally try, more and more, to be like him. He was a giant, a towering figure, in his virtue and character.

The Bible says the fruit of God's Spirit dwelling in you is love, joy, peace, kindness, patience, goodness, gentleness, and self- control and other virtues against which there is no law. By the time he died, my father had these things in his life in abundance. So he died happily, certain of the knowledge that he is going to heaven. He had surrendered his life fully to God.

God was kind to me that I could meet him on the day before his death and attend his funeral. There were many people at his funeral but what I remember is that he was laid in a sepulcher next to my mother so that both were "not separated in their death", like David and Jonathan, but reunited, after many years as my mother had left him early and many years he had gone on alone, but without faltering despite it. Here was a man and what a man, a brave man, the like of whom you will seldom find anymore, in this harsh world. There were a lot of men like him in his generation, I am certain, but they don't make men like them anymore.

Dad published three books or more. One was a detailed Bible Quiz Book, of which we don't have any copies left. The second was an assimilation of hymns and songs and selected passages from the Bible for singing and reading when comfort was needed. And lastly, a collection of published articles in various Christian magazines. An article he wrote just before death was also published in a magazine after his death. He was a systematic reader of many books, but he found immense pleasure in reading the Bible all over again and again and hence the book, Sweeter than Honey, was compiled and published and became rather famous as many people read it and get spiritual solace from it. This writing ability of his and my mom's, his wife Sara's, has also influenced his children and grandchildren, many of whom are also excellent writers. This memoir itself could probably not have been written if not for this gift that he passed on to me.

Bio:

Dr. Koshy A.V. is presently working as an Assistant Professor in the English Department of Jazan University, Saudi Arabia. He has many books, degrees, diplomas, certificates, prizes, and awards to his credit and also, besides teaching, is an editor, anthology maker, poet, critic, and writer of fiction. His latest poetry book Wine-kissed Poems, with Jagari Mukherjee, is an Amazon best seller. He runs an autism NPO with his wife, Anna Gabriel.

When I was an expecting mother

Brindha Vinodh

As I sit down to pen down my memories a little down the roads of nostalgia, I must confess that this is an emotion that I have dared not to share with a lot of people hitherto. It is very tender, close to my heart and intricately embedded.

However, what makes me write today despite getting goosebumps, is the fact that with many middle-aged women going through emotional turmoil during pregnancy, my case could invigorate their languid frustrations, not to ignore the tremendous advancement medicine has undergone in India.

Let me go down the journey like this. In the wings of time, I fly backwards like a humming bird, by half-a dozen years, to 2014, to be precise. I was pregnant with hopes and aches of happiness for the second time at the age of 32 (no points for guessing my age now, ha ha, I am not an actress to not reveal my age, a light one before venturing into the serious stuff).

My elder daughter was already six. I knew my fetus was growing within from the upsurge intertwined between the hunger of two creatures. The day my ultrasound revealed two placentas, the eyes of my family lit in anticipation of twins, only to discover it was ephemeral.

"We thought they were twins, but the other placenta is an empty sac. It's a single fetus," the words spilled by my gynecologist echoed through the night as I submerged in thoughts of mirage, a mermaid in a sea of turbulent waves. Thus began the first setback of my pregnancy.

The advent of second trimester crept with news to keep sinews strong, a new term learnt in my ladders of maternity,

"Grape like vesicles". "It's either the vesicles grow or the baby grows. The vesicles tend to multiply and the uterus has a space constraint," said my gynecologist, Dr. Vidya Chaya.

To put it in a layman's jargon, only one placenta had a surviving fetus and the other placenta was mere vesicles that seemed to nourish all the nutrition. It was a tough situation where the survival of the fittest would continue. The vesicles multiplied when compared to the constant growth of the fetus.

My trepidations belittled the words; would my womb succumb to those vesicles? Dr. Vidya advised me to go for a second opinion to Mediscan, a leading scan centre in Chennai, India.

It was more of a research-cum-scan center dealing with genetic engineering. They explained to me that mine was an unusual case and could lead to three possible encounters. Being a student of Econometrics and business studies, I was not used to sophisticated medical parlance. So, I finally came to comprehend that a test needed to be done to figure out the fetus had the chromosomes intact. And even if it did not, it was too late as per medical ethics to terminate the pregnancy.

The bitter truth gnawed in to engulf me in envisages of portends... 'Amniocentesis', a test of needle injected into the uterus to see if the chromosomes were intact, was the one that I underwent. With a five percent chance of abortion, I agreed to it with a heavy heart for it was a forced choice.

My prayers knew no boundaries, my family knew no new fears for we awaited with aches of angst to pass each day in edges of hopes; we were spiders in cobweb waiting for clouds of illusions to clear off until the reports were negative which meant we breathed positive air yet. It was finally discovered that mine was a case of "Mesynchymal Dysplasia (PMD)," an unusual case of partial molar pregnancy. The fact that made it even more unique was that it occurred with twin placentas, the other placenta, luckily the one with the fetus, not harmed. The ensuing weeks moved in inches like a tortoise, each day pushed until week-34!

Finally, in the last two weeks of my pregnancy, zephyrs blew in shades bright for my countenance sported a smile, a curve that could straighten things out. With the blessings of the Almighty and the good wishes of my husband, my parents, in laws, close relatives, and of course the innocuous wishes of my elder daughter, on a beautiful Wednesday afternoon, my second princess was welcomed by this world, a mother was born again!

Aren't women warriors?

PS: PMD is a rare case of pregnancy especially with twin placentas and research is going on in medical labs throughout the world.

Bio:

Brindha Vinodh is a postgraduate in Econometrics. A former copyeditor and a freelancer, she is a writer within. Her poems and short stories have been widely published in magazines, e-zines, literary journals, and she has contributed to several anthologies. She currently resides in the United States of America with her husband and two daughters.

The Grass Grew High and Seeded Her with Doubt

Candice Louisa Daquin

*[**Author's note:** This is the story of my paternal grandmother. She married young to my grandfather, who told her a few years into their marriage he regretted marrying and tried to persuade her to give both my father and his brother to relatives. As an artist and prodigy from a young age, my grandfather believed he had been robbed of his chance to study under a master, and trapped into domesticity. Despite this being a choice he made. My grandmother, a woman of her day, did not have the financial choices to leave and start a life of her own, and spent many years under the boot of his disappointment. Upon his suicide, she temporary fell apart, only to rise up, a phoenix reborn. She went on to buy a small home, selling their large house and land, and lived on top of a mountain with goats and dogs and cats. An eccentric, talented woman in her own right, she inspired her granddaughters deeply and remains in their hearts forever. This is her story.]*

When her husband, sleeping forever in blue room, switched off the light one last, certain time, and daylight brought horror with toast and ghosts, already inhabiting her hinges like spectators to a wake before dying began. He skipped the last part and went straight to his place among the hills; only there in quietude and undisturbed roll of thick grass, could he spill onto page, the water colors of his imagination.

After they carried him away, cold to the touch and longer than any blanket they had to hand, using her favorite plaid, still with dog hair from the dog that died seasons before, the cats came and ate some of hens left by the fox, who annoyed the ducks that swam, in ceasing rings on silver water.

She sat at the wood table, her varnished hands motionless, the collar of her nightgown muddied with something

The Body of Memories

indiscernible. For hours she did not move, her sons were absent, arranging as men will, the process of grief in static form, whilst she fed the ducks who mostly ignored her, and noticed another broken egg by the side of the pond, a low mockery of her feelings, hemmed and constrained, wishing to slip into water and be lost.

Soon, the sun rose, the house clock still ticked, his paintings nailed to the whitewashed farm walls, an obscene reminder of his absence and his disregard for her. Her body was as blue as his pills, some she had found underneath the eiderdown, scattered like pollen, staining the white sheets with little blue smudges. *I don't know if baking soda will get it clean*, she wondered, rubbing at the cotton with her thumb and sucking it free of sting.

Crane flies crowded the steps to the attic; she climbed up stiffly and unlatched the black lock at the very top where the stairs grew thin and treacherous. Half thinking, she could fling herself down, and possibly meet him by dinner time, she knew she'd snap her wrist and ankle and it would throb and hurt despite any pill, because the cold never left, it climbed inside her and ached like a grain of sand.

In the attic she found the rest of his work, the pictures of young women, splayed and naked, glorious in their youth and artistic rendering. She wanted to add them all to the big bonfire he usually built in the back garden, and laugh at his impotent horror as they caught light and were vanquished. But that seemed small now, as so many petty jealousies did, and instead she gathered them together, and put them behind cloth. She would preserve his infidelities by default, for the sake of his being an artist, but not have to be reminded of it, have it stuck in her face, an obscene reminder of the doubling of loss.

Light from the steeple and above the tall trees, filtered in through the tiny attic window, catching color like a kaleidoscope, moving shadows out of their turn and she moved through the attic to the very back where she kept her hidden bottles, all amber and innocent at first glance, maybe art supplies, maybe empties, but the nectar of them bid closer inspection, full and ready, her hands clasped two and made the descent.

Back in the kitchen, the infernal Augur chuffing smoke like a wheezing addict, the smell of last night's pudding still sweet in the air with a slight sickness, she closed the blinds and gave herself over to the first drink. Shockingly, and before very long, his absence was a welcome one, the walls did not seem to close in, the day was neatly blocked and avoided and a far ringing phone could be imagination. She sank lower in the chair, a stiff thing of wicker they'd purchased for little at a sale, like most things, bought out of cheapness than like, yielding nothing in the years they sat, straight and silent with one another, listening to the clock count down the days.

Her beans and cucumbers and radishes and rhubarb outside needed picking. There was a wash to be done, the cats scratched at the back door for late breakfast despite their success in catching a swatch of voles by the wheat field behind, and then she had some jarring to do of late summer jams before they turned and grew white beards making them good only for the bees.

But she did none of those things. Her husband had died. No, her husband had killed himself. The fine tall dark eyed-dark-haired man of her youth, the one who bent his head to her in acquiescence when she said she couldn't sleep with him unless marriage was his intention, and without pursing his lips or skipping in heavy breath, he said he wanted her to be his wife and she lit up like a hundred fire flies, when day sleeps.

It wasn't how it turned out, and she knew, because her mother and her grandmother had said that things rarely did. She had two sons, and they grew like her husband and her

The Body of Memories

vegetable garden, away from her, in sharp angle. At times she wanted to rip the phone out of the wall and hurl it toward the compost heap in hatred of how it only rang when the church needed something or a neighbor had too many cabbages. Rarely was it family, rarely was it her husband when he travelled and said he'd check in, and she strummed the wood like an impatient basketball player, stuck on the bench.

He didn't call on his long visits into the city, 'seeing his agent' he'd fumble, and she knew his agent was a woman, younger than her, taller than her, thinner than her. He didn't call at night when he said he would eat out at the local inn, where they'd have a thin soup served in tin bowls and a plate of cheap pasta for artists and the like who usually walked instead of taking buses, to save enough for cigarettes and cheap coffee.

He didn't call when he got to his inexpensive lodgings, because probably he was never there, and she wouldn't find out because then it would be true and she'd have to confront him. The last time she did that, he called her bluff, said he would leave to be with (what was her name that time?) and began to pack. She flew into a cyclone of repent, pulling on his sleeve like a child, reminding him of his promises and responsibilities (thank God the children were still at home) while watching his eyes, once bright and direct in following her own, glazed over and watched the wall, in askance.

She imagined the other women and she saw herself as a mad jackdaw, unable to break from cliché, to be free of her envy and her spite, brewing in her like potent yeast. She saw the infirmity of her position, yet also, the female within her yearned to revel in the passions of her gender. She didn't have to be imprisoned by this man, she could board a bus, with a threadbare ticket in her teeth and shout from the top of her lungs: "I'm going away and I'm not coming back!" With her own printmaking skills, her love of writing, her keen intelligence, why couldn't she? And the other women? His other women? They could go hang.

As simple as that was, it was complicated. Like the knots in her grandchild's hair as she beat on the side of the porcelain bath and sang:

Cigale, ma cigale,
Allons, il faut chanter
Car les lauriers du bois
Sont déjà repoussés. (Nous n'irons plus au bois, French children's song)

We'll go to the woods no more, she thought, imagining him dancing with his high-ladies, their watermelon lips, glittering shoulders, whiskering ankles. She thought of herself, once an artist's model, once considered *la reine du bal*, now feeling withered, forget-me-nots, put away beneath pressed paper, dried of life. Her granddaughter, the next generation, red-faced, bright-minded, perpetually in trouble, she would do just fine, she didn't care if she were safe, she hung from trees by the barest of finger and yelled at the fates to come for her.

The knots in her own knitting, unpicked with stiff Winter fingers, only to be re-threaded, a little like life, except you cannot unthread some of what you do, she thought, the echoes of them around the house, a silhouette of him in the doorway, lean as ever, lying as he left, finally looking happy. What was it about her that squeezed the happiness out of him and left him a dry rind, she wondered, just as the stain of her words rebuked and scolded, reminding it is too easy for us to blame ourselves for another's misadventure?

Perhaps the other woman who didn't attend the funeral threw herself off a haystack or the **Pont des Arts**, oh the irony of that. Perhaps she wore a yellow dress the color of bunting and Spring cake and crocus and cried like a fox at night, the terrors of her loss as she drowned. The redolent glamor of her absence caused many imaginings, over the plucking of

The Body of Memories

stray white hairs in the unforgiving morning light, seeing the sink of her chest as she let the poison in. *No good comes of envy or regret,* her piano fingers told her, tinkering to play on ivory; *no good comes of imaginings, when for all you know, she is as boxed and sealed as you, in her hermetic grief for his passing. Only you possess something she does not; less regret, less loss.*

When you hijack a person's love and you know it's a fantastic illusion, treading water resentfully until a time they will fly out when the cage is inadvertently left ajar, it's not as if you do not know what you do, or feel the crush of knowing you are not chosen, not wanted, not necessary. But in a mad way, you do it anyway, holding on despite yourself, losing in the desperation, your own instinct and self as much as the prisoner feels they too are lost. And both without what is necessary, two people sit for years, at the same place, far away, and too tired for fury. It is often the little things that cause a row, often the big things, like those giant stones they saw once on a holiday (was it Spain?) so giant and unyielding in the fields, as to be ignored by the people spilt around in distracted sunlight.

At some point the boys would return. They would ring on the door bell because they no longer lived in the house, and she would hear the ring and not answer, because they should come in unbidden. But they didn't want to live there, and she now did, alone, with the bottles that glimmered in the setting of sun and shone red against her fingers. And the grass in the back of the house, grew so high that year, when he died of his blue pills and his moldering heart of paintings and blackness, she didn't even get it cut, and from the seeds, the most incredible wild flowers grew, springing up overnight, covering the fields, surely a magic trick, she couldn't be certain.

But from the window where the rhubarb grew tall and masculine in its crimson jackets, she could see deer eating the red and yellow flowers in delight and doubting things, feeling her pulse, reedy and fast like the tick of wild things heart, she thought she saw herself walking among them, as she was before they trapped each other, before she lost her reflection, when she was young and filled with lightness and her fingers clasped living things, and she was not sitting in a chair, becoming less and less with every breath. When she was part of that world and not given over to the slipping shadows of this one, in its slow recoil toward nothingness, mocking her in his face, his tread, his absence.

With each turn of sun dial she saw herself becoming the hypocrite she had detested, mourning a man who snipped her out of his life with every stroke of his brush. Even the painting of her, ugly in its rendering, something disquieting and coiled about her mouth. She didn't like the way he looked at her, even less the way he imposed his nipped fury in his caricature. She wanted to see herself the way her granddaughter did, a bonny, gleaming eyed thing, her playmate among the damson trees, the woman who could heft child and bag of rhubarb together and run nymph-like back to kitchen door.

In the quiet of his shifting dissolvement she found beauty. The peacock blue of her dining room and how midday sun caught the wallpaper and lit it with a blue flame. The farmer who smiled over his shoulder as she ran, fleet footed, for the bus. The taste of elderberry honey on her lips at night, as she read the books she wanted to read without query. A close fit of tweed and wool against her slim waist, sewn by her own tarnished needle, still capable of tailor. With each pulled onion the skin folded into chapters and she found herself, nestled there, between the beginning and the end.

Eventually, through drop of snow, gust of hail, shaking of roots, when the Summer came and her granddaughters came to visit her, father's dropping them off thankfully without so much as an enquiry into how she was, she touched the wings that had sprouted like ideas from her narrow shoulders. Their bewitching softness, belying a strength she gathered in her

The Body of Memories

skirts, breathing in the verdant open fields, their song of life, life, life! With possibility, shimmering like fever around her, she lifted her girls to her cheeks and breathed them in. Feeling their plump little bodies hot against her own calm, she knew, like this season's seeds, they would grow strong, they would grow strong, they would grow strong. And so ... might she alongside them.

Bio:

Of Sephardi descent, Candice Louisa Daquin immigrated to America and trained as a Psychotherapist. In her spare time, Daquin works as Senior Editor at Indie Blu(e) Publishing. An ardent equal rights campaigner, Daquin created SMITTEN This Is What Love Looks Like, an LGBTQ anthology of love between women, which won Finalist in the National Indie Excellence Awards. Daquin's last collection of poetry, Pinch the Lock, was published by Finishing Line Press. Daquin's work is widely published and she recently co-edited The Kali Project, Invoking The Goddess Within, with Megha Sood, a collection of poetry and art from Indian women. www.thefeatheredsleep.com

The Passing Over

Chaitali Sengupta

The best part of looking back is that it also enables us to look inward. When we're looking back, even the harshest memories in their profound unfairness bring some solace, as we turn those pages from our past. That is, perhaps, one of the strengths of writing a memoir. We revisit the moment of grief when we're done with the mourning, and yet carry the burden of loss. In our otherwise vibrantly throbbing world, the fragments of grief remain.

Looking back, I see the overcrowded past, looping over and over, trailing like footprints on the snow, stamped with many regrets; stuttering, like a garbled echo, of what could have been. And from the sepia-colored past, one happy image shines forth. That of myself, standing in the small kitchen garden, encircled with the bright spring marigolds, and talking to my Nanna- my grandmother. Due to some family situations, I lived with my grandparents as a young child, and not with my parents. I missed being with them, just as an eight-year-old would, but my loving grandparents, especially my life-loving Nanna, is someone who defined my childhood days, away from my own mother. I remember our days together, bright and sunny, specially wrapped with exquisite moments.

However, Nanna was sick, a patient with asthma and some serious lung complications. The demonic disease was hell-bent on deducting her quota of breaths on this earth. The sore lungs in her hollow chest were often overpowered with stubborn pain. There would be days in her life, full of wait and worry, when her raspy breaths and clattering bronchial spasms would tear apart our nights. when she could hardly catch her breath. And although my Nanna was not the one to whimper and moan about her adverse health, my gentle grandfather, a learned schoolteacher, during these days would talk about creating a box of memories with Nanna.

"Why?" I would ask.

He used the Bengali word then. *'Chole Jawa'* (to pass away, to leave.)

"Where to?"

"To a better place where she wouldn't suffer so much."

I remember I was so scared that I gave a terrible wail and ended up saying, "That sounds scary. And I'm afraid I will forget her if she never returns, I'll be lonely..." I said, amid my muffled cries.

We're never alone, he said then, not even in our darkest moments.

Sometimes, when you're young, some moments linger just long enough, to last for a lifetime. This was one such moment, etched in my mind, to be a permanent part of my being. Perhaps it was this moment when my mind started to grasp that there existed another reality. The reality of death. My Nanna's death. The thought brought a deep ache inside my stomach.

It seemed near, for although the doctors tried to bring as much relief to her tired, infected lungs as possible, the disease persisted on, like a headstrong child. Later, I'd realize that it was not only the disease. The crimson in her body flew, but the will to carry it further was gone missing. Each day, on my way to school, I'd think of ways to bring her back to life, if she went away, finally, walking through death's door.

And so, on that dripping morning, almost a year after my first discussion with my grandpa, when Nanna called out to me and smiled at me, it raised my spirits. I thought she was improving at last. With emotions brimming inside my heart, I sat near her, talking to her about how I had spent time with Sandhya, my school friend from the house opposite to us, helping her decorate the crib of *Bal Krishna*. On Nanna's query, I replied that it was the day of Janmashtami, the birthday of Lord Krishna.

Throughout that morning, Nanna was unusually talkative. Her eyes bright and smiling, as if she held a deep secret there, she talked of old memories, of her little home in Rajshahi, in Bangladesh, her parents, her friends with whom she swam in the pond. She talked of grandpa too, of those very few happy moments in their life, when my mother was born. Gaily, she talked about the day she was married, so suddenly, that when Grandpa brought her to this ancestral home, his relatives were all shocked.

"But they had accepted me, although they never felt comfortable with me."

Mere remembrance brought a light of happiness on Nanna's face, but it made me anxious. Wasn't Nanna in the grip of terrible pain till yesterday? How did she carry on with such a long conversation then, when it would have been difficult for her to speak a word? Was this the glowing of the candle before it was snuffed out forever? The thought, like a needle, forced inside my brain, as I hurried Nanna to stop ruminating. She needed to preserve whatever little energy she had. Our cook hastened grandpa to get up and bring some vegetables from the market so that she could prepare our daily meal. As grandpa got up, Nanna called after him. Her face looked unusually bright, as if the afternoon sunlight was glinting there. She expressed her wish to eat *maccher jhol bhaat* (Rice with fish stew) 'Bring fresh fishes,' she called after him.

But hours later when Grandpa returned with the fresh fishes, after having searched every fish market far and near, she was breathing shallowly, and the doctor had sent his assistant to get hold of oxygen tubes, as her condition continued to deteriorate.

The Body of Memories

I felt the earth turning beneath my feet, and yet time stood at a standstill. It was a dismal day, and water, like tears, dripped continuously across the windowpanes. Nanna's eyes would sometimes travel outside the window, focusing on a lone *shalik* (Indian myna), with its pebble-smooth head, that sat on the branch of the flamboyant *gulmohor* tree, with its scarlet flame-colored flowers. The tree she herself had planted, when she came to this house, as a young bride, her bright eyes wide with dark *kajal* (kohl) and she a mere girl of fourteen. The plant grew up, hearing the sound of the *sankha* (the sacred conch) she blew, every evening at the altar of her Gods; it continued to grow, accepting water from her young, wheatish hands, and stood growing under the mellowed rains. A tree that knew the tale of her heart and love, its vermillion-red flowers, like her innocent hopes and small dreams. The sun, now, behind the clouds, the raindrops nestled on the leafy boughs for a while, quivering, slipping and sliding, before drenching the lonely *shalik* bird. Hearing a call from its mate, it flew away then.

In the depths of Nanna's tired eyes, I could detect a smile. Her eyes closed slowly; it was as if, she too, had heard the call. The call of death. For long, I sat holding her worn hands in mine, watching her breath flicker ever more feebly, until the last moments approached, slowly, unhurriedly.

What else do I remember from Nanna's last journey? I pile up my memories, turn them around, and there I find her-still warm, still very much alive. One memory passes into another and the one that stands out, I'm certain, would never grow wings.

Nanna in a bright, red bridal *sari*, getting ready for her last journey, as the sun broke forth in its splendid last glory. The crimson of the evening, almost as blossom red as that big dot of vermilion on her forehead. As red as those scarlet bangles, lying limp against her fair wrists. Never had she looked prettier, never so at peace. As she was laid out on the floor, my heart thumped. And then the canvas changed, the vision blurred and in Nanna's face, I saw mirrored Goddess Durga's visage, just as sad and as sorrowful on the day of immersion. Perhaps, it was then, that the hard knot near my throat melted. And the tears coursed down, unrestrained.

That year brought a new season in my life: the season of grief. A deep sadness followed me for a long time, but time, eventually brought a sense of healing to my young heart. I survived, grew stronger, turned mature, but Nanna's *"chole jawa"* (passing over) has stayed with me, altering me significantly. Like a half-buried memory, it existed, mapping up to the texture of pain, marking my identity.

Bio:
Chaitali Sengupta is a writer and a poet by passion, a financial analyst and a language teacher by profession. She's a translator and volunteer journalist, based in the Netherlands. Her literary & journalistic articles have appeared in both Dutch and Indian media houses. Her debut book of prose poems **"Cross-Stitched Words"** has been published in 2021 (Setu Publication, USA). She has translated two works from Bengali to English "Quiet Whispers of our Heart" and "A thousand words of heart" (Orange Publishers, 2020 & 2021, Kolkata). Her works regularly appear in print and online journals like, *Muse India, Indian Periodical, Eindhoven News, NPO.nl, Borderless Journal, Setu Bilingual, The Asian Age, Different Truths, Verse Visual.* She has co-authored for numerous anthologies, most recent one being the prestigious international anthology *The Kali Project: Invoking the Goddess within, (Indie Blu(e) Publishing, USA,* and *Earth, Fire, Water & Wind* anthology (Authorspress, New Delhi.)

The Body of Memories

Lockdown Story

Debraj Moulick

Hello! My Ghost.

If I survive, I will be a survivor.

If not, I am going to haunt you like the creatures of Ramsay Brothers' production. But if you read this one, I might spare your horrible life. Could you just tell me, what is the use of this life? Sooner or later, you are going to perish, why the f (aww, I won't use the other alphabets) are you so scared of death?

Ah, I get it- A family to feed? Old parents?

If it is making you afraid of death, then you better die. Wait! Do I sound like a pessimistic animal? Don't you think this life is a curse and this struggle for existence is exhausting?

These are the thoughts inside my brain. You want to use some kind of adjectives like hopeless, suicidal blah! blah! Do it, I don't care.

Now what do I do to deal with these feelings?

I pour it out, I imagine stuff- I compose poems, I write short stories and try to perform them. The streak of creativity is keeping me grounded.

There is no pattern around here; it is a pure example of putrefied conscience. What do you expect from a sensitive (am I worthy enough to be branded as a sensitive one?) individual aged 30 years? I have been staying with cockroaches, rodents in my small apartment in the city of Bay, away from my parents, relatives. This Indian counterpart of Wuhan is dealing with an alarming number of pandemic cases, my acquaintances have shown their true colours and my friends have left for their respective hometowns long ago. My flatmate is also in his native place, enjoying the warmth of family life. I have been a loner and a worshipper of solitude, oh yes, that bliss of solitude infused by the literary theories of the great romantic poet William Wordsworth, ah snap! During the initial days, the lockdown was an enjoyable, but now it is creeping like a creepy beetle insect inside my brown skin. What is the use of our system? What is the use of scientific advancement? Oh! Dear God, please have an avatar again and save our bodies (soul is always there, I know) from this capitalistic pestilence or a natural wrath against humanity. There are so many theories about the origin of this germ, which one is real?

What is the use of writing so many things over here? I cannot leave my workstation and enjoy the homely comfort in my hometown. Do you know about the concept of marooning a pirate on a small island with a small bottle of rum and few bullets? Well, just think of it as a metaphor. I cannot leave this city and I cannot take my life, I guess I don't have the liberty to end my life also, Oh! I guess death is the only freedom and I don't have the audacity, I don't have the autonomy of ending my own life.

Ah! I remember the words of another great romantic:

'I fall upon the thorns of life! I bleed![1]'

I don't know why I am being so negative about my existence?

At least I am still breathing; I am having ample food in the kitchen. Ah! Snap, the rodent is playing with food particles.

Working from home, cooking, cleaning and yes, motivating myself for the daily chores is taking a huge toll upon my cognitive map. It is really tiring, I am exhausted because of no sleep till early morning, I am drained out of living in constant fear of getting affected with the virus. What will happen to me? I might lie down as a piece of flesh in a medical ward, for there is no one around here. I am 500 miles away from my home (make it 2000kms). I would be rotting

The Body of Memories

in a distant place with other corpses. The thoughts are real, I cannot escape such thoughts, and those demons are really taking a toll upon my health. I am sorry my bard, I couldn't stick to your wise words:

'Where the mind is without fear and the head is held high;[2]

My mind is full of fear; no science, no religion is able to console me.

No one will remember a dead man without credentials, no one will shed a tear since death is the new way of life, it is the new normal. My anxiety is normal and yes, the ghost of death is coming for all of us.

Ah!

"We Poets in our youth begin in gladness; / But thereof come in the end despondency and madness.[3]

Do I need to visit a psychiatrist? Now, the places are crowded, phone lines are busy and I am one hell of an egoistic & a male chauvinistic prick, I am living in a bubble that depression is not men, not for me. I am doomed.

Disclaimer: This is an original piece of writing.

References

1. Percy Bysshe Shelley's 'Ode to the West Wind'
2. Rabindranath Tagore's Gitanjali 35
3. William Wordsworth's 'Resolution and Independence'

Bio:
Debraj Moulick works as a Lecturer of English in K J Somaiya Polytechnic College, Mumbai. He is also concurrently pursuing research as an M.Phil Research

Scholar in Department of English, University of Mumbai. His area of interest includes the Violence and Bloodshed in Films & Literature, Science Fiction, PostColonial Studies, Mythology, Language studies and Marginalized Literature. A full-time bibliophile and movie buff, he is also a bilingual poet, composing and reciting poems in English and Hindi. His poems are part of various anthologies. You can catch up his poetry recitals in YouTube. He also writes official book reviews, film reviews among others, in his blog: https://debrajdpaideia.wordpress.com/

In search of myself

Elvira Fernandez

> *Two roads diverged in a wood, and I—*
> *I took the one less travelled by,*
> *And that has made all the difference.*

Teaching was and is still considered a noble profession which not many would take up as a first choice voluntarily. I look back and I feel proud to say that I come from a family of educators. What could be more natural than my slipping into the role even before realizing it? Over the years I have come to accept that though teaching is a fulfilling experience, it can at times be the most thankless and underpaid service. Many a times, what you do is taken for granted and even criticized viciously. If you work diligently with the desire to achieve the best then you can add to the already bubbling cauldron- peer jealousy and rivalry. Now, you have the perfect recipe for stress and other stress-related disorders.

The earlier you step into this field, the faster is the chance of a burnout. With no promotions in sight, a feeling of saturation begins to set in and you feel you're stuck on a plateau, because you've seen all there is to see and you can now only go round in a circle. Although learning continues for the simple reason that you constantly come in touch with the youth, but as an individual you feel 'caught up' in one place.

I was lucky that before I reached that stage of saturation, an opportunity to branch out presented itself. I grabbed it with both hands, and staying 'rooted' to the place, I started reaching out to the alumni of the institution. Soon, with the help of two of my colleagues, I was able to start building up an Alumni body, investing in it thoughts, ideas, efforts and much more. The venture grew and flourished, bringing in much appreciation and of course criticism too, initially. With the passing of nine years, many of the old critics got transformed into allies and a whole set of new ones were born. I can't stop laughing whenever I think of this. Each time we would learn from a previous experience and apply the lesson to a new event, the next set of problems would show up, to teach us more lessons. When I took up this mammoth task, I was told by a few committee members that this Alumni Body wouldn't last long, they quoted the earlier examples. I thanked them for their support and persevered over the years. I learnt that perseverance and determination can get you through the worst of times. A deep faith in the Almighty Father cannot be negated from the list of essentials.

I remember one of the Alumni meets; as the date for the event drew nearer, I could sleep only three to four hours a day. I, along with two of my colleagues was struggling with things, having no support from the authorities. I had innumerable calls, emails and messages to reply to each day, apart from taking classes, planning tests, conducting and marking them. To add a cherry to the cake, I came down with viral fever and had two relapses. When I look back, I've no idea how we managed to get through those trying times. By the grace of God, the event was a huge success. The Alumni bid goodbye with effusive praises. The words of appreciation in spite of all the obstacles soothed the pain and suffering. It boosted our confidence in loyal friends and good teamwork.

With one peak scaled and new records set, what was next?

Since I had joined the institution, students would approach me with requests for various kinds of written materials like – essays, debates, scripts for plays, prayers, etc. One colleague in particular, a well-wisher, who watched the steady stream of students walking to and fro suggested that I should compile all these works so that in the future I could publish them. Each time he suggested it, I would laugh away the idea saying where was the time to think about publishing books as I already had a lot on my plate.

But time changed, and much changed with time. I came face to face with a not-so- pleasant phase professionally. Around the same time a friend began working on a series of English textbooks. He requested me to help him out with a colossal project of planning and penning a series of English textbooks. We would discuss, and I would put down in ink certain stories and poems as per the requirement of the blueprint. After reading a few pieces, he insisted that I should think about putting my pen to paper seriously. He said that I had the imagination, creativity and flair for it. You bet, I didn't take him seriously either, to begin with. Then I wrote a very descriptive piece intending a collection of short stories. When I shared it with him, he suggested that I should create a protagonist and have the story revolve around him or her. Feeling inspired, I deliberated over a number of options. Gradually the idea took root and blossomed into 'Magic at Ferns and Blooms'. By the time I showed him what I had done, I had penned sixteen chapters of the twenty-one-chapter long fantasy novel. He was aghast! Till date I remember that moment of intense surprise! I seized the opportunity of asking him to be the Editor. I shared with him my plan of penning a trilogy; he liked it. I wished to have coloured illustrations in my books and thus began my search for an illustrator. God intervened once again and guided me to the person, perfect for the task. Three of us, together as a team, brought out a series of three books – The Ferns and Blooms Trilogy (Magic at Ferns and Blooms, More Magic at Ferns and Blooms & Goodbye Ferns and Blooms) in a span of three years.

Success always follows earnest preparation. I remember how hours were invested in discussing plots, possible solutions to dilemmas, edits and the resultant pictorial representation through illustrations.

During these years of misfortune, my efforts multiplied, as I desired to bring out the best in me. Since I had been buried like a seed, I had only one option to germinate like one, to rise stronger and brighter than before. I was determined that I was definitely going to answer the setback with a clamorous comeback. And I did!

'If you can dream it, you can do it'. Life taught me that however adverse the situation maybe, things could surely get worst, after which they would without a doubt, get better. Every struggle helps to draw the best out from deep within us. Hence, the ingredients for success according to me are: inspiration, desire to dream, dedication, perseverance, good friends, hard work, willingness to experiment, acceptance of failure, desire to try again and openness to constructive criticism.

Today, from where I stand, I know...

> *The woods are lovely, dark and deep,*
> *But I have promises to keep,*
> *And miles to go before I sleep,*
> *And miles to go before I sleep.*

Bio:
Elvira Fernandez is an English Lecturer and an avid reader of all kinds of literature, but Children's Literature, Fantasy and Romance top her list. She is an Indian author who loves to write for children. She has written short stories, plays, poems, content for some academic books and e-zines, apart from doing some editing assignments. She has won several awards – including the first prize for her English essay in a competition organized by AINACS in 2019 and the Editor's Choice Certificate for her story in the AILC 2020 organized by the Creative Post.

Her love for Nature, children and her pets find expression in her writings, especially in the Ferns and Blooms Trilogy, a

The Body of Memories

fantasy series. The first two books of which have been recognized as an Enchanting Series of Books by Nissim Prize for Fiction 2020.

Finding Bibhabati Devi: Queen of Bhawals

Gopa Bhattacharjee

"Are you sure my friend belongs to our anti - family? The Bibhabati Devi family?"

When my uncle confirmed, I had goosebumps. He is my friend, and been beside me during the most difficult phase of my life. How can history repeat itself?

In the present Gazipur district in Bangladesh, the *Bhawal Rajbari* stands as a testimony of time and history. This *Rajbari* (palace) has been a silent storyteller of several incidents. The Rajbari is built over acres of land surrounded by huge walls even today. The Rajbari belonged to my ancestors, the Bhawals of East Bengal.

While in Uttarpara, Hooghly, a part of West Bengal currently, the huge zamindar pattern house that I often passed in my dad's car during my childhood days to go to my *mama bari* (mother's maternal house) in Seerampore is the house with whom our ancestors fought a case for 14 years. It seemed unbelievable; it still does. My friend, a relative belonging to the clan of Bibhabati Devi, lives here.

Well, we belong to families that fought a famous case for 14 long years against Bibhabati Devi. The famous Bhawal Case which is still referred to in the context of modern day court cases. We were on the side of Raja Ramendra Narayan Roy who was allegedly killed by the conspiracy of his wife Bibhabati Devi and a doctor named Asutosh Dasgupta. Later, a stark, bitter truth was revealed. That night, the dead body bearers couldn't burn the Raja's body due to heavy rains. The Raja was alive. He lost his memory and roamed as a *Naga Sanyasi* for almost 9 years. Later when his memory relapsed, he came back to the Bhawal estate for

The Body of Memories

justice. He fought the case for 14 long years and ultimately won. Later, six months before partition, he died and his descendants had to leave Bangladesh due to the partition. We belonged to his sister's side who supported the brother, the Raja of Bhawals.

I kept repeating one question after every story telling session I heard from my elders about our ancestors. What happened to Bibhabati Devi? Where is she? It was unknown to me for years. Whenever I asked my elders, they would shrug their shoulders and I would often find resentment in them. I grew up with a strange, unexplained hatred towards that family as stories were unfolding to us.

History remains under the soil; it's true and is excavated at the right time, when it wants. I met my friend through a common friend of mine and we never discussed about our past history of families. Suddenly, in a casual discussion with my uncle, I came to know that the zamindar house which belonged to my friend's ancestors is where the relatives of Bibhabati Devi live till now. I was absolutely awestruck. When we both came to know our family history and the legacy of our forefathers, we couldn't believe the intricacies, the enmity between two families that was brewing for generations. Here we both were facing the history of our ancestors, but after so many years as friends and not as enemies. We weren't born during that era and naturally, we both didn't know what would have happened. Would we still remain friends or enemies? It would have been like a script written like the famous Aamir Khan, Juhi Chawla starrer movie ' 'Qayamat se Qayamat tak.'

I was always curious about the lady whom history couldn't forget. She betrayed her own husband. But here I was in front of my friend who is still one person I would call in times of distress, in my desperate need for advice. One good friend, rare nowadays. He belonged to this Bibhabati Devi's family and they have their own history to reveal. She spent many years in this house near the Ganges in Uttarpara. I think it has changed my whole perspective towards seeing reality. But there were still questions that kept haunting me.

Should I probe further? Or keep history as it is? It still lingers in my mind. Keeping in mind all that history has endured, I dedicate the following poem to my readers and ancestors.

[Bhawal Rajbari...Image courtesy: the author]

Bhawals of Bengal

The old Banyan tree whispers to me,
"Come near,
A story is there for you to hear.
See this spot a hundred year,
An enlightened *sanyasi* with long hair
Came and sat your progenitor.
Villagers thronged with wonder in mix
Names from yesteryears surfaced his lips.
Followed his inquisitive relatives,
His sister recognized his eyes clearly
Despite the Naga adornments and ash's smear."
In Jaidebpur Palace was long-suffering
The Bhawal king amidst betrayal and poisoning.
His own Queen outlined the deal

The Body of Memories

Knelled news of death in Darjeeling.
"Time and fate bestowed on him a new incarnation,
The King was back for retribution.
He sought justice under the British Crown.
Twelve years of strong fight,
And verdict emerged on his side."
But now lovelorn, this magnanimous half-broken palace
Lay in ruins with sand from pebbles.
The banyan tree standing in his might
Questions my thoughts—
What is left of the Bhawals in Bengal?
What did they gain?
Acres of estate wasted, left unclaimed.
A storm arose, my eyes misted.
I saw my ancestors standing scattered.
"Its history that you hold as sand,"
they said,
"But our honour lives in you to abet
You are the progeny of a fearless creed.
Remember, deceit falls quick as dominoes, even in dark.
Only truth withstands like a Bhawal Monarch."

Bio:
Gopa Bhattacharjee, born and brought up in Kolkata is an entrepreneur by profession and poet by passion. She completed her Masters in English and has been a part time teacher trainer in CMTC for many years and also a lecturer in IGNOU. She has been the guest poet in many poetry meets in and around Kolkata. She is one of the leading actors and co-producer of 'Kolkata Cocktail', the short poetry film presented by ICCR. Her poetry has been published in various national and international magazines and journals and also in an anthology named 'Muffled Moans Unleashed'. She has been the featured poet at the American Consulate, Kolkata Lit Meet 2020, *Nagar Kirrtibas* and many other cultural meets in and out of Kolkata. Her poetry book UNTURNED VERSES was published in Kolkata International Book Fair 2020.

Return to My City

Gopal Lahiri

Weeping, the laughing,
The power of love came
Into me and I became
Fierce like a lion, then
Tender like the evening star.

Rumi

Yes. It has begun from here. I can remember vividly. The city turns grey day by day. The landscape of the city is now an index. There is no denying that crumbling walls are eyesore. How can I express my attachment to the city through the people who live it? The milk van still drums in the early morning. The first tram takes you to the river bank. The road forks off into two and is still covered with gravel.

Here is a road in the morning fog. Here is a road in noonday glare. Then suddenly the streets are damp, washed and combed under the street lights, the city is clamped by the rain, the rows of mango trees stand tall, with its fruits that hung low. The city grows on me.

And the old railings on the veranda are still there. I can remember the mahogany smile of the girl next door. I forget her name but her song 'The stars in the sky do not respond to my call' haunts me even now. 'do you even know what it has been without you…all these years.' There are ruptures in the ceiling and the mystic alphabets break away in numbers. I have noted everything in my diary.

This narrow lane, this yellow pavement whispers in silence. A patch of dark shadow lies on the window sill, The breeze sways on the green grass in the boulevard. Before the setting

The Body of Memories

sun slips on the horizon, the sound of the hidden whistle floods in.

Some holy pigeons flutter, black cats shrunken and run deep into the rugged interior of the heaped dry soil. The long line of benches invites long footsteps, unexpressed desires. Evening lights put its words into the world of vessels filling with sighs and moans.

The lonely *Gulmohor* tree is now branching in the mist. Lights begin to sprout around it. This alley, this dusty pavement is known to all, Now, everything has changed- even the colour of the grills, the dust and debris. The unexplained smile and the rumpuses resonate in the triangular park.

In its hollows and fullness, in its lows and highs, the memories cruise along. The evening glow reclaims my childhood ever so softly. Those tiny birds are flying now, from one tree top to another in drunken glee. Crows lengthen the vowel, managing to keep the anxiety out of their voices.

A shadow of time waits with my words, lighting up my mind in myriad colours. The voice is hardly above whisper. Speak, say something. Does she talk ever? Can she stand at the dark corner of the room, with dim light filtering through the skylights? Can I borrow the happy times from fruit sellers' handcarts?

I lit a cigarette. I am out of breath. Neon lights glint on the street, catching the beams at will. Cars, bikes and autos speed down. Pedestrians walk up the street. But inside the park the recollections of voice pour in amidst the palpable silence. Why can't my memory fail? Why that song sounds like the sounds of fireworks? Why the notations hide the anguish? A long shadow crosses over those tall buildings and drops my last letter on the doormat.

The cool breeze washes over my face. For all its softness, the blister of moonlight weaves around my shoulder. I know something like this is waiting to happen- more or less expected. The fugitive winds tell it's not you. The brick-coloured building shines in time-lapse survey. Do you really have any address? Do you cry in higher notes? Come night, the city membrane grows thick and an assembly of stars toss sermons with dust follicles for an entire mass of old barns.

I am waiting here to memorise the song 'The stars in the sky do not respond to my call'. There is the light, the unhurried air. Let us not row over the twilight, its colour of love never completely leaves the bone. The breeze now brings the smell of the narrow corridor, the wooden floor, the long curtains. All those high octave notes thin to your lips breaking into a chip poem. There must be some stories behind the stillness to know if you still exist. The stills are never still, the song is never song. Let go the passing clouds.

I know that in all of these places where the colour blooms and a part of me stands there still, till a few drops of rain wet the soil and I cup my hands, follow it out, as I do always break into a song, 'The stars in the sky do not respond to my call'.

Bio:
Gopal Lahiri is a Kolkata- based bilingual poet, critic, editor and translator with 22 books published mostly (14) in English and a few (8) in Bengali, including four jointly edited books. His poetry is also published across various anthologies as well as in journals of India and abroad. He has been invited in various poetry festivals. He is published in 12 countries and his poems are translated in 12 languages. He is the recipient of the Poet of the Year Award in **Destiny Poets**, UK, 2016, *Setu* Excellence Award, 2020, Pittsburgh, US and **Indology** Life-Time Achievement award, West Bengal, India.

The Body of Memories

Didima

Indrani Talukdar

Didima is what I and my siblings called her. While they seemed to adore her, I did not entertain any illusions of doing so. Visits to Allahabad, my mother's natal home, were never anticipated with pleasure. The reason was simple: I hated being picked on, especially in the presence of my cousins and siblings. Yet, apart from nursing resentment, there was little I could do. Being the eldest girl child (my maternal aunt's daughter's being less than six months my junior didn't count) of my generation cast me as the repository of censure. Where other children in the house were allowed to make merry to their hearts' content, I would be called away to lay the dining table or roll out the dough for chapatis. The rebukes, delivered with a sharp edge, only served to fuel anger. White, impotent anger against which I found myself helpless.

The feeling of helplessness revisited me to hold me in its grip on being packed off to Allahabad for my Masters.

'Why couldn't I live in the university hostel?' I protested to my parents. They shook their heads in cold abnegation, stonewalling me and my protests. A free-spirited eldest offspring needed to be tamed by the family's formidable matriarch prior to entering the marital trap.

There, I knew it! Being deported to my grandmother's was nothing short of a conspiracy. A conspiracy preparatory to setting me up for the marriage market. Talk about a calf being readied for slaughter. My Masters (in Psychology) was simply a pretext.

And I wasn't wrong, for prospective grooms were systematically lined up and scrutinized. Rejecting the chinless wonders was going to prove an uphill task; I acknowledged this irrefutable fact with a plummeting heart. Needless to add, as time went on, my fears were proved right.

Being paraded in a saree (not of my choice) while prospective in-laws filed past in an interrogative mode became a matter of routine. My unacceptability did not seem to matter.

My reaction was simple: Why oh, why had I chosen Psychology for my Masters? Had I dug deeper before broaching the subject to my parents, I would have known that Allahabad University was renowned for its English and Psychology departments.

An MA option in my hometown, Dehradun, was ruled out, owing to circumstances. So the fat was in the fire and ready to burn. My astrological chart pointed to an exile. And Allahabad, more specifically my grandmother's house, felt like an exile in every sense of the word. Partying with friends and dancing away the New Year became a distant memory. As did trips to Mussoorie and Kempty Falls, treks up to the Rispana River, and soaking up the raging monsoons of Dehradun. The familiar was getting relegated to the unfamiliar, and vice versa. Plus, there was a culture shock element to deal with. Allahabad, known for its poets and litterateurs, was also more conservative in its attitude towards women. Eve teasing being more severe in east UP, it did not take long for my jeans and skirts to get mothballed.

Inside the classroom, my brogue Hindi became a butt of jokes as I tried to clone the slanted *purabiya* accent of my classmates and new-found friends in a bid to fit in. Returning 'home' to a despotic environment provided scant relief.
Yet relief came, from rather unexpected quarters.

It all began with crooning Sa-Re-Ga on my tanpura one early morning. I had forgotten that it was time to serve the early morning tea. Phoolkali, my grandmother's maitre d', who came to remind me, was gently chided by Didima "not to disturb didi *ji*." I heard her saying, "Let her sing, we'll manage the tea."

It was what I called my 'aha!' moment. Music proved to be my tunnel of escape. It meant a holiday from housework (the marriage market forgotten temporarily) and... bullying. Singing bhajans or ghazals was strictly banned; it had to be pristine Hindustani classical music or nothing.

A percussionist was hired on a monthly basis, all thanks to Didima who made no secret of her disapproval towards women who wanted to join the workforce. More encouragement came my way as I perfected my notes.

My grandmother's house was an enormous quadrate fenced by lawns and guava orchards with the servants' quarters lining the backyard. Phoolkali's son, Chote, would guffaw loudly hearing 'didi *ji*' going through the motions of Sa-Re-Ga-Ma at the crack of dawn. Obviously, I didn't inform him about the significance of the Bhairav family of ragas at that auspicious hour.

Beginning with Raga *Ahir Bhairav* in the morning and ending with *Bhairavi* in the night became second nature to me as Phoolkali single-handedly continued to roll out the chapatis in my grandmother's sprawling kitchen with no help from me. How many Indian families allow their marriageable wards to indulge in musical *riyaaz* in lieu of housework? It was not until much later that I came to appreciate the sentiment.

The Hindustani pantheon of melodies corresponds to time cycles and seasons. I learned about forty-four types of *Malhar*-based ragas (melodies) sung exclusively during the monsoons. Also that the formidable *Megh Malhar* symbolized the peak of the monsoons, and that Lord

Ganesha, the obstacle-expunging deity of the Hindus, favoured *Raga Hamsadhwani*, a Carnatic import.

Didima ruled the roost in her Allahabad citadel till she grew too old and weak. The beautiful villa in which my mother had grown up with her siblings was sold to a builder who tore it down, along with the orchards, and built a mall. The gates, I am told, are still standing. I have not seen it so far. I don't know if I shall.

Once, on meeting Didima at my eldest uncle's house in Gurugram where she lived till her death nine years ago, she told me how much she missed my marathon singing sessions. I did not mention that the sessions were inspired by compulsion, not so much by impulsion.

Today, I look back upon my time in Allahabad as one that was imbued with music. Today I know that aspiring for a musical career, be it playback singing or teaching, would have invoked my grandmother's blessings.

Today, I wish I had...

Bio:
Indrani Talukar has a Masters' degree in Communications' Studies from RMIT University in Melbourne (Australia). Currently employed as Senior Editor at the Institute of Rural Management Anand (IRMA), she has worked as a journalist in India and Australia. She won First Prize at the Greater Dandenong Short Story Writing Competition in Australia as well as a Rotary Exchange Fellowship to Argentina besides penning three novels, a novelette, and a book of short stories for children, one of which was selected for publication by the Rajasthan State Board. Her poem - THE RIOT – was ranked Number 1 Star Finalist in the Voices.Net International Poetry Contest in 2012 and her short story "The dowry" figured in the long list of the 2019 OWT Short Fiction Prize. Her debut novel, WHEN THE LAMPS WERE

LIT (2008) appeared as an e-book serialized by www.indianwoman.com, based in San Jose, California. Her second novel – THE SOUND OF SECRECY – was published in print by LiFi Publishers (New Delhi) in 2016, while her third novel, THE COLOUR OF POPLARS, was published by Spring Books (New Delhi) in 2019.

A Sojourn to Remember

Ipsita Ganguly

The mountains glistened golden in the sunlight. The snow-capped Himalayas looked ethereal from the plane as we flew parallel to the Kumaun and Karakoram ranges crossing the country from East to West.

I was off to the ancient land referred to as Trigarta of the Katoch kings in the Mahabharata, the seat of Indus Valley civilisation, Vedic civilisation, the battlefield of Alexander and Porus, the heart of Sikhism, and one of the major hotbeds of Indian nationalism, the land of valour and the only other state, other than Bengal, to have been brutally divided and its people cut into two in our War of Independence!

Punjab~ The land of Punj (five) Ab (waters)

The flight lands in Chandigarh, the Union Territory that serves as a capital for both Punjab and Haryana.
One of richest, cleanest, and most planned cities in contemporary India, my first impression of Chandigarh will always be marked by the feeling that I was gulping in fresh air! The air felt healthy here. And so did the green look of the city. Le Corbusier, the French Swiss architect who designed the city and its Capitol Complex with the High Court, the State Legislative Assembly and the beautiful Hand Monument had taken inspiration from the ancient indigenous and the contemporary and designed a masterpiece.

Elements like the ramps in the high court and the Shadow monument take inspiration from ancient forts or the play of light and shadow of Jantar Mantar. And yet the look is postmodern and breathtaking. The Hand Monument, a symbol of the city upheld the spirit to give and receive and the hand moves to the direction of the wind. The most spectacular part of the Capitol Complex undoubtedly was the giant enamelled door, made out of many panels, each panel telling a story, be it of religious unity or the length of the shadows in different seasons.

Another brilliant mascot to the city is the creation of the Nek Chand sculptures found in various parts of the city. Nek Chand ji was a road inspector for Public Works Department in the 1950s. He collected waste material from demolition sites all over the city as Chandigarh was being redesigned and rebuilt by Le Corbusier, and used his artistic sensibilities to convert waste into art. Acres and acres of land was converted to a village with sculptures of humans and animal and wells and springs and rocky pathways. This was his imagined kingdom of Sukhrani near the Sukhna lake, spread over 18 acres, today known as the famous Rock Garden of Chandigarh.

Post Coffee and Sunset at the Sukhna lake, I was embraced in the warmth of friendship and poetry and whisked off for a delightful Italian meal by friends of friends who I was meeting for the first time, although it felt like I had known them forever. Pancham and Nosheen's sweetness was my welcome into Punjab.

Chandigarh is also home to beloved Lily di and Colonel Swarn. And an opportunity to convert a virtual friendship into reality. So here I was, ensconced in the friendliest elderly sisterly affection, wrapped in *churni's* of love, exchanging our books, just before setting out on a humongous lunch of Dal Roti Butter chicken in the famous Pal Dhaba. We are Indians and our language of love is indeed Food!

Colonel Swarn and Lily *didi* gave me the rare opportunity to visit the absolutely gorgeous Chandi Mandir Cantonment, which is the Western Command headquarters.

Amidst the tanks, choppers, aircrafts and the train that served as the headquarters in the Indo Pak war, a year after our independence, stood out the Sarva Dharma Mandir~ a common place of worship for all religions. Oh, how the civilians all over the world need to understand that religion should unite people and encourage goodness in all. And that should be the only use of religion.

Equally momentous was our visit to Nada Sahab Darbar, before I was lovingly put on the train to Jalandar and set off to visit the heartland of the land of five rivers!

Some memories stay etched forever.
Some random connects happen and linger on
Some things just come your way and live on.
And some strangers remain with you, in your heart.

One such memory, one such connect happened with me on a certain train ride from Chandigarh to Jalandar quite unexpectedly.

Just as I boarded the train and took my seat, I saw a lady seated next to me. There was nothing extraordinary about her and yet she left me with an outstanding impression. Harminder Kaur, my companion on the train to Jalandhar was a stranger who felt like my very own.

There she was, to the apparent eye, the simplest of souls...
And embodying a spirit of steel and gold!
She softly told me with iron resolve, that she has a son in Chandigarh and another in Germany and grandchildren in both places, and hence even though her husband does not like travelling, she does... and how...
She travels alone, all over the world.
That day she was travelling back from Chandigargh to Jalandhar.
But from California to Europe she travels all over, meeting

The Body of Memories

a sister here or a friend there, taking in new places and people.

Harminder ji looked after me like a fond elder sister, absolutely refusing to let me pay for coffee, treating me to chips, telling me all the while that I was a guest of Punjab. She waited with me even after we reached the station, till the time that I met my friends, and only then, did she bid goodbye
Could I have had a warmer welcome to Punjab?
My head bows in respect and love to the spirit that she embodies!
The Spirit of the truly liberated Indian Woman!
Who proudly, happily says she has two grandchildren and both are girls!
The power of simplicity!

Harminder ji, grandmother, world traveller, embodiment of warmth and hospitality, living life as an example, carving out her own identity and upholding her independent spirit even while she remains dutiful to all others.

And so I reached Jalandar and met my dear friends Brigadier Shome Banerjee and his lovely wife Suman.
And was warmly whisked into a military jeep and driven to Kapurthala where Brigadier was based.
This beautiful old town in the Doabi province of Punjab became the epicentre of it all.
The Heart of the Heartland.
A rustic real revelation.
A historic old town founded in the 11th Century by Rana Kapur, from the Royal Bhattis of Jaisalmer in Rajasthan who then later converted to the Ahluwalia Sikhs.
This was a princely state in British India.

It is around this lovely Punjabi town that there are so many holy shrines at a distance of 1 to 2 hours.
And unlike the better-known cities, Kapurthala embraces

you with what it is... the beauty and grace of a living town going about its daily chirpiness... without the frills of extra touristic overtures!

And when this beautiful real living piece of history is graced by the presence of friends, the warmth of their beautiful homeliness, the fragrance of their garden flowers and home-grown vegetables and fruits, a stroll through the maze of gullies of the town (the small gullies of heartland India tells its stories), the place embraces you in manifold ways.

I also had the privilege of savouring cantonment life, first and real time, thanks to Shome.
To stay as a guest in the Officer's Mess of the 68th Armoured Regiment was an experience of a lifetime. Nowhere else is nationalism, dedication and discipline lived every moment than within those who put our national protection before their lives.

I come away thinking...about the responsibilities that we the civilians need to take towards nation building. We are a young nation and we too have a duty. We have a duty to build the value system and culture of Independent India. An inclusive culture of integrity, dedication, service to mankind and truth.
The culture quotients for which India i.e., Bharat has been known for ever.
And if each individual can strive towards that goal of inclusiveness, integrity and dedication, we may make our nation proud!

You cannot be in Punjab and not get in a highway evening. A long drive ...
And then delicious dinner at a Highway Dhaba!
Albeit a Five Star Dhaba called Haveli near Jalandhar!

But it's what you encounter en route...
Like the almost full moon
And the well-meaning young *Sardarji* who took it upon
himself to teach us how to defog the car
More than once, he made us draw up the car to the side and
taught us the methodology.
Just like that
Just out of goodwill
Made us believe that goodness exists
Right here
Amidst us
On the highroads
In a Sardar heart.

The moon shone brighter than the LED lights
The oil glowed on the *baturas*.
Life was bright and beautiful and rustic and fancy
A paradoxical reality
Almost a mirage ... on that Highway

Punjab celebrates valour and national pride.
Something that I would like to see everywhere and in
abundance.
People known for bravery.
And bravery for the right cause is beautiful.
So there is a celebration of national pride everyday at the
Retreat Ceremony at Wagah Border.
Grandmothers, granddaughters, people in wheelchairs, and
even foreigners celebrate our nation, India.
It's a fervour and its joyous.
And then there is the War Memorial Museum, a must visit
to absorb the history of the nation and its wars as one
passes on from gallery to gallery and ends it with a 7 D
Animated movie on War History.
Jalianwala Bagh is a very important sacred ground,
sharing the legacy of Indian Nationalism and our fight for
Independence. A visit to pay tribute to those who gave their
lives for our today is but a duty for us. Although I do wish

that both the War Memorial as well as Jalianwala Bagh were better maintained with Son et Lumeire shows and a place where we could keep flowers for our martyrs as well as souvenir shops selling books and memorabilia about our wars and martyrs.

Last but certainly not the least, a visit to Amritsar has to be relished with its delectable *chana kulcha* and deliciously creamy lassi.

But then of course, came the most defining part of my sojourn and made it unforgettable.

The sight of Harmandir Sahib or Golden Temple as it widely known takes your breath away.
Golden light emanates everywhere, and it is easily one of the best sights in India. The Golden Temple is serene as it is beautiful. It is bright and it is calm.
It is busy and it is at peace. The spirit of *Seva* is writ large. It is not just the beauty of the structure; it is actually the beauty of the spirit at Harmandir Sahib.

Amritsar
From the wholesomeness of the Langar served to one and all, to whosoever seeks it, irrespective of caste, creed, religion, to the chants of
"Jo Bole So Nihal
Sat Shri Akal"
which means that he, one who says (the above) will be filled with divine joy
That God (*Akal~* The one above and beyond time) is (the real) Truth!

"Waheguru ji di Khalsa
Waheguru ji di Fateh"
which loosely translates to the people of God (Those who follows Godliness = Khalsa)
The Victory of God

The Body of Memories

~ If the people follow Godliness
Then they will be victorious
And that will be the victory of Godliness!

'Nar i Narayan', says Sri Ramkrishna, which means
Narayan i.e. God resides in Mankind.
'Satyam Shivam Sunderam' and 'Satyameva Jayate' says
the ancient Hindu scriptures.
What is true is Shiva i.e. God and is beautiful and sustains.
May Truth i.e. God always be victorious.

The tenet of Service to the Godliness in Mankind
And the victory of Truth i.e. Godliness is upheld by all
religions, be it Hinduism, Sikhism, Buddhism, Jainism,
Brahmo Samaj, Zoroastrianism, Judaism, Christianity or
Islam.

There can be no greater teaching irrespective of which
religion we follow.
Whether we call our God ~Ishwar or Allah or God or
Waheguru!
Aum, Ik Aumkar, Amen or Ameen are different ways of
calling upon the same Spiritual Oneness.
Do your job with sincerity to God, whatever be the path
you chose to follow at the end, you go back to the same
elements and become one with the same spiritual oneness.
Hence use Religion for good work, and that is the true use
of Religion.

If each one of us can do this
If each one of us can realise that Religion is just a path to
reach a common destination of spiritual oneness
Then truly we will have Godliness in the world.
Serve not only through donations, serve with your being.
For God resides everywhere
In every element
In every Church, Mosque, Gurdwara and Temple
And God resides also within each man.

As I flew back from Amritsar, this spirit of Harmander Sahab resounded, just as the warmth of strangers like Harminder ji and other friends lingered into today.

Bio:
Former Hotelier, Business Consultant, Author, Travel Writer, Heritage Enthusiast, Poet...Ipsita Ganguli has worn, and continues to wear many hats...but above all, she has, and will always be a student of the myriad experiences that life holds out. Ipsita writes...because she "must".

Her poems have been published in several national and international e zines and anthologies. She is also one of the main characters of the poetry film 'Kolkata Cocktail'. Her solo compilation of poems 'Of Love, Longing and Random Pondering' is available on Amazon.in and in select stores all over the city.

West Side Story and Lao Tzu

Joyce Yarrow

My older brother Rick and I grew up in the Southeast Bronx. Our most vulnerable years were spent ducking and dodging violent encounters with the two street gangs – the *Fordham Baldies* and the *Scorpions* – who warred over control of our neighborhood. On my first day in elementary school my classmates told me not to wear certain colors on certain days if I didn't want to risk having my head shaved. Of course I believed this, since the *Baldies* and *Scorpions* had total control of Roosevelt, the high school Rick attended. He'd be in the middle of math class when a greaser with slicked-back hair wearing a black leather jacket would burst into the room and call out his buddies to go rumble in the park. An hour later they'd come back, some of them dripping blood in the stairwells. Nothing the teachers could do about it.

Years later I had a good laugh when I saw the romanticized version of our chaotic existence so neatly portrayed in the musical *West Side Story*. Don't get me wrong. I loved the costumes and the song-and- dance. Carol Lawrence (Maria) singing *There's A Place for Us* may have been my first clue to the existence of another world beyond the empty lots and elevated train tracks that defined my universe. A world where people sang away their troubles and their friends laid on a harmony or two. It's just that they got it so wrong.

Take, for example, the obligatory street fight. Unlike Maria, I was not exempt. If you've ever been singled out for bullying by the kid with the toughest rep in your class who brands you as a "stuck up snob" because your Bronx accent isn't thick enough, then you won't be surprised that my first reaction was to stay home and fake illness. After a few days, my Mom forced me to go to school, unaware of what that meant for her secretive daughter, who crept like a frightened hamster along the backways to and from school. My classmates soon got sick of waiting for the showdown and threw Sandie and me into the center of an expectant circle they formed on the sidewalk. Sandie (who eventually became the protagonist of my novel *Sandstorm*) threw the first punch. She never got in a second. A rage like I'd never known before propelled me forward to grab her, push her down to the ground, and roll her off the curb so that half her body ended up beneath a parked car. Damned if I can remember the model. What I do recall is how terrible I felt. This was not a victory—it was a surrender to everything my mom had taught me to detest. "Use your mind and outwit them. Only stupid people fight," she liked to say.

[Childhood photo of the author]

Ironically, Sandie and I became best friends after our knock-down, drag-out fight. But I'd earned her respect at a cost unwillingly paid. Like Billy Goat Gruff number three being forced to be the one who fights the troll.

Did this shape my view of the world into adulthood? *What am I most afraid of today and is it coming after me in search of a fight?* I exclude disease and the loss of close friends and family members, since that's a given. I'm talking about the inner monster of fear we carry within us, whether we admit it or not. The kind of fear that was planted inside you without your knowledge and can destroy you at any moment if it chooses to do so.

My biggest fear was unthinkingly gifted to me by my parents, who were blinded by their obsession with practicing "total honesty" with their offspring. I'm sure they were entirely ignorant of their crime. I was seven years old when they told me that there was no God, that death meant total annihilation, and life was a random experience with no meaning. Period. No room for argument.

For nights I dreamed I was being buried alive and came awake screaming as the dirt pellets rained down into the grave to hit my face. From that point on, I refused to attend funerals and when a friend of my mom's I'd felt close to died, I slipped into a depression that seemed totally incurable. Until I met my first boyfriend at the age of thirteen.

Tommy was three years older than me and I'm lucky he didn't turn me onto drugs instead of introducing me to the taste of well-aged Scotch and the classic poetry books he "liberated" by not stopping at the cash registers of the numerous bookstores we frequented. Tommy only stole the best—Brendan Behan, Dylan Thomas, and other Irish geniuses he loved. He had me reading Shelley and Rimbaud at the perfect young age for their beauty-soaked words to turn my head. I even set William Blake's *Infant Sorrow* to music when I got my first guitar. I was well on my way to leaving behind all things Bronx, in particular teased hair, people who believed bomb shelters could save you from radiation, and anyone who read Nancy Drew. I wore my hair long and straight. I later learned the other kids in junior high school were a little afraid of me.

At sixteen I moved to Manhattan to live with another, older boyfriend and started writing poetry inspired by bus rides through the Lower East Side. My work was playful-yet-serious, influenced by my first formal writing teacher,

Kenneth Koch, who urged his students at the New School to experiment. Koch's only rule was "no dead bird or lost love poems." Good advice. Although looking back, I wonder if he reinforced my existing skill at marshalling words to keep my true feelings at bay.

I continued to devour books, among them works by Jean Paul Sartre and Celine, and other existentialist writers that I imagined, like me, had their first glimpse of life's meaning stolen away at an early age.

Enter Lao Tzu, a sage who legend has it disliked word and was forced by some border guards to write down his wisdom before they let him disappear into the wilderness for the last time. I would never have made Lao Tzu's acquaintance if not for the fact that music has a way of transcending words too.

I had just turned twenty and was toting my guitar and little else around the city, crashing at friends' houses, when I was taken in by a group of young musical geniuses who shared an apartment on the Upper West Side. There was an opera singer, a philosopher, a playwright, and a piano player with whom I began to write songs. I was thrilled when a few of our compositions were recorded by some better known singers.

It was the pianist who gave me his very own battered copy of the *Tao Te Ching* (Book of the Way). He will remain anonymous but he knows who he is. I read a little bit every day and slowly but surely the pervasive metaphor in the book, gratitude for the selfless water that benefits everyone with no thought for itself, came alive in my life.

The Body of Memories

[Joyce the singer]

How I left behind the frenetic pace of New York City and moved to a log cabin on a hilltop in West Virginia is a story in itself. For a year I practiced letting nature Herself become my teacher. It was like discovering a different person within me, one less distracted by externals and capable of embracing solitude without feeling lonely.

Upon my return to the big city, I found I had changed and New York of course had not. The world seemed oblivious to this twenty-something whose song lyrics were as ethereal as her voice. My poems, however, were written from a more surrealistic perspective that attempted to capture the intensity of the times. One such effort was published in *Ghost Dance*. It took me a few years to appreciate that my three poems were printed alongside the work of the then obscure poet, Charles Bukowski. Here is one of them:

THE HISTORY HOUSE IS ROCKING
-I-

the world's 5 greatest
composers were beating their
clean fingernails in grammatical
order at the young musician
who plays the triangle and
comes from one of Pirandello's
sulfur permeated towns
and the blue haired singer who
waits for him after every performance

and as the rhythm of the orchestra
moves towards the wallpaper
on his grandfather's porch,
the small grey house where
the blue haired singer
practices is being slowly
filled with a new beat

and one morning they decide
we must buy some music for
our bed and that morning
the admirals all put on their
sunglasses and that evening
the light iron sound of the
triangle could suddenly be felt
though never again was it heard.

-II-
they met a sprawling nude who
hurriedly dressed in the clothes
of the new
abstract sound of
electrical churchbells
and joined the unconscious
political history of each

new hardheaded dance
much later these three were to encounter
audiences of screaming physicians
pursuing them with a noise to
make bartenders cry.

-III-
right now historians in lavender
shirts are exploring
the geography of soul

music seeps from the top drawers
of bureaus encasing the toilet
articles of a million
potentially unemployed parachutists.

You may be wondering what all this has to do with Lao Tzu. I'm not sure myself. Perhaps there's a hint in the sage's words, "Not knowing is true knowledge." Although my parents' atheism was a dogma that they practiced religiously, they did give me space to decide for myself whether life serves a higher purpose or not. There are many days when I'm on the fence about this. Today is not one of them. The birds outside my window are busy building nests or modifying the ones from last year. They have faith in the seasons and their reason for being. Why shouldn't I?

Bio:
As a child, Joyce Yarrow often fell asleep to Afro Cuban rhythms drummed on the mailboxes of her Bronx neighborhood. At seventeen, riding the bus through Manhattan's Lower East Side, she jotted down poems soon to be published by a literary magazine in Brooklyn. Joyce continued to write, while exploring new places and other ways of life, including a formative year on a farm in West Virginia and signing with the world music ensemble, Abrace. Yarrow set her Jo Epstein mystery series in New York City, Russia and the Caribbean and co-authored the

novel 'Rivers Run Back' with Indian journalist Arindam Roy. Her latest book 'Zahara And The Lost Books of Light' was inspired by a sixteenth century Ladino song and is also a tribute to Ray Bradbury's Fahrenheit 451.

Stolen Threads, Stolen Memories

Jharna Choudhury

My sentences are malleable, like my feeling about home; brittle, changing, quick love. It needs stronger words of tenderness uttered by dear ones, like firm bamboo sticks tied to creeping plants. Whenever *ma* brings me a cup of tea with words like *"thanda hoi jabo, khai lua"* (drink it before it gets cold), I feel steady enough to hold on to the beauties life has to offer me. My mother leaves the room, and I am still sitting by the window light, in an Édouard Vuillard setting, with my yarns, crochet needles, pin holders, jars of spools, embroideries and two imagined companions, who smile at me once in a while. It has almost been a year since I saw his faded and blurred paintings in MOMA, which left me hanging in thoughts. I brought Vuillard home because there is this homeliness about threads, not pure domesticity, but warmth, desire, and a possibility to imagine unique narratives through the act of embroidery. There is an unorganized mess around me, on my table lies a glass jar, painted black, and my eyes turn to it when I take breaks from my satin and chain, as if that small closed container matters, matters so much to me!

Some winter nights, I would open the jar and spill its content on my bed, light my fairy lights and enjoy counting nostalgias, in the shape of broken buttons, hairpins, and mostly threads, shiny, rugged, torn, beautiful. I have collected them over the years and I feel good about it, because every single piece means a person to me. When I touch the loose threads of my mother's *nakshi kantha* saree, or the white button, now turned yellow, from my father's sleeve, my aunt's old *mekhela* fragment, *muga* silk yarns, my niece's first bandana, beads from my grandmother's broken necklace, I feel at home, and this is a home that I have stolen for myself to cherish.

My home in a jar also contains articles belonging to strangers I have met for conversations or crossed paths with. Some are parting threads, some are first meet, first coffee, first walk, long drive threads. I have rolled the constantly unfurling, winding, pieces from woolen sweaters or cotton scarves, in my fingers, like tiny whirlpools in a lake and hidden them in my room. My brother does the same thing with stones of varied textures; some of my friends press flowers inside their books, petunia, marigold, rose. I steal threads, to weave my personal history of little things, like an explanation of how I reached here or why I want to rescue memories from exhaustion. Sometimes, I am one crimson sunbird stealing sweetness from beautiful people's sumptuous springs. Often, I make a ball out of these threads, imitating *ma*'s *ladoo* making hand movements; and what I am left with feels like a handful of "knowing and loving".

I also pick and choose, flaming reds glued on a canvas, patterned into *gulmohar* petals; black and grey threads for body hair, yellowing sun on the horizon beside turquoise-blue water, shades of earth spread out on a school project art paper, and everywhere, every time, my thread colours are available. I am always occupied with my scissors, fixing and mending. I am a dressmaker to my niece, measuring her tiny waist, dressing up her dolls, giving them noses and eyes and whatnot; and when *ma* quietly keeps the kitchen towels next to my sewing machine, I receive her unsaid message with a smile; mend, love, mend, love, decorate, sew and make it look pretty. In return, she would give me shredded threads, honest threads, from old curtains, table runners and more.

By my window, the two Vuillard girls are still weaving secret passages through the thinness of my threads. I ask, "Why have you coiled up the shreds like small moons on my work table?" They look drowsy to me. "Don't you sleep at night?" They are quiet! Their tongues are soft sculptures, and I am suspicious that they are littered shadows of my mind.

The Body of Memories

"Did you say something?", *ma* stops in the doorway every time.

"No, not a word!", I reply.

Ma picks my recently finished embroidery piece, "three women" she says, and widen her eyes to configure that this is my room, this is my window, my bookshelf, and here, one two three women. "Is that you?" *ma* asks.

"Yes, you can distinguish me from my mole!"

"And this woman in a saree? This younger-looking girl? I love the embroidery piece! Their faces are so real. I can almost hear them breathe."

"I always have company, *ma*. I am never lonely when I work with my threads. I feel…"

"Happy", she adds.

"Yes".

But I meant "I feel that I not sick anymore; the people I see are not trying to make me bandage myself to the walls, unlike when I was eight years old. These are kind people. They just move around my room, help me decide my fabric type, the shape of my tulips. They do not strangle me. They are muses, embellishing spiral leaves. Their eyelids are heavy from threadwork."

"You can make a tapestry someday", *Ma*'s eyes gleam.

"I will", I nod, "It will be a fiction swaddled in the privacy of my room".

She understands. She always understands that fictions are real things.

I get back to my hand-embroidery, this time I am making an oriole. I open my special jar of threads, when nostalgia breaks in. I remember how my aunt held my hand and helped me tie my first knot. "There you go, now make a box...straight running stitch", she said. Now when I turn back, I see how well I have manoeuvred my way out of that box. My embroidery is more than maiden flowers; it is my diary of mildew, shapeshifters, resistance, upheavals in the porticoes of my imagination. However, in this complex world of round trees and multi-headed faces, my home is a simple cup of lemon tea.

I often think to myself, this, what I love doing, is it safekeeping, homekeeping or memory-keeping? This motivated assemblage of threads is so difficult to categorize into a hobby. It is a mere abridged version, when people tell me, "I love your hobby and what you create, are they called embroideries, those little designs that you make?"

I then desperately want to answer, "No, these are my concepts of home! These are stolen moments, recreated by stolen threads and I love it; I love to take my threads out for a picnic, take them out for dinners. These are also my days of gigantic fears and hours of mourning. Inside closed doors, there is always a party of dead and living people who are connected through the colours of my silk and cotton. Come, see, tonight at 11.30 pm?"

Bio:
Jharna Choudhury, 27, from Assam, India, is an embroidery artist, aspiring poet, PhD student working on grotesque bodies. Her creative writings have been published in *The Assam Tribune, The Sentinel, Muse India*, also forthcoming in *The Little Journal of Northeast India* and the anthology *Unsent Letters- From the South Asian Diaspora*. Previously covered by *Shawatales*, Ladakh, in a talk series 'Hand-Embroidery & Storytelling', she insists on making narratives via threads.

Can I call you Ibi?

Kamalini Natesan

Ibiso was a Dutch American, who I met at an exhibition, which had a book reading by Marshall King, in the neighbouring hall. Nothing works like laughter, and we were introduced in a moment of humour by a common friend who had invited us both. When you laugh together, you bond. It was something the writer had said, that we'd all found equally funny. Apparently, he had read something about himself, that humored him greatly, as it did us.

She said she was an old dame who had had her day, but I saw her as a sixty-year-old youth, and she saw me as an old soul. We connected over the meaning of art, and what reading books meant to us. Dressed in a black skirt and a lemon-yellow tee, with a pretty scarf around her throat, I thought she looked the part of sculptor par excellence. I was in a regular tee and a pair of faded jeans, the quintessential tourist. We went on to become buddies, swapping anecdotes about what we considered a slightly off-the-trail life. Hurdles we learnt to cross every time we stood at the edge of one, was the other thing. I was at the threshold of a new career as a writer, and she, a forever-sculptor; we struck gold.

This unlikely friendship was born out of simple compatibility, or because we were at the right place, at the right time- in Madrid, Spain. The excitement in the air was palpable, and there we were, side by side, giggling at the author's innuendos and tongue-in-cheek humour, we both had come to associate with him, through his writings. We were united in our admiration of this 'big, tall guy', who had come 'all the way' from New Zealand.

Later we downed three cups of coffee each, and bonded, Ibiso and I.

Her name made me smile. "So did your parents name you?" I'd asked as soon as we were comfortable.

"No, actually I was named Iris, but as soon as I had the balls, I asked to be called Ibiso. A dog I had loved, bore that name. I wanted to be Ibiso, that's the story," and she giggled, "does it sound odd to your ears?"

"Well, I suppose it's as good a reason as any to name yourself," I had said out loud, and giggled along.

"And you can call me Kay, although I'm certain my parents would disapprove," I said with confident chuckle.

This sealed our friendship that night.

We didn't talk very often, but when we did, we unhooked a can of ideas that fluttered above oceanic waters, dividing our physical worlds.

We both laughed a lot together, during our subsequent conversations over WhatsApp. She was of Dutch origin, but considered herself American, and returned to California. She had two grandkids, whom she adored. Living close to her sons allowed her to babysit the grandkids when moms and dads were away working, fetching them from school, feeding them etc. She spoke in great detail about the lives her sons led, leading theirs surreptitiously, when described thus. The deep affection she bore in her heart, reverberated over the phone line, encasing me in her life. Her own unique life, which she tried to make sense of, every day, was special to my Indianness. Weekends were spent sculpting. I listened and absorbed. Our cultures drew us to each other, rather than drawing us apart.

I was fascinated and quite taken by her sense of independence, at sixty years of age, while I struggled with dependencies of all sorts- my kids, my husband, my friends, my mother, my sibling and her kids. I both wanted out, and in. I learnt that it isn't possible to have it all, and we must choose to live with frayed edges, as long as the garment we wear is made of stern stuff.

The Body of Memories

"Can I call you Ibi?" I asked her a few months later, and I'm not sure why.

She was elated, and I was granted permission right away. I was the only one to do so, ever.

Over the years that followed, we bonded over her grandchildren's antics and their short-lived distresses and joys, and my children's progress as much as my own. Her first husband hadn't been perfect, but they had remained friends. She thought she had learnt enough from one marriage to get remarried. Tragically, her second husband left her with a child, and died early on, from heart disease. She continued to miss him dearly. Her sons were the only relations she invested in then on.

Instead of drowning, Ibi pulled herself out of a situation which could've been far more tragic, and taught herself to sculpt. She engaged her angst and grief and bundled all her energies and gave them meaning, transferring it into her creative endeavours. When I asked her why she chose this particular form of artistry- i.e., sculpting- she told me how she needed to feel the transformation of what she held within- it had to have tangible form. I understood.

I grasped from our exchanges, that coming into one's own is not an end in itself- it's a voyage into ourselves, a scape that transforms all the time. Love was not about giving or taking. Love wasn't about erasing oneself either; it was about melting into many different shapes and then remolding oneself into something one might recognize later as an original.

I also understood the practice of exploiting my various attributes to sharpen mind muscles, and letting go of that which scraped my insides. Novel spaces were allowed to emerge, and form of their own will.

"Kay," she had said one morning, "don't analyze who said what, and why- try the face value system, it truly works."

I learnt from Ibi, that it was possible to acknowledge newfound elations in the smallest of triumphs, use them to fuel us. She was wise, and kind. She made me believe I was wise too. Ibi told me one day, as I heard her smile, that she too learnt from me, that she envied me my, 'spontaneous joie-de-vivre' which she severely lacked.

The transfer and exchange of energy that passed between us, lent my days bounce and energy, whenever we communicated.

Ibi's age, and the difference that lay between hers and mine, was anything but in the way. We met when I was forty, and she, sixty. Our friendship lasted all of ten years. We met, perhaps, only four times, but in the interim, we wrote each other long emails, sprung conversations that went back and forth over an entire week sometimes. They were invigorating and awarded my days with fine reading material. I found reasons to pick her brains, and vice versa, and it was inexhaustible. We laughed, we cried and swapped tales. Her grandchildren were her life. When her son moved away, from her neighborhood to a different state, she was heartbroken. As luck would have it, within a year they moved back because the kids wanted to be 'near gram'.

Her thrill was palpable, even as she tried to conceal her overwhelming mirth. I find it impossible to forget her breathing on the phone- it was hard, and it spelt a universe of love.

I learnt to let go from her- to cope and to fill my days with creative activities. She never let me down. I hope I didn't either. There were a couple of months when I didn't write back, being taken up with my child's move to university. I retired into a sad place. It is she who threw me a thread, which she tugged at, gently, and drew me back out, helping reinstate my natural bounce.

The Body of Memories

Ibi's corny sense of humour, and the ease with which she turned my woes on their head, showing me their lack of worth, was her greatest attribute. She illuminated my qualities, and threw a spanner in all my complaints. She did not, however, minimize the reasons for anxiety, but subtly taught me to flip them, to help me see these as learning opportunities. We ended up agreeing that I was given to exaggeration.

Ibi's sculptures are moving, and I remember prodding, demanding her to reveal sources of inspiration. She muttered, "You know Kay, I'm no award-winner, or a master of her craft, but every time I finish a piece, a sense of fulfilment pervades my being. This is what drives me, this flow I am in, when I sculpt." Flow was a word that stayed with me.

I pondered over my own sense of worthlessness on days, when nothing moved, at least not as I wished for. I was no one without my appendages, my relationships, my family-so I began to redefine and redraw my own sense of worth from her words and her reasons for turning into a sculptor.

Ibi, my friend, left an imprint upon me that is impossible to ascertain. Ours was a friendship that was natural and beautiful. I am grateful for it, and perhaps the difference in our age, made us both equal and unequal. The foundation of a solid friendship like ours, was a lightness of being that we perceived and encouraged in one another.
I miss you Ibiso. I miss you Ibi.

Bio:
Kamalini Natesan, originally from India, currently resides in Bangkok, Thailand. She is a French teacher, blogger and Indian vocalist (Hindustani Classical, Sangeet Visharad); author of debut novel 'Naked Beneath the Midnight Sun' (Olympia Publishers, UK). She has published short stories,

travelogues and poems in online literary magazines: ColdNoon, Oddball, Café Dissensus, Twist & Twain and The Curious Reader, as well as some print media. She has also published an essay in an anthology on differently-abled children: 'Twilight's Children, Chronicles of Uncommon Lives', and three short stories in an anthology with 6 other authors ('A Life in Transit'). She speaks many languages, German, French, Spanish, Bangla, Tamil, Oriya and Hindi.

Author website: https://kamaliniwrites.com

To Fond Memories and New Beginnings...

Kanina Sarkar

The past few weeks have been replete with retrospection. Some looking back, some reminiscing. Even as we raised a toast to new beginnings.

My eldest was transitioning from elementary to middle school. You heard that right. Not graduating from high school and going off to college. Not transitioning from bachelorhood to marriage. Not a major life event to most. Still, to my mommy heart, big enough to indulge every now and then, in a few moments of recapitulating, pondering on fond memories. And because first time milestones of our lives, in whatever sphere, always have a special place in our hearts, my thoughts often went back to that first year of public school. To that one day in particular...

It was the 27th of August, 2014.

The day was special in myriad ways. It was the fifth birthday of my firstborn. It was also his first day of kindergarten, his first foraying into public school. It was also the day when I returned to work after a four-year hiatus.

That morning I clutched the hand of my brand new five-year-old and entered the school cafeteria. We had been told to wait there for the bell to ring and then we would see our respective wards to their classrooms. In fact, we were instructed by the school to follow this self-same routine for the first week, until the children got used to their new surroundings. I was tense and apprehensive as we waited ... my little man putting up a brave front next to me. We rose as the bell rang and I held on to his hand with utmost protectiveness, walking him to the classroom. As we stepped outside the cafeteria, he let go of my hand. I looked at him quizzically, but he said nothing as he kept walking next to me. I tried to hold on to his little hand in an effort to offer him some reassurance and support. It was a big day, after all, a day that would carve out a path to future learning and development, and would be, in many ways, the basic foundation for growth. But he was firm in his determination to avoid my hand, even as he looked up and smiled. My little boy was trying so hard to fit in ... almost as if drawing from some secret source of knowledge, which told that he would be on his own from then on. And my heart broke into a million little pieces that day, sensing his brave display of courage, and his newfound sense of freedom. I realized that day that he had already initiated the process of letting go, unbeknownst to himself.

It was a long day and seemed to drag on with little sense of purpose or fulfillment. I felt lost and at odds with myself with a vague feeling of restlessness. I had invested so much of my time and energy into this little being that has been the center of my equilibrium thus far ... and all of a sudden I was losing my balance as I groped desperately for some semblance of support and familiarity. Life would change manifold and this would be a good change, I told myself firmly. Even then, I couldn't wait to pick him up from school that day and give him a big, giant hug. I had a little birthday celebration planned in my mind, before I would have to leave him with his dad to begin the first day at my new evening job as an adjunct faculty at a local community college. It has been a well thought out decision to be a stay-at-home mother to our first-born and in ways more than one, the experience had enriched both our lives. We had had a beautiful 'routine' thus far, as we visited parks, went grocery shopping and did most things together. That routine of five long years was about to be broken as we embarked on new adventures, to teach ... to be taught .... in a more formal setting. It was with some nervousness that I had decided that I would pick him up from school during that first week, before he could start traveling on the school bus. The doorbell rang just as I was about to walk out to my car. An

The Body of Memories

older elementary kid from our neighborhood stood outside the door.

"Did you not know you have to be at the bus stop to pick up Rijoy?" he demanded.

"I was just going to drive to school to pick him up."

"But he was on the bus, and the driver wouldn't let him off!" the boy wailed.

I waited with bated breath, just long enough to ask him the bus route and then flew to my car as I prepared to track down the school bus. I followed the route around the next few stops and found the bus, just as it was on its way out of our housing community. I honked like a mad woman, parked the car at a crossing and ran out to the bus, waving frantically all the time.

"My boy is on the bus", I panted as I climbed up the steps. And sure enough, there he was, sitting quietly on a seat near the exit. He looked at me and smiled, and my heart swelled with happiness and pride. Apparently, he was none the worse for his little adventure! I grabbed his hand, helped him down from the bus and into the waiting car, parked at an awkward angle. As soon as we got home, I gave him a big hug and asked him if he was okay. As I set about preparing a snack for him, I explained how there had been a misunderstanding and I would be there to pick him up from school the next day and for the entire week, until he was more comfortable with his surroundings.

"But I want to go on the bus. I love it! I'm not scared,' he said indignantly. And just like that, my little boy, the youngest in his class, grew up a few inches, not in size, but in his maturity and thoughtfulness on the first day of public school.

He's had a great innings at school these past six years, made good friends and has had some wonderful teachers, and I couldn't be more thankful for that.

"Who is your favorite teacher?" I would ask him at the beginning of every grade. "My teacher now", he always replied, referring to his then class teacher. But how is that possible? I wondered. "I can't help it if I like my present teacher even more than my last one", he would say with remarkable alacrity, far beyond his tender age.

It had been a great six years for him, and for it to come to an end, without saying his goodbyes did not feel right. The kids transitioning to middle school and high school had missed the last few months of spending time around their beloved friends and teachers, not to mention the hallways and classrooms of their known territory. Any change is stressful, especially at that tender age, but to leave the first establishment of familiarity, apart from their homes, must feel bewildering and strange. It was not totally without a sense of sadness, then, that we prepared to drive him to the farewell parade for the fifth graders arranged by the school.

A new 'normal' which he had resigned himself to, courtesy the virus. Yes, he did miss his last walk down the school hallways as a fifth grader in his elementary school, and needless to say, the yearbook signing too. What he gained was an army of teachers and school staff cheering for him and the others as we drove around the school parking lot. The fire truck put their sirens on and the school mascot danced about merrily as the teachers waved their last goodbyes. Oh, what a show!

When I asked him how he felt, that evening, he said he was sad not to have seen the inside of his beloved school one last time, but he was excited for what the future would unfold. There was my son, sounding all grown up and ready to face the world head-on, a little beyond his years.

And I'm glad you got that right, my boy. For, the essence of life is to move forward and not to dwell in the past, but to linger long enough to smile at those cherished memories. We are excited for you too, and can't wait to see what lovely surprises life has in store for you. We will watch out and cheer, sometimes from afar, but never too far to reach out. And we will hold these memories close, to remember and to cherish, forever.

Bio:

Kanina Sarkar was born and raised in Kolkata and that will always be the city after her heart. She completed her BA and MA in English literature from Calcutta University and also holds a diploma in Public Relations from Jadavpur University. At present she resides in Dallas, TX with her husband and two boys. She has a full-time job in finance, but loves to write whenever she gets a chance. She also loves jewelry making, container gardening and reading.

My Parents Used to Say: Lessons Learned Just By Listening to My Parents

Kelli J Gavin

Eat your vegetables so that you will grow big and strong.
Sit up straight or you will be hunched over by the time you are 40.

Make your bed every day. It will make you feel better.
You are never too cool to wear boots and a winter jacket.
Dry your hair before you leave the house, or you will catch your death.

My parents said a lot of things to me growing up. Some useful and some half-truths mixed with myth. Some so comical and far-fetched, I still laugh thinking about them. But some of the things they said were meaningful, heartfelt, and so extremely important.

"You were born in Minnesota and will be raised here. Figure out a way to love it."

As a young child growing up in Forest Lake, Minnesota, my parents were at a loss when it came to raising me. I loved being outdoors in the summertime. I enjoyed harvesting vegetables from the garden, running in the fields, biking on the dirt roads and exploring the woods that surrounded our home. I found humor in stealing as many raspberries as I could fit in my mouth and feeding stray cats because they always seemed to make their way to our home. My sister and I would play for hours in fallen tree forts and with the dog in the backyard. We would build makeshift homes in the woods, gather pretend supplies and enjoy water fights and hide and seek until after dusk.

The Body of Memories

Winter was another story. I hated the cold. I hated the wet. I hated the ice. I hated winter. Go play outside? Why would I ever want to do that? My socks would get wet. I didn't have sufficient snow pants so snow would go up the back of my too thin jacket and I would fall apart. The time it took to warm up in our very rustic basement next to our not up to code fireplace would sometimes take all night. What was the point? Boredom often set in. Apparently, now as an adult I have learned that boredom often leads to naughty behavior. Naughty behavior leads to punishment. Punishment leads to being upset. Being upset leads to parents doubting the punishment in the first place.

After such an incident of punishment, my dad sat me down. My dad has these amazing kind, bright blue eyes. Now, even in his middle seventies, his eyes still shine brightly.

With a deep intake and exhale of more air than was necessary, my dad began carefully. "Kelli. I love you. You are an amazing child. I want to talk to you. Have you noticed that you often get into more trouble in the winter months? I think I know why. In the summer, you are outdoors constantly. Your mom and I have to beg you and Angie to come in each night. It is a different story in the winter. You hate being outside. You say no each time we encourage you to even go out for a half hour. Then you confine yourself to staying indoors all day. Your mom and I feel that you have started to think that your boredom is an excuse to do anything you want without asking. You are touching things that are not yours, making mess, destroying projects in the works, taking food from the root cellar and opening jars just for fun. You know these things are wrong, but you continue to do it."

He paused for a moment and then continued. "Kelli, you were born in Minnesota and you will be raised here. You need to figure out a way to love it." I stared at him. I guess

I wasn't really sure what he meant. "Tomorrow after breakfast we will begin."

What was it that was about to begin? I guess I was still upset about being punished earlier in the day, and I chose to stay silent.

The next day was Saturday. My mom had laid clothes out for me and had pancakes and eggs waiting by the time I woke up. I sat down at the table and watched as my dad sipped his instant coffee. We ate in silence. But then as we both finished eating, my dad asked, "Are you ready for an adventure?"

We suited up in all of our winter gear and my dad even gave me an extra pair of his heavy wool mittens. We exited the house in silence and I followed him as he entered the woods about a block from our house. "Today, we will explore. First, I want you to find three things. A bird. A fallen tree. Animal tracks."

Oh. Okay. I could do this. When I found the cardinal, we spoke in quiet voices about how much Grandma Re loved cardinals. He told me to notice the quick turns of his head, the way he pecked at the air. We discovered many fallen trees that day. Even pondered why the good ones couldn't fall closer to our home so we could make a fort in them. And as we progressed on our walk through the woods, we found animal tracks aplenty. Rabbits, deer, possibly coyote. My dad encouraged me to touch each of the spots where the animals had left their mark. He asked me about school, about what figures I saw in the clouds, about friendships and voice lessons.

My dad told me that my Saturdays would no longer be my own. I would now be in his employ. He told me I would need to get ready for the day, eat and then do any chores my mom requested of me. Then I would be helping him. I was dumbfounded. What did he want me to do? His requests

The Body of Memories

were odd at first. 10 small pines cones, 10 medium pine cones, 10 large pine cones. Something beautiful. Tree barks in three different colors. A sign of spring. For each accomplished task, I was paid 50 cents.

My boredom, my naughty behavior, the punishments ceased. I was given a job. I was on a mission. I was employed. I was earning money. Spring quickly approached; the snow began to melt as the crocuses and daffodils made an appearance. The temperatures got warmer and my excitement for summer reached an all-time high. The last Saturday of the school year was upon us. My dad caught me early that morning. I met him in the garage after chores. I saw a large metal trash bin with the lid on. Every item that I gathered per his request that winter was in there. It then dawned on me. My dad taught me to love my surroundings. Even when it was cold, even when there was ice. Even when my feet got wet and I shivered. He taught me to love the beauty of creation that surrounded me. He taught me that boredom was no longer an option.

That summer, I turned 10, and that winter, my dad only revisited the troubles I had experienced the prior winter. He explained, "This winter, I will not receive any reports from your mother about poor behavior. I taught you this past winter how to keep yourself busy and how to enjoy your surroundings. This winter, you will teach the kids in the neighborhood. Two Saturdays a month, you will create an activity or a scavenger hunt. Locating items, exploring, drawing pictures, timed or untimed. It doesn't matter. It is up to you. But you are now in charge of winter adventures for all the kids off Humber Street."

Clever man my dad was, he disciplined me, guided me, encouraged me, taught me and then pushed me to do the same for other children. For some reason, all the kids in the neighborhood began to behave that winter. They spent more time out of the house. They learned to love Minnesota in the winter and all that it had to offer.

"Always sleep if you are given the chance."

My dad worked the majority of my childhood for 3M Corp, installing and maintaining Corporate Alarm Systems and as a self-employed Home Improvement Contractor. He was very good at both jobs, great with people, knowledgeable and hardworking. He was an asset to 3M and a good businessman once he became self-employed. My dad worked what I thought were strange, long hours. He would leave as I was going to bed, work all night installing alarms and return home as I prepared to leave for school. He would take two Excedrin, eat a large bowl of oatmeal or farina and crash into bed.

He would sometimes still be sleeping when Angie, my sister and I returned home from school. My mom would meet us at the door with her finger pressed against her lips, "Your dad is sleeping, keep quiet. I have a snack for you and Little House on the Prairie will be on in 10 minutes."

Our evenings were filled with lots of whispering. Dinner dishes were saved until dad woke up when cuddles and bedtime stories seemed so exciting. My dad always looked tired. Always. Even after a good 8 hours of sleep. He struggled with the nights and days and back again and just tried to be as present as possible when he was awake.

Angie and I sometimes found we wore out our welcome with our mom. Mom tried her best, but she was trying to do it all. She worked part time, was always home to get us off the bus, and was very involved in helping at my sister's dance studio (so that lessons would be free). She would observe my sister or I moping about.

"Angie, I know you are bored. I got you some cardboard from work today to make more rooms in your basement Barbie Village."

"Kelli, let's play dolls. I made a new scarf and booties for your Cabbage Patch Doll."

Our mom knew our moping was because we missed our dad. He was exciting and funny and silly and enjoyed everything that kids enjoyed. Even though he was there, I missed him.

I struggled with this. One afternoon when Angie and I returned from school, we increased our speed when we saw our dad was awake and waiting on the front porch. Hugs and kisses and animated stories of our day were freely shared.

Dad had us sit down, and when we finally settled and told him everything there was to share, dad broke in. "Oh, daughters of mine, I wanted to talk to you this afternoon. I know that I haven't been home or even awake much lately because of my work schedule. I am working very hard right now so that we can save money for the winter. Work is hard to come by for me in the winter months, and having a cushion is important. To pay for food and gas for the car, the house and clothing. And I know that I don't get the chance to spend much time with you on bike rides and just playing anymore. But something I have discovered is that you should always sleep if you are given the chance. Now that I focus on trying to get a good solid 7-8 hours of sleep each day, I enjoy my job more and I am more productive. I also have more energy when I am not working and can enjoy our time together as a family. So even though I miss you guys all the time and maybe you miss me too, I still want to tell you guys that for the rest of your life, always sleep when you get a chance. Your mind, your body, your family, your employer will be happy you did."

As an adult, my dad's words can still be heard, but also understood. When I worked a split shift at the bank for two years, 5:30 a.m. to 8 p.m., I had three plus hours off in the mid afternoon. I always laid down to rest and often would sleep two hours. When my son was tiny and had been up six to eight times the night before, I would take a nap when he did in the afternoon before leaving for work. Now that my kids are older, I work when they are at school. But on Mondays, I get home 45 minutes early before my son's bus, to ensure that I have time to rest. I wake up when he arrives home, get up and conquer the rest of the day. No, I don't always sleep when I lay down, but I often feel rested, physically and mentally and ready to take on, whatever comes my way. It also makes me wonder why children fight sleep. Why? If you are given the chance to sleep, don't you always feel better when you get up? Never fight sleep. Always give in.

"Just love him. Love him like your life depended on it."

At two months old, my son Zach started to cry. Not really cry, more so just scream 6-8 hours a day. In addition to the screaming, he was up no less than 6 times per night. Projectile vomiting 2-4 times a day and constant diaper changes disabled me from leaving the house even on the best of days. I was exhausted, unhappy, and felt like I was failing as a parent, as a mom. I was trying to make our family "work" on about three to four hours of sleep a night. It wasn't working. Nothing was working. My husband was amazing and did everything he could to help me, but nothing seemed to change with Zach.

I would call upon my mom when things got really bad. I had slept about 12 hours in 4 days and I became a weepy mess. Josh, my husband, called my mom this time and asked if she could come and stay for a few days. To take care of Zach, maybe do some laundry and the dishes and cook a meal or two. But mostly, I know he called her to take care of me.

The Body of Memories

My mom arrived with so many bags, I thought she was moving in. Photo albums, baby books, notebooks, journals. I strongly believed she may have packed everything she owned. She walked in, stashed her belongings in the corner and took Zach right out of my arms. She wanted to know when he last slept, when he was last changed and how much formula to put in his bottle. She explained that she didn't want to see me for at least two to three hours. She would have dinner going by that time. She wanted me to rest. To put earplugs in and rest. She wanted me to take a long hot bath. She wanted me to read a book. She just wanted me to have some time to myself. I thanked her, hugged her and kissed Zach and walked upstairs to my room crying. This was hard. I was tired. Oh so tired. I think I may have fallen asleep as fast as my head hit the pillow. I slept. I slept for three hours straight. I woke up confused, unsure what day it was, and panicked for a minute, not really sure where Zach was.

When I walked down stairs after taking a quick shower, the smell of dinner was so amazing. I was starving. I questioned if I had even eaten that day. I rounded the corner and saw that the entire main floor was clean and there were three baskets of folded laundry in front of the fireplace. The dishes were done and there in my mom's arms was a content, sleeping baby. "He ate, he slept, he peed a lot and he even told me a story. The story of his tired mom who can't do it anymore. He told me to tell you he loves you and to never forget that. He told me to tell you that it will get easier. That these days are hard and long, but you are a great mom and things will get better." Tears rolled down my cheeks. My mom stood and put Zach in the bassinet. I hugged my mom, and thanked her.

My mom had laid out two photo albums on the kitchen counter. She warmed a plate of food for me and encouraged me to take a look. The beauty I found in those pages. Babies. My grandmothers, my mom and my dad, my sister and I, aunts and cousins. So many wonderful stories and memories. The notebook? My mom kept a journal after I was born. Entry after entry I read. *~I am tired. I haven't slept in two days. Was I meant to be a mom? How am I going to be a good mom to these two girls when I can't even seem to take care of myself?~* My mom had all of the same doubts when I was a baby.

She smiled when I met her eyes. "Kelli, you can do this. It is always hard at first. Just love him. Love him like your life depended on it."

I remember these amazing times with my mom from 17+ years ago like they were yesterday. My mom passed away over 7 years ago, and I miss her so very much. Zach, now over six feet tall and 17 years of age, is amazing. Diagnosed with Autism at a young age, I felt even more challenged at being his mom. But what do I do when I feel overwhelmed, unqualified as a parent and discouraged? I just love him. I love him like my life depends on it.

"Life isn't fair. You will not always get what you want. Sometimes, that is a good thing."

I began singing when I was 9 years old. First at church, then in small local and regional competitions. I moved onto state, then joined traveling singing groups and enjoyed all that it entailed. I was known as the vocalist amongst my friends at school. I enjoyed the attention and the accolades. I found my calling in high school with musical theater productions of Because Their Hearts Were Pure, Carnival, and the role as The Mother Abbess in The Sound of Music.

I was not sure what I really wanted to do with my life. I did know that I wanted to sing and see how far that took me. I went to Crown College in St. Bonifacius and was very excited to recreate myself as I began my adult life. Upon arriving at school and after getting settled in the dorms, I was excited about auditions for Chamber Choir and possibly the traveling music group I had always had my eye on. Auditions went quite well, I thought. I was well prepared with three songs and sang all the scales which showed off my powerful soprano voice.

With great disappointment, I wasn't admitted into Chamber Choir, but to Women's Chorale. And I didn't make it into the traveling group either. But wait. I was the accomplished, well trained vocalist. There had to be a mistake. I went back and checked the posting a second time, just in case I had read it wrong. Nope. Women's Chorale. I walked calmly back to my dorm on the first floor and lost it. I couldn't stop crying or catch my breath. I felt sick. How was I going to tell my mom and my friends? I had talked a big game and shared all of my lofty ambitions before I left for school. I got myself in check by dinner and went to grab a quick bite, determined to return to my room and call my mom.

The moment I heard her voice, I wept. I explained what happened. She was quiet for a bit and let me cry. She let me work it out and share my heartbreak. "Kelli, life isn't fair. You will not always get what you want. And sometimes that is a good thing." Why was it that my mom, all 5'4'' of her, could drop these truth bombs all the way from Anoka County to me in Carver County?

"Did you ever think that possibly there was something bigger and better in store for you? That you will learn from this, grow from this and come out more driven and determined in the end? You have been blessed beyond measure in this life. You have always gotten what you have wanted. Now you will learn what it is like for the rest of us." We call those Jo Cook-isms.

And of course, she was right. My mom was always right. I was able to receive an amazing amount of encouragement and training from Dr. Klempay in Women's Chorale and grew immensely as a vocalist under the tutelage of two private voice teachers. I had fantastic opportunities through referrals to sing at huge fundraisers, weddings of epic proportions and corporate sponsored events. I am not sure if I would have even said yes to any of those requests if my time was consumed by Chamber Choir or the other music group. I also had the benefit of learning at 18 that you don't always get what you want, rather than struggling through that truth at 25 or even later. My mom telling me that not getting what I wanted was a good thing, was a foreign concept back then, but is now an everyday truth. When I didn't get that bank job that I really wanted, I found a better one at an insurance agency as a bank consultant. When I didn't get the medical test results that I wanted, I made changes that affected my overall physical wellbeing and I have improved significantly. When I was told to not carry any more children, I became content and discovered that I had a heart full of love for the two kids I was already blessed with. And when I got rejection letter #156 from the Blinder's Journal, I started writing for the local paper. Indeed. That is one of those good things.

These life lessons were not always easy lessons to learn. But they were lessons learned just by listening to my parents.

Bio:
Kelli J Gavin of Carver, Minnesota is a Writer, Editor, Blogger and Professional Organizer. Her work can be found with Clarendon House Publishing, The Ugly Writers, Sweatpants & Coffee, Zombie Pirates Publishing, Setu, PPP Ezine, Sweetycat Press, Passionate Chic, Otherwise Engaged, Flora Fiction, Love What Matters, Printed Words and Southwest Media among others. Kelli's first two books were released in 2019 (I Regret Nothing- A Collection of Poetry and Prose and My Name is Zach- A Teenage Perspective on Autism). She has also co-authored 17 anthology books. Her 3rd and 4th books will be published

in 2020 and 2021. Kelli is currently writing a book of fiction short stories.

Her blog can be found at www.kellijgavin.blogspot.com

From a Daughter to a Father: A Memoir

Lopamudra Banerjee

The concoction of mustard oil and canola oil is a queer one, and it has been through trajectories diverse, unsettling. The concoction scampers through the folds and creases of the chicken being cooked; the way the kitchen spatula works to let the chicken pieces with bones and the big potatoes and chopped onions and minced garlic soften and turn succulent with the killer combination of the oils and the Indian, rather Bengali spices.

A dash of salt twice, a pinch of sugar once, just the way that a father's sharp, indulgent tongue had always relished it. The tongue of a father that became embittered from time to time too, hashing and rehashing those queer indictments and lingering words of admonishment that would be best explained, perhaps, as 'a father's legacy for his daughter', at once unnecessary and inevitable.

"I won't cook, ever in my life!"
"Won't cook? How would you get a husband if you don't?"
"I don't want a husband...I will rather have servants cook for me."
"Servants? Are you sure? You can't get a glass of water for yourself, pampered overtly by your mother! Servants will only tell your husband to drive you out of the house!"
"It's not your house, or your kind of future that will be mine, it's the kind of future I would build myself."
"Build yourself! I see...but with what? With two pennies and your English education?"
"If that's what you think, yes, English education and two pennies it is!"

In a damp, enclosed kitchen, moist with the aroma of sweat and smoke and an assortment of Bengali spices, the mother has cooked her way to her erratic husband's heart, the husband and the daughter colliding from time to time in the house, burning in their differences. In an open kitchen, ten thousand miles away from West Bengal, in the quiet suburbs of a mammoth southwestern city in America, a daughter chops some more onions in a white cutting board placed on a granite countertop, her back facing the cooking range and the ovens where multiple food items are being cooked. For the moment, the skillet cover has to be opened, to add the extra onion slices and a couple of red and green chilies.

A teaspoon of mustard oil bought from the Asian grocery store is added to the concoction, the oil that dances in the body of the brown curry that the father has relished during his first and last trip to the alien land to visit his rebel daughter.

"*Chamatkar* (Splendid)!" The father exclaimed while tasting the chicken curry with his fingers.
"You know, the roasted Cornish hen you make is even better!" He said again.

The daughter, trying to get into a domesticated skin by now, with spurts of rebellion still showing when she washes baby clothes, throws away soiled baby diapers, bangs the front door shut to walk past the corridors, looking at the miles of snow and the wind drift outside the huge glass window at one side of the corridor. The husband of the daughter whom the father had envisioned as a staunch chauvinist long before he met her, works on chopping onions, whipping eggs, making waffles in the kitchen. The husband who had once been drawn to the dark, shaded eyes of the daughter, the gray shadows that flirted with the opaque white of her being, making her a miasma of wayward thoughts, hard aspirations and an irrefutable energy, often misconstrued.

The world that she has wanted to build, with her 'two pennies and English education' reared its head stronger every day, but there has been an unspoken 'want' always, the want of words never spoken between the two that could bridge continents, the want of childhood wounds, adult scars never attended to, sleeping in their graves.

Only that now she is a parent too, and these wants appear in new forms, new avatars when her own girls prance and preen in the light and shade of the room, when she sucks full throttle their words and the little nuances of their incessant fights.

What is she fumbling with, then?
With the aimless words that have swam in her consciousness like numerous small fishes swimming in the water? With the act of getting caught in the weeds of her cantankerous thoughts since her girlhood days? With the cacophony of the strong, odorous storm of the dual of words, or with the calm after the storm with which she has signed pacts since forever?

***

"It's an educated Brahmin family who came to see her. Why was she brimming with anger, tell me? Who does she think she is?" The mother is summoned, to throw light into the whims of a rebel daughter. The mother trembles with fear, lest the daughter gets more severely punished for the act. 'I....I don't know, maybe office stress." She tries to cover up. Within seconds, the daughter storms into the room.

"I give a damn to a Brahmin family, I hate being who I am, bearing the legacy of forefathers believing in casteism and racism, and god knows what else!"

The Body of Memories

"How dare you speak like that about your forefathers, your grandfather or his father? Don't you know we are Brahmin Pundits, and how much the people here revere us?"

"All I want is to be free…free from the shackles of caste and creed and race! And I want to achieve…"

"Achieve what? By trampling over forefathers' ideals of centuries? Do you think you can ever be greater than them in any way?" Her sentence is cut midway. Both the father and daughter tend to their long-nourished narratives of differences. One hole in the wall, one dint in the surface, and it all gushes out, unabashed.

****

And it has gushed out, spilling over the courtyard where the father has uttered his Slokas in Sanskrit, invoking all the Gods he could remember and his ancestors, long dead, his face smeared with the thick lathers of his shaving cream…it has gushed out, the incessant outcome of neurotic words exchanged, words twisted and turned over and over again, by a difficult love. The daughter, often craving to be the soft petals of a blossoming womanhood drenched with the rain of filial love, but ending up being a roaring, raving storm, bearing a torrential rain without a prelude, or even without a closure.

"These acts won't be tolerated in my house, as long as I'm alive."

"So do you want to imprison me, suffocate me with your blatant, meaningless rules? You'll find no luck trying that with me!"

"Do you want to live your entire life doing what you think suits you, when it really doesn't do you any good?"

"Give me one concrete example! Will you?"

"One example? I can give you thousands. For the start, your argumentative nature…your opposing every single rule in the household!"

"And you…you impose those rules, don't you? Have you really thought what I have sought for? Have you attached any importance to it, whatsoever?"

"Your audacity is hard to bear…you've never learnt to stay within your limits."

"And why should I learn that, pray? To remain in your good books, which is a waste of my time anyway, since I am perennially a wrong-doer in your eyes?"

…Words, sentences and their queer algorithms whoosh past her mind's window; she leans against the railings of the train's window, crossing those surreal miles of nondescript train stations in search of a home away from that temperamental father's home. A home where her mere belongings of a few clothes, a desktop computer, a saucepan for boiling rice and eggs, a bar of soap and milk chocolate to ward off depression would be enough to sustain herself for months, and even years, hoping against hope that men she has had befriended in turns, will emerge as chivalrous saviors, as father figures in the garb of soulmates, or partners for life. Men, who come in her life as sweet acts of serendipity, then drift away, lured by sweeter tides, but then she lets her impossible dreams dangle in the wind of her subaltern realities.

Words, sentences which have again, lost their shores, on the cliff-edges of an evening when all differences nurtured and their meanings have gone for a toss. The father with a bruised, bandaged head and the daughter with sweaty, trembling hands holding his belongings, a tattered khaki-colored bag and a black umbrella, try crossing the bustling city streets. The daughter had stormed away from home twenty-four hours ago in a fit of anger, empty-handed, with an empty stomach.

"You're sure you won't need any food on the way?"

"No…will just have dinner once I reach home."

The Body of Memories

She looks wistfully at the street vendors selling sweetmeats and *pani-puris*, thinking of the lunch which her mother had prepared the day before and laid the table with, the lunch that she skipped while going out of the house in a wild rage, the episode of her nervous breakdown in her institute a few hours later, aggravated by her empty stomach.

Curious, well-meaning, concerned faces...faces brimming with news, mouths pregnant with messages to convey at the seminar hall of the old, rusted institute, where she remains unconsciousness for a while, floating over fluffy, benign clouds, pulled by a father on one side, and a daughter on the other. Wait, it might as well be a chariot, a winged one, and the tug and pull of it appears so surreal...
In the real world, she is lying on a hard, makeshift table, and expert hands check her pulse and her heartbeat. She opens her eyes with a concerted effort, with labored breath, asks for water.

"How are you feeling now? We've informed your parents. Your father is coming to take you home, he's on his way by now."

The father, a tattered parent torn between his threatening patriarchal, chauvinist legacy and his turbulent sea of anxiety for the daughter, lying unconscious miles away, in yet another part of the city. The father who banged his head and fell down, unconscious, collided by a bus while crossing the busy street in a desperate bid to reach the institute where the daughter lay, unconscious.

The winged chariot dangles in her eyes yet again, as the daughter's furtive eyes meet the father's a couple of hours later, the father escorted by a couple of men from a nearby hospital to the institute, where the daughter has waited.

"Why is his head bandaged? What happened? And all this blood in the head?" She asks.

"It's a long story. First rest, you both, then you'll listen."

Yes, she fumbles for words, sentences which have again lost their shores, dashing against the cliff-edges of the evening, as they both cross the bustling streets.

****

At 12.30 am, half-an-hour past the midnight hour, the amniotic fluid inside the womb has exploded, and the heavily pregnant daughter wipes some of the water trickling down the cushioned chair where she sat with her laptop and academic deadlines after a late dinner at the family dining table.

"I told you not to be so utterly careless about your movements and the timings of your meals. Look what you've done now. It's more than two weeks early than the expected date of delivery." The mother toiling in the kitchen till the wee hours of the night, comes up to the table.

"It's nothing. Sometimes, I have low bladder control these days."

The pregnant daughter argues zestfully, wiping the cushion of the chair with a tissue, while a Bengali soap keeps playing in the television at the living room, soundless, amplifying the midnight silence in the room. Was it the same soap that played on the television in the noon when the mother was cutting the vegetables in the room for lunch, when a petty scuffle between the father and the daughter brewed again and turned into a volatile fiasco? The dual of their words reverberated in the walls and the ceiling of a new home in a new continent where the parents had arrived, to welcome the birth of their grandchild, the seed of a new generation.

The vegetables and the fish smattered with turmeric and salt and pepper and Bengali spices spluttered in the skillet in the cozy cocoon of the kitchen, but the daughter had made a quick, sharp exit from the room, from the home already, with her invincible temper and her empty stomach. Well, almost empty, since she had consumed only half-a-cup of tea and some spoons of oatmeal in the early morning, trying to be a good girl following the doctor's commands.

"Hate to be in a quarrelsome family with a quarrelsome father bossing over me since I've started to know the world. Can't it be a bit different, just a little bit different here, in this other part of the world?"

In the university where she studies, the daughter loiters impatiently in the huge hall of the Student's center, the cafeteria, thinking whether having a cup of café latte would break her resolve to fast for the entire day, as she had sworn at home.

"What new happened again now?" The husband queried over the phone.

"Ask them…rather ask him, who started it all today since morning!"

He knows it is part of the same web of stories woven around the father and the daughter, stories of mismatched tunes and loud outbursts, stories of pent-up storms and gushing, incessant rain. It had been a staple news to him since they had met online, since he understood during their daily rendezvous that he would remain by her side, and one day, it all might sink into oblivion.

A life, apparently different than his, slashing through the rigmarole of life with anger as her weapon of choice.

Anger has boiled on the surface for a long while, even as she has sipped her café latte and nibbled on the blueberry muffin in the cafeteria, anger that has slowly settled in the vicarious pores of her heart and the bulging stomach, unable to hold the baby any longer. Anger, that has lurked in the shady nooks of her being even as she comes back home in the evening and has eggs and toast, putting on an old Bengali family movie which the family can watch together.

Anger is the slight tingling in her heart as the husband decides post-midnight that she needs to be taken to the hospital through the emergency door as her water has really broken technically. Anger, the fraternal twin of a difficult love waxes and wanes. The husband waits inside the car as the father comes to the daughter and touches her forehead and stomach lightly, with vigorously shaking hands making gestures of prayers, chanting a healing mantra in Sanskrit with his quivering lips.

……Inside the apartment, two months later, his quivering hands hold a soft bundle of an infant that the daughter has borne after a difficult labor. He keeps cradling the baby as she continues to whine and refuses to take the milk bottle after she has finished with her usual quota of two ounces.

"*Chup, chup, Shona, chup, chup* (Quiet, my darling, be quiet) …" He utters time and again, but the infant's wails skyrocket, an extension of the daughter's rebellion pitted against his tough love, but this time, there was love leaping from his body and his consummate senses, blossoming into a nameless, welcoming realm. Love that sprouted from a porous state housed within himself, a hunger to look for love that was tame enough to give in when tough love surrendered. Tough love had softened, melted into wishful oblivion with a huge sense of entitlement. The infant girl and the music of her incessant cries, the music of the progeny of his progeny was the reality of their rebellion, the promise of a truth, never uttered.

■■■

It's a different kitchen, two new homes later, an enhanced kitchen turning old and worn-out again, and the smell of the cooked chicken curry wafts in the kitchen and the living room, mingling with the smell of incense and sweets offered to the father, or rather his framed photograph that the daughter has kept in the living room, along with a framed photograph of her mother.

The concoction of mustard oil and canola oil is a queer one, and so is the smell of incense and flowers picked fresh from the front yard of the house, kept in front of the framed photographs. The mind of the daughter traverses through paths, zigzagging through continents, unsettling.

A dash of salt twice, a pinch of sugar once, she reminds herself once again, as steady and insistent as her rhythm of rebellion that has held her strong, levelling life, death and everything in between.

It is the third death anniversary of the father, and she has worked her way through the chambers of her turbulence. Life, that has brought along with it surges of travel-scarred, naked memories. Death, that has opened the floodgates of more memories, but in the end, brought a deep calm. Or, has it, really?

Bio:
Lopamudra Banerjee is an author, poet, translator, editor with six books and four anthologies in fiction and poetry. She lives in Dallas, Texas with her family where she also teaches Creative Writing at Richland College and Texas Christian University. She has been a recipient of the Journey Awards (First Place category winner) for her memoir 'Thwarted Escape: An Immigrant's Wayward Journey', and also a recipient of the Woman Achiever Award (IWSFF, 2018), the International Reuel Prize for Poetry (2017) and International Reuel Prize for her English translation of Nobel Laureate Tagore's selected works of fiction (2016). Her nonfiction essays, fiction and other writings have been published in various journals, e-zines and anthologies in

India, UK and USA. She is also a consulting editor for Blue Pencil Publishers, India and an associate editor for Life and Legends journal, USA. She has been a featured poet/writer at Rice University, Houston and co-produced the poetry film 'Kolkata Cocktail' directed by Shuvayu Bhattacharjee, where she has also been one of the lead actors.

Her works are available on her website www.lopabanerjeewrites.com and also in Amazon.com and Amazon India.

Of Sunshine Amidst Blue Clouds

Kokila Gupta

Lying on the couch basking in the afternoon stillness, I was flipping through the yellowed pages of my grandfather's copy of 'Twelfth Night' when a few dried petals of rose fell from it. Paper thin, crusty, satin smooth... the dunes of memories shifted, a lone linnet trilled somewhere, a lambretta vrroomed past the residential building, however the jarring notes of traffic were muted down to a pleasant buzz at the ninth-floor apartment.

The pesky sun smiled wan, its tepid light wrestling through curtains to filter in just enough to warm my toes... mellow warmth tingling through my body, transporting me back to similar languid days when curled up with a book in some sunlit corner of my ancestral home, I'd read my way through holidays - summer and winter both.

My posture reminds me of how I was teased about being born in *Marjar yoni* and of my love for the aroma of fresh boiling milk, having a kitten like pointed face, sans the whiskers. Of course, my nature of playing with tumbling woolen balls, curling up anywhere in sunshine into an instant deep Zen meditation like sleep was contributed to my 'feline' astrological qualities!

Another memory that struts up close on the heels is how during school breaks, Saturdays at my grandparents' home were reserved for *Sham-e-Shanichar,* the formal *mushaira* with a fat tallow candle doing turns of being placed in front of esteemed *Shayar* guests, glowing and flickering with an ochre golden light as they read their poetry. As a child I used to drift off to sleep soon after the Moon entered inside the *Mushaira baithak-khana* peeping through the barred embrasure; the cadence of verses filtering in my dreams.

Not only the visuals, but my olfactory receptors too can ferry me to the realm of reminiscences... the tranquil fragrance of frangipani, petrichor from the rain-soaked earth, the smell of *chapatis* puffing up on flame, mint leaves and cinnamon sticks, all bring back a surge of memories... whispering in magical notes to the atrophied mind igniting sleepy cells with a scented spark.

I reminisce the mornings full of fragrance of cardamom ginger tea wafting through the huge ancestral mansion in Ghaziabad, due to immenseness of which my maternal great grandparents got the moniker *Mahalwalas*. I reminisce the evenings bringing balmy air with *Harsingar* scents filling *baradari* (the courtyard with twelve thresholds or door) with a vinous exhilaration.

While in Ghaziabad, a huge part of my holidays was spent with me firmly lodged inside a brick alcove above the staircase, where firewood used to be stacked with a few Pran comics and Maxim Gorky's "My Apprenticeship" and "My Childhood" under my pillow. The alcove was illuminated by the slanting sunrays throughout the day, and for most of the evening till the daylight, used to dissipate in befriending the dark.

On other weekends, when my Catholic school observed holiday, I used to tag along with mom, my single parent and a Lecturer of Literature, to her college where the library was my ultimate and much sought-after refuge. After the half-day teaching schedule was over, the entire college was my playground, its gardens like *Charbaghs* of heavens and the beautiful teachers with swish-swash of their satiny silk saris, my muses.

The disciplined, dignified lecturers used to shun their fearsome masks and laugh like blooming founts of colours as they'd scatter in the gardens to correct notebooks and examination sheets and I, who had undertaken the solemn duty of matching seasonal flowers with their saris, would pin a bud each in their variety of coiffures.

What an array of hair styles I was introduced to!

My abundant future knowledge of makeup and looks had its roots in those flower- matching sessions.

After three hours of enjoying reading in library under Mrs. Dhar's strict monitoring from behind her thick glasses, those next three hours of sauntering around, meandering through giggling teachers used to intoxicate me with a lethal eclectic combination of beauty and brains!

Heady on their wit, sharp tongue, knowledge and beauty, I used to look forward for Saturdays.

However, I owe more than that to those diligent ladies!

Back then in 1980s, they were my BBC channel. There was nothing going on the global firmament which they did not know. Masters of their respective subjects, they used to crack academic jokes and were hands down responsible for not only making me multifaceted, but discussions with them sharpened the arrows of witty sarcasm. In fact, my own mom was the most respected in that arena!

Never again in my life I experienced such a collection of youthful ladies bubbling with zest for life, for work and a healthy, hearty interest in everything they did, all at one place!

Without my realizing it back then, those delicate looking teachers strengthened my emotional backbone and nourished me with positive 'come what may attitude', readying me to face life full on.

The secure childhood was punctuated by Russian stories and verses of Bihari, Bhushan and Subhadra Kumari Chauhan as lullabies. My childhood self was soaked with scent of old books and libraries, dotted with homely scenes of pickles and jams in jars kept in a straight line with military precision under the sun for ripening like carnival lanterns on a string. I remember the gleaming blackboard full of glittering wisdom in white chalk, mummy's modulated voice filling in the drawing room where she used to teach anyone who cared to know anything about literature, the toddler cousins and playmates, all nurturing my soul with a secure joy of a happy childhood, imprinting all my winter afternoons and beryl summer evenings with a beautiful nostalgia.

The other evening as I was sipping warm coffee raindrops lashed at the glass pane of the bay windows, leaves romped around with wet wind, the grass susurrated under the effect and I was whisked away to days when monsoon used to pour down with such ferocity as if it was an exclusive performance for our playground!

Water coming down in sheets making it impossible to see the child standing next to you was something my 11-year-old mind considered the best time to play football!

Kicking mud instead of ball and giggling with the feeling of earth being washed away in torrents from under our feet, taking away slippers and all in its mighty wake was my idea of hygienic organic fun. Surprisingly, my friends' parents did not see eye to eye with my brilliant rain sports and my mates were yanked back under huge and equally useless umbrellas.

The moment the last child was sabotaged by un-empathetic guardians, I returned home accepting my defeat. I vividly remember mom opening the door with two badminton rackets in her hands!

Seconds into the match and the shuttle cock was nowhere to be found and by the end of it, I was sitting in her lap getting drenched to the core.

It was hard to discern what soaked me more and what was mightier, the pelting rain in the backyard, or her unwavering affection.

Phrases float... Mrs. Massey from my Missionary school prophesizing, "She'd be a writer someday, the way she reads and quips!"

When our sports teacher was on leave, my knack for impromptu story creation had saved her many aspirins by keeping the class spellbound for many a sports periods.

Returning home in an open rickshaw, I had to continue that story demolishing kingdoms after kingdom and 'siring' princes and buffoons left, right and center! Somehow, much to the chagrin of my five-year-old listeners, I always stayed clear of magic elements in my story - the vanishing slippers, the time travelling turban, the talking horse... as at that ripe age of seven, I felt that magical props rob the conflict, the challenge out of a story!

Those days. And nights!

Despite being an ardent fan of golden sunshine, the *ko mo rebi*, I was and am a nyctophile too who feels that light always is not propitious and can be too candid or bright to hurt vision. At times one needs to be in phantasmagoria annihilating harsh reality nurturing hope and dreams in shadows.

In my childhood, knowing my love for natural shades, everyone knew the exact places to find me in all the different cities we lived in.

In Hapur it was the rhododendron bushes near bougainvillea and *madhumalti* vines, in Modinagar I was pulled out from under the pomegranates and guavas in the backyard, in the Ghaziabad home I was found in the red brick alcove in the staircase or the attic, in Dehradun on the swing on the Banyan tree near the hills, in the quaint hamlet of Dakpatthar catching fireflies from the hedge of Colonel uncle and while in Pune, I'd be lounging in the pebbled gardens surrounded with hordes of palm fronds, coconuts and arecanuts or in the copse of bamboos.

All these places were ripe with sounds of silence and had the hallucinating kaleidoscopic quality of an optical illusion.

From the treasure of memories, another one giggles bright when much later, in my mid-teens there was this evening when I was verbally instructed to find a certain Professor's quarter near Bank of Baroda branch in my hometown.

I duly pedalled my cycle there to found the lane bathed in darkness flanked by a residential garden fringed by huge dense trees bequeathing further opacity under the veil of crepuscule on one side and a neat unobtrusive belt of doll houses like homes on the other, all drenched in an eerie silence with weak lights in form of dangling naked bulbs.

Apprehensive about what to do next, I was wondering when a 20 something lad emerged out of nowhere and asked me if I needed to go somewhere. Reluctantly, I told him, house number 18. Without any further words, flicking his finger to follow him, he ambled on.

I trudged behind him, burdened with my cycle and bag when a few minutes later I saw the house with 18 written in black paint inside a yellow circle under a pale lamp on the boundary wall. I called him to thank him, but he was already beyond earshot; I tried calling a bit louder this time, but he still went on!

Parking my bicycle on the road, I ran up to him and blurted out gratitude explaining that he should stop as house no. 18 had been located.

Ignoring me, he still walked.

Mad with frustration, I ran right up to him blocking his way in a confrontational manner almost spitting out a thank-you and asking him to stop!

The Body of Memories

With complete calm and a poker face, he replied, "Miss, you must have found your no. 18, but I still need to reach MY home which is yet ten more yards away from here. "

Flabbergasted, I stared at him while he muttered a polite thanks and vanished!

Oh! how my folks hollered with laughter when I told them and how this has been told and retold and remembered many a times till then! Tears of mirth still roll down my cheeks, remembering the dumbfounded expressions on my deflated face that day as in my mind HE thanked me once again for stopping pestering him!

I remember it for another reason. It was the day at Professor Arya's home when despite not wanting to be a doctor, I pursued Life Science and ended up doing the coveted Masters in Immunoparasitology. The day marked the start of a beautiful lifelong relation with the branch of study I love and respect.

I cherish the sunshine of those days, always dissipating the blue clouds; on tough days a canorous voice reminding me these moments reside within, tiptoeing around in beatific tranquility or swirling and twirling with quintessential chutzpah of impish moments.

Unlike many, I enjoy my solitude, sipping the silence... busy in my own inner world where faces and images glimmer like starry pinpoints on the canvas of mind... imparting wisdom anew with each recap of the event, drenching me with bliss.

I caress the textures of moments bygone, grainy with raspy laughter or silken, embroidered with satin thread of dreams; dreams, preceding hopes, prevenient to memories.

Because dreams are the gossamer footings taking hold of which delicate hopes construct a strong edifice of impressions. And Time, the eternal gypsy loiters on. As I introspect and reminisce, the daylight bends one last time to

bid adieu and am left wrapped in the cashmere of ethereal
past serenading it.

"Memories bloom
Like a yellow wildflower on a lone stalk,
Or a sunbeam posing dainty smiling with
Burnished gold
The smell of old books
Swirling around enveloping,
 A flurry of fairytales and anecdotes
Yellowed brittle pages of Grandpa's diary
About saffron blooms in purple fields
Laughing rivulets spanning miles
About fireflies dancing like glimmer of hope
Of trembling hands which write

Of *zardozi* silks in the trunk
Blankets of lullabies forgotten
A bale of old letters from mountains
Fetching fragrance of ripe apples and plums
Scent of coffee brewing fresh
Spilling out from window on cobbled streets
on a winter night
Silver keychain with tiny bells dangling
from amma's *pallu*,
The bright vermillion on her exalted forehead
Cavalcade in heart
Chockablock with images

I on a swing with dad pushing it from behind
Mom laughing nearby, daisies blushing pink in dulcet light
Summery scents turning autumnal in mind
Blowing in wind like dandelion seeds
My tiny hand waving goodbye to him
Tryst with death, untimely demise
His words, his love
Like flint stones
Ignite dreams of sun kissed pastures

The Body of Memories

Bordered by russets and mauves of autumn
Framed by snowflakes
Etched

Life in retrospect gleam
With gilt edges
Nudging to live to the fullest
Depth counts not the length
Alone yet never lonely
Soliloquy of past reign
As silence stirs melodies of
Quietude"

Bio:
Born in literary environment of 'Aatmavat Sarv Bhuteshu',
with poems as lullabies; philosophy as bed time stories,
Kokila Gupta was brought up amid mountains and valleys
nurturing a deep love for nature and simplicity. She chose
Immuno-Parasitology as her studies and later resigned from
a Government job to pursue her other interests. Her latest
professional role was as the Head of Department (Life
Sciences) in an Intermediate Institute in Himachal Pradesh.
Her prose, poetry, musings or Haiku, all express a natural
affinity for life in mundane spontaneity. Her poems and short
stories have been published in many Anthologies, Online
Literary Portals and International Literary Magazines. She is
a lecturer by profession, an artist by nature, a reader by birth,
a traveller by passion and a writer by choice.

Those days...

Madhu Jaiswal

I as a child was a docile and introvert person who used to confine herself in a shell. It was way tough for me to express myself and speak out with others what was going inside my head. Girls of my age used to drool on so many things in their teenage days and here I had none to share my feelings with. I was skinny and dark who felt ugly and useless. Being an average person, I wasn't up to the mark on any scale. Be it studies, looks or other skill and co-curricular activities. It was tough and kind of suffocating for me, but I had none in whom I could confide and share what I felt. Although I had few friends in my class, but they too were just like me, dull and unnoticeable.

I used to find respite in painting and reading. Painting was a liberation for my heart. The zigzag sketches and colors of my paintings, somehow deployed the inner me. Nature allured my heart and mind and I could easily depict those things via the stroke of my paintbrush and vibrant colors. Myriad thoughts invaded my heart and mind, I used to connect them with the rising and setting sun. The beauty of dusk, the azure skies, the singing of birds. All these were my expressions of joy when I felt solace. Often I used to gaze at the starlit sky counting the stars and trying to configure a story, contemplating about them in my mind. Other thing that I liked was reading. It let the inner me dream and decipher a new world where no-one was there to judge me or let me feel inferior because of my looks or ability. I was an avid reader and would read and try to grasp things that I couldn't understand sometimes.

Quite later in my life I realized that I had inferiority complex during my teenage days. That was the reason why I used to hide myself behind others. Having zero confidence, it felt as if I was good for nothing.

The Body of Memories

I used to be in awe of those who took part in various competitions and co-curricular activities in school and emerge winners. I couldn't even stand up and answer properly in class. Whenever my class teacher tried to send my name for quiz competition, I would be blank and fumbled for words in front of others even when I knew the answers. Same happened if I dared enough to take part in debate, although in my mind I could recite the whole thing quite aptly. The words would just get stuck in my mouth, my heart beat raced and I felt humiliated as others laughed and hooted behind. Every day, I dragged myself to complete my task with zero enthusiasm and no motive. I barely existed for others in class.

That day two years back, when our social group visited the girl's orphanage for celebrating Christmas in December, it all came back rushing to my mind. There I found a dark-skinned, timid girl standing in a corner. Her big eyes lit up when the song played on the music system as we sang Christmas carols and most of the girls joined. She just stood there watching everyone dancing and enjoying with eager eyes. Our eyes met and I insisted her to join others saying,

"Tumhara naam kya hai? Aao agey aake tum bhi perform karo sabke sath." (What's your name? Come to the front, perform with all others in the group.)

"Nhi madam, mujhe ye sab nhi aata." (No Madam, I can't do all this). She replied, bashfully.

Somehow, I could feel that she wished to do all the things what others were doing.

I held her hand and let her towards the girls in the center of the room where others were dancing on the beat of the song.

"We wish you a Merry Christmas!" Holding her hand, I sang along.

"Chalo abhi sabko karna hoga, koi bahana nhi chalega" (Come on, everybody has to do it.) I said, with a steadfast voice.

At first, she resisted. Then gradually she picked up as we all cheered her with our clapping and whistles. As the music changed to a fast dance number, she danced enthusiastically, making most of the moment.

We were literally in awe when she danced her heart out. Though all the girls there were not very talented, but it felt heartening to see the little angels enjoying, especially Tia.

Yes, that was her name. Her eyes shone with brilliance when we all applauded her, and she grinned ear to ear, red with all the appreciation.

I said, *"abhi kitna acha perform ki aur nakhre kar rhi thi ki mujhe nhi aata."*

(Just now you were performing so nicely, why then did you say that you couldn't do it?)

She was like, *"mujhe laga mai kharab karungi to sab hasenge mujhpe."* (I thought I would perform poorly, and everyone would laugh at me.)

I saw in her a mirror image of my own childhood. She was unaware of her skills, having no confidence in herself. A gentle push and she was in. A bit of appreciation and cheering did the much-needed magic.

As I reflect back on the days when I was a loner myself, it pains me to think how things are around us. We all are bound by our limitations, our self-made prejudices regarding the way a person should be. God created this beautiful world. Aren't all creations of lord beautiful in their own way? Only we impose infringements on them, and those create shackles that impede their growth.

In a class-divided society, we think we need to fit in to be the perfect one! But why do we need to be perfect? Why can't people accept us the way we are? All these thoughts used to ransack my mind and it felt suffocating.

The situation never changes, it's our mindset that we need to incur change upon. For me it proved correct. When I was at my lowest, a few true friends showed up and their acceptance of me uplifted my soul. The motivation of doing better paved my path towards a better tomorrow. I don't say that it completely changed my world, but yes, it did make a significant change in my attitude and my perception towards life.

A bit of appreciation and acceptance goes a long way. I learned that lesson long back but it comes handy all the way to breathe a new lease of life again. Tia's happy and glowing face reflected that Midas touch of a compassionate heart which would be her guiding light.…

Bio:
Madhu Jaiswal is a bilingual poet and social worker hailing from Kolkata, India. She is associated with The Impish Lass Publishing House, Mumbai in the capacity of an executive editor. She has 7 anthologies as an editor to her credit. Her creative contributions have been published in various national and international anthologies and she often gets featured in prestigious e-zines. Her poetry was recently featured in the prestigious anthology Aatish 2 alongside various stalwarts. Also she bagged third prize in Beyond Black Sakhi Annual Poetry Awards 2019. She is attached to a social group named Share A Smile and volunteers for social cause and upliftment of destitute individuals.

Spirit Sisters

Mary Ann Sestili

I never saw my mother cry in public - until Almarente died. Then she wept. My mother, Esther, believed that in grief, one should not cry in public, rather should do so in private. She practiced her mantra even as she schooled me at my father's wake, "People don't come to see you cry. They come to pay their respects, not to see you cry."

Pizzoferrrato, Italy

Yet, there she was – weeping. Sitting small as a sparrow in an oversized winged chair at Elachko Funeral Home in Pittsburgh, Pennsylvania overwhelmed with grief at the death of her cherished spirit sister and soul savior, Almarente (Casciato) Cirelli. The Cirelli family was preparing to leave for the cemetery and wanted Mom to ride in the family car, but we couldn't find her. I went from room to room and found her alone, head bowed, hugging herself mourning her beloved. I approached her cautiously, but somewhat alarmed. "Mom," I said. "The Cirelli family is waiting for you to go to the cemetery. They want you to ride with them,"

"I can't do it," she said. "I just can't do it." Eventually, Almarente's son Joe took her arm, "Comare (Godmother), please come with me," and he walked her to the car.

These remarkable women – my mother and godmother - formed an admirable life relationship that has prompted me to wonder what kept their bond intact through marriages, children, depression and even death?

They could have been twins. Born one month apart – Almarente on February 27, 1913 and my mother on March 23, 1913 - in Pizzoferrato, a Middle-Ages mountainous land in Italy's Abruzzo region, they shared a common Italian surname – Casciato, and grew up in women-centered homes as their fathers left Italy when both were very young. My grandfather, Nicola, left my grandmother (Antoinette), his two daughters, (Philomena, five years old and my mother, two years old) to work at the Jones and Laughlin (J&L) Steel mill joining by 1910, the estimated 1.5 million foreign-born inhabitants who settled in Pennsylvania that had become an industrial colossus.[1] His plan to rejoin and accompany his family to America was interrupted by restrictions imposed by World War I. Almarente's father, Carmen, abandoned his family when she was three months old. That event preceded her future heartache when her mother left Italy to remarry in the United States leaving Almarente, then seven, in her grandmother's care.

Constant companions in their hill town, the girls and friends gathered in the piazza, walked to school, church, to and from their homes and to the surrounding wheat fields where they, with the adults, worked to supplement their households. Although I have no photographs of their early years, I imagine them wearing modest clothing, long stockings, sturdy shoes, simple skirts, and kerchiefs, arm in arm, running, chasing one another and squealing in laughter, trying to stay out of trouble while at the same time cheering one another on to be a little naughty.

In 1922, the all-female band left Italy for America. With few precious possessions and only a glimpse of the unknown, they boarded the Columbo and sailed in steerage class for approximately three weeks before embarking at New York's Ellis Island on July 4, 1922. Mom spoke often of this voyage and recounted not only the exhilaration but the hardship of

sickness that so many passengers experienced. An excellent visual of the steerage experience is shown in the famous 1907 photograph by Alfred Stieglitz who while traveling first class with his wife and daughter on his way to Paris, memorialized this scene.[2] When the women embarked, an official changed Mom's name from Pasqua to Esther as her baptismal name was not considered to be American. The closest

Figure 1- STEERAGE by Alfred Stieglitz 1907

name American-sounding name to Pasqua (meaning Easter) was Esther.[3] Seven years had passed when my grandmother, mother and Aunt Phil re-met my Grandfather and two years since Almarente, had a less than cordial meeting with her mother – that became a prelude to a lifetime-strained relationship.

As nine-year old emigrees to Pittsburgh, PA, Esther and Almarente's companionship was uninterrupted. Living only three modest houses apart in Panther Hollow (an Italian enclave for recent immigrants), they exchanged a country home for a city one, learned a new language, and were introduced to America's culture. As long as they had one another, they felt safe joyfully embracing their new lives with gusto. Temperamentally, they were true Pizzoferrato daughters, exhibiting their region's characteristics of fierce determination, conscientiousness, diligence, and dependability. They were taught to never praise yourself for something you would ever do, expecting us, their children, to do the same.

Figure 2 -Cirelli Wedding. Esther, Cirellis, Paul Pasquarelli - 1933

While marriages – Almarente to Charles Cirelli and Esther to Max Sestili in the 1930's - and children born into the 1950's thrust them into roles as wives and mothers, and while their physical proximity to one another changed, their sisterhood remained steadfast. They committed to support one another and automatically extended this commitment to us expecting us to support one another in all of our life stages.

We served as one another's sponsors for baptism, confirmation, and marriage, beginning with Almarente and Charles standing as my baptismal Godparents. They wove us into a tapestry of love and commitment as we went back and forth, up and down, here and there, in our homes, at school, church and in the community. These magnificent women - Esther and Almarente - were the weavers – they were our Mothers!

I n preparing this article, I was struck by the number of photographs (most of which were taken by my Godfather (Charles Cirelli) that show us growing up. Two from our early childhoods show us together for birthdays and other family events.

Figure 3 - Max and Esther Sestili Wedding, 1936

The 1940's and 50's were difficult times for families and for women in particular. Most women married when they were in their early 20's (as did our mothers), carried out most household chores of cleaning, cooking, caring for children - all without automatic conveniences, and managed the family's daily life even as society continued to suffer from the aftermath of the Great Depression and deprivations from World War II.[4] When Life Magazine published an article that documented the lives of American housewives, Mrs. W.L. Mann in a letter to Life Magazine wrote: "I'll bet hundreds who read your article threw up their hands and said, One woman could not do all of it." [5] Almarente and Mom, no different from the wives and mothers of that area, did do all of it. By the early 1950's Almarente had three children and Mom not only birthed seven children (a daughter died the day after her birth), but experienced at least three, and perhaps four miscarriages.

Roman Catholic women felt an added burden. If couples chose to follow the tenets of the Roman Catholic Church, they were required to abide by the papal encyclical, Casti Connubii (translated - a chaste wedlock) issued by Pope Pius XI on December 31,1930 that espoused three purposes to marriage: produce offspring, grow in conjugal faith and show benefit from the sacrament of marriage. [6] Abortion was forbidden, and contraception was considered to be

The Body of Memories

intrinsically and one that violated the law of God and nature. Catholic couples had to be prepared to create life each time they engaged in intercourse or practice the Church-approved Rhythm Method (the Natural Family Planning Method) .[7] Many couples found this method to be unreliable. While I never heard my mother discuss this topic when I was growing up, but on a visit home as an adult, my mother confessed, "I wish the Pope had not talked about the Rhythm Method. It didn't work."

Figure 4 - Cirelli and Sestili Children in their childhood – 1940's

As the oldest of six children, my impression was that Mom was always pregnant. I don't mean to imply that she did not want the children she bore. On the contrary, I frequently remember her saying, "Dad and I always wanted a big family." I understand that. But, to have to be prepared for a pregnancy to result each time the couple engaged in marital intercourse, and with no legitimate way to intervene, must have been stressful.

One incident is seared in my memory. We were eating dinner. Dad, having just returned from a labor-intensive day as a landscape gardener, was in his seat at the kitchen table as we in ours. Mom was serving us. Suddenly she left the kitchen, called my father and in what seemed like seconds, Dad, carrying my mother over his shoulder, as he would have carried a burlap sack of leaves or gravel, hurried through the kitchen and said to me, "Call Mrs. Robel (our neighbor) and tell her to come and be with you kids. I'm taking your mother to the hospital." I can't – or don't want to remember what happened after that – but I do remember that I prayed. "Dear God, please don't let my mother die." In retrospect, I suspect she was hemorrhaging – from a miscarriage, or other gynecological condition - I don't know.

Several years later, when I was 11 years old, my sister Mary Esther was born. We were thrilled. We had a sister after having three brothers in a row. Tragically, Mary Esther died one day later. My father called our pastor, Father Connare, who traveled to the hospital to baptize and name our sister. My mother, like all mothers at that time, was kept in the maternity ward for about nine days. We took it for granted that she would be coming home, but not then and certainly not after any of Mom's miscarriages, did we talk about loss or grief or trauma. Nothing was explained to us - not by our dad, not Mom, nor anyone in the family because it was just not done. We were told Mom needed a little rest. She looked tired, but otherwise fine and she sounded OK. Most importantly, she was home and sad to say we expected our lives to continue as they had. I suspect that similar scenarios played out at my Aunt Phil Sestili's house when her beloved Rita Angela died two months and three days after her birth (Aunt Phil always remembered the exact amount of time) and when Chris, Aunt Viola's beloved little boy, lived for

The Body of Memories

only a few hours. These brave, heroic women continued with their lives and cared for their other children.

While women of this generation neither discussed a child's death or their sadness from miscarriages, it is heartening that now some women are beginning to courageously discuss the sorrow they and their families experience from these tragedies. Among the women are Meghan Markel [7], the Duchess of Sussex and Chrissy Teigen [8], American Model and television personality who, using their notoriety, have bravely and candidly described the physical and emotional pain they experienced. They and others, such as the women and men quoted in Pooj Shah's article What Happens in Relationships After Miscarriage? These Couples Taught Us spoke of their grief, loneliness and in one mother's comment – guilt.

By 1958, we were six children and while my parents shared business and financial responsibilities for their 10-year-old newbie landscape business, Mom continued as the helmsman running our active and hectic lives. Did the home, children, business, perhaps medical issues overwhelm my beloved mother? She – a strong Pizzoferrato girl – a girl from a region when translated means iron – had a mental breakdown that so incapacitated her, the doctor urged my father to admit her to St. Francis Psychiatric Hospital for treatment. Dad, reminding the doctor that he had children at home who needed their mother, brought her home, only to have her incapable of carrying out her role as mother and wife. She lost interest in everything going on around her, was depressed, unable to prepare food, had limited interest in eating, could not make decisions, was listless, sad, could not concentrate and needed help.

In spite of family's attempt to care for her and address her needs, it was Almarente who saved Mom's life. Even with three children of her own, Comare Almarente became my mother's helper, protector, advisor, and soul savior. There was little discussion of what she would do or how she would help. Every day for about two months, she and her family moved into our Dawson Street home where she cared for all of us. That meant leaving her home each morning and coming to take over our house doing all the chores - cooking, washing and ironing clothes, getting kids ready for school, caring for two families - while my mother, not able to function, sat comforted by a blanket that lay across her legs and watched TV. My mother confided during my visits that "Comare Al saved my life. Had it not been for her, I may have ended it as I contemplated how I was going to do it. The only thing that stopped me was thinking of all of you kids."

Now, I can only imagine the stress that she experienced caring for a house, a new family-owned business, six children and especially the death of a newborn baby. She spoke to me of that birth a few times in later years recounting how difficult it was to remain in the maternity ward of the hospital for nine days (the hospital stay at that time) without a baby. Her baby had died, but the other mothers were receiving their babies each day. She also told me that she suspected something was wrong with the pregnancy as it appeared to her that the baby had – as she said stopped growing at about six months. It is not hard to understand how the accumulation of these events shifted her from being a strong, independent woman to one who experienced profound depression.

Over time, although it did take time, Mom was able to enjoy a normal life again when she regained her sense of humor and her joy, especially as we became adults, and when her grandchildren were born. I believe that the role she played with my Dad – her true love and life-time partner- in establishing Sestili Nursery [10] – were fundamental in her healing. Above all was her abiding faith and devotion to her Church and the practice of her religion.

Figure 5 - Almarente and Mary Ann Sestili ~1977

Mom's relationship with Almarente remained resolute. Ironically, later when Almarente's health declined, Mom reciprocated to help her sister gain back some health until her death on May 12, 1979, 20 years before my mom's death. They never left one another. Their memories, lives and spirits live on in our families. May they rest in peace.

Figure 6 - Almarente, Sister Maurice Whalen, Esther - 1978

References:

The Steerage is a black and white photograph taken by Alfred Stieglitz in 1907. It has been hailed as one of the greatest photographs of all time because it captures in a single image both a formative document of its time and one of the first works of artistic moderns.

My grandfather, Nicola Casciato, was among the immigrants who came to the United States for work with the Jones and McLaughlin (J&L) Steel Mill. Stories from PA History. The Peopling of Pennsylvania: The Creation of a Multicultural Society. Chapter 3: Huddled Masses 1865-1930), http://explorepahistory.com/story.php?storyId=1-9-23&chapter=3

Sestili, Mary Ann. "Storytelling: Ellis Island could lead to a new name as well as a nation." Pittsburgh Post-Gazette 22 Apr. 2011:2. I wrote this vignette based on the story my mother told of her voyage from Italy to the United States in steerage class on the ship, Columbo. I imagined her as a nine-year-old girl.

http://www.post-gazette.com/pg/11112/1141102-294-0.stm

Mrs. America: Women's Roles in the 1950s (From the Collection: Women in American History) https://www.pbs.org/wgbh/americanexperience/features/pill-mrs-america-womens-roles-1950s

A Day in the Life of An American Woman, Amanda Uren. "In 1941, LIFE magazine sent photographer William C. Shrout to document the lives of one of the biggest single demographics in the U.S.: the 30 million housewives who did most of the washing, made beds, cooked meals and nursed almost all the babies of the nation, with little help, no wages and no other jobs." https://mashable.com/2015/05/10/housewives-1940s

Casti connubii (translated as On Christian Marriage) – The papal encyclical proclaimed by Pope Pius XI on December 31, 1930.

http://www.vatican.va/content/pius-xi/en/encyclicals/documents/hf_p-xi_enc_19301231_casti-connubii.html

Rhythm Method for Natural Family Planning: The rhythm method, also called the calendar method or the calendar rhythm method, is a form of natural family planning. To use the rhythm method, a woman tracks her menstrual history to predict when she will ovulate and helps a woman determine when she is likely to conceive.

Megan, Duchess of Sussex, Reveals She Had a Miscarriage: Calls For Compassion In A Polarized World. Caroline Davies. The New York Times, November 25, 2020. https://www.washingtonpost.com/world/2020/11/25/meghan-duchess-sussex-reveals-she-had-miscarriage-july-calls-compassion-polarized-world/

Chrissy Teigen Publishes Essay About Pregnancy Loss. Sandra E. Garcia, New York Times, October 27, 2020 https://www.nytimes.com/2020/10/27/style/chrissy-teigen-pregnancy-loss-essay.html

Sestili, Mary Ann. *A Life Together That Changed Pittsburgh's Landscape,* Western Pennsylvania History, Spring, 2019, Vol 102; Number 5, pp 34-47. Describes founding of the Sestili Nursery 75+ years ago.

Bio:
Mary Ann Sestili, a native of Pittsburgh, Pennsylvania, writes about life events growing up in a large Italian American family. Sestili's vignettes and stories have been published in the Pittsburgh Post-Gazette, The Washington Post Sunday Magazine section, and the Western Pennsylvania History Magazine (published as through the John Heinz History Center). Sestili is a graduate of Carlow

University in Pittsburgh and the Catholic University of America, D.C., where she earned a Ph.D. in the biological sciences. She lives in Potomac, MD with her husband, Anthony René.

Poetry in the Time of Coronavirus
Megha Sood

I still remember the afternoon of March 13, 2020, when I started following the official site of the New Jersey Coronavirus Dashboard and the number of cases started to escalate like mercury on a hot thermometer. My nine-year-old was in the school playing and socializing with his peers with no fear and awareness about the pandemic. As his mother, I was fighting a world of anxiety and panic, as the familiar world around me was transforming bit by bit, bracing for an incredible disaster. I requested the school for a day off as I was too paranoid to send him to school the next day and my fears were realized when the mayor ordered a state lockdown the very next Monday.

What happened after the next three months was nothing anybody was prepared for, not at least in the span of the last 100 years. The sudden realization of the lockdown, coupled with the anxiety of the new *insane* normal we all had to get ourselves prepared for, characterized the next few months. The instant change in the daily routine from driving my kid to school to just making him sit in the next room along with my husband setting up our third room in the house as his office came as an unexpected change. I could see the excitement of going to the final year of his elementary school diminishing in my son's eye as I started setting up his reading table. Suddenly our world was confined in the three-bedroom apartment of our high rise in the densest part of the city.

Though as a poet and an editor I mostly prefer to stay indoors near my writing space but sharing the same house with three people in different rooms screaming over their virtual screens has become a constant battle for all of us. Initially, my son was really excited by the prospect of remote schooling and the idea of getting up later than usual for school. But spending eventually four to five hours of screen time started causing him digital saturation. I could see the frustration in him popping at unusual times for unusual reasons. He started having more meltdowns. I contacted the school to cut down content as it was nearly impossible to achieve the same level of productivity in remote schools versus actual schooling. To my surprise, the school agreed and reduced the volume.

This pandemic also came as a mixed bag of emotions for me. The negative aspects of it are the cancellation of the local poetry reading events, which were a great source of networking for me and also gave me a platform for my content. The cancellation which I regret the most is the week-long poetry festival in the neighboring town which I was headlining for the first time. Now in retrospect, I think that It was the right decision as it would have become the next cluster of infection.

Poetry in the time of coronavirus has been a blessing and curse in equal proportion. The good part was that now I was able to attend any poetry event irrespective of time and location. Any event was just a click away on my computer. I don't have to juggle my chores and run like headless chicken driving my son from one class to another after school. Now, I could easily accept an invite for a poetry event in Brooklyn happening simultaneously with my son's Taekwondo class without blinking an eye. The sad part of it was everything looked and felt isolated, the joy of hugging and meeting your poetry friends in person and seeing faces of your audience lit up during a poetry reading was now replaced with the ZOOM gallery view with countless clueless faces staring at you. Working around your way in the ZOOM application has become a quintessential skill these days. Otherwise, you look like a mouse stuck in the maze, clueless and trapped.

Reading poetry in front of a zoom screen never gives me the same level of satisfaction as compared to a room full of cheering and a live audience. I compensate for this fact with

The Body of Memories

my zoom sessions by snapping fingers and typing positive comments in the chat window. A performer thrives on appreciation and feedback.

Also, there is a deluge of submissions for the anthology I'm co-editing for my literary journal. The anthology celebrates the 100 years of the women's suffrage movement in the United States. This gives me the necessary distraction from the pandemic news. I was immensely affected by the stories of people going through the pandemic. My poetry gave me that essential cathartic release and as a result, I started writing poems as a way to document my emotions.

Several poems penned by me during these quarantine times became my creative outlet for my anxiety and fear about the pandemic. I also collaborated in various crowdsourced projects, and my involvement in the poetry events increased by many folds as more of my literary contacts shifted to the virtual platform.

I am now able to attend and meet more people through this virtual platform which earlier was not possible either due to locational disadvantage or time conflicts with my son's extracurricular classes. Earlier it would have been impossible for me to connect to the Jersey City Theater Centre because of my lack of experience in performing arts. But because of the incessant need for sharing the perspective of poets with the rest of the world, I got this fantastic opportunity to be a panelist in the Online Series *"Voices Around the World"* curated by the JCTC Artistic Director Olga Levina. Due to this online event, I was able to share the space twice with the world-renowned theater artists. I also crossed the 400+ published poems mark in the month of April. This brought me face to face with the fact that every cloud has a silver lining. No matter how grim and bleak the current ongoing situation appeared, we as writers and poets were thriving and everything around was acting as a creative stimulus.

This pandemic has been nothing less of an emotional rollercoaster for me. There are days when I am really excited about poetry acceptances or my winnings in State and National level Poetry contests, and then there are days I am really sad and depressed. When someone lost a family member to coronavirus in my writing community, it became a personal loss to me, instilling an unknown fear of losing my own. I have been calling my mother and my siblings more often than usual. All my phone calls have been switched to video calls from the regular voice calls. Anxiety morphs and molds into a new shape every day.

April being the National Poetry Month was extremely productive and busy. WNYC Studios gives prompts to their listeners as part of their annual *#PausePoetry* contest to celebrate National Poetry Month. One of the prompts was *"Lessons Learned"*. Articulating something of value from my pandemic experience was a rather challenging task, that too, in a refined, metaphorical way in the genre of poetry. Then the next day I received unfortunate news of my close friend's mother passing due to cancer and him not being able to visit her due to the flight cancellations and border closure. I was dreading making the condolence call, but I finally braved my fears and made the call. What came out of that 30-minute call was the response to the prompt *"Lessons learned"*. The poem luckily got selected for the prompt and was mentioned on the Morning Show of the WNYC Studios. The hidden grief in his voice was overlapped with both of us talking about the trivial stuff like groceries and virtual schooling. The grief in me rose to the surface and gave birth to my poem" A Condolence Call".

Excerpt from the poem "A Condolence Call"

"Grief sits like a day old soup in my kitchen unless the anger stirs it
rattles and boils it. Grief rises to the surface and chokes me

I hear the loss of a mother. My friend's mother, over the phone
It's a condolence call yet I can't seem to join in his grief

Sudden loss disjoints your body, the pieces don't seem to fit anymore
Body and language are extricable. Our tongue moves in the way

our body can't decipher in grief. I can't seem to form a legible sentence
our conversation keeps coming back to the grocery, the loneliness of

being stuck in a condo looking over the lush green deserted parks.
I don't want to bring back the conversation of the dead and dying.

Another truth that became more apparent during the time of pandemic is that the role of caretaker as a mother surpasses any other role in your life. Following the pandemic and the lockdown, I cook more often now that my family stays home at all times. Bored with the monotony of home-cooking, I also have started trying new recipes from my mother's cookbook. Looking at the satiated smile of my family after a well-cooked meal has been one of the good things that have happened recently. I get to spend more time with my son compared to the four hours I would normally get. We also have started going for walks in the morning, weekly hikes, and have started exercising together as a family. This has added a new level of bonding between all of us. This forced confinement in our house due to pandemic has been a blessing in disguise as we get more time than usual from the earlier hamster on a wheel routine.

I also gave a haircut to my husband and my son and to my surprise it came out pretty decent. I have heard the horror stories of the bald spot, but I successfully managed to avoid that. That first haircut gave me such a sense of achievement. I realized that I'm now capable of doing small fixes around my house, whereas earlier I was immensely dependent on the handyman for these fixes.

During the times of the pandemic, I also discovered there are significant happenings around our socio-political surroundings that I needed to ponder on. The introspection was not only centered on the virus and its consequences, but also on racial discrimination and injustice which is unfortunately embedded in human history. Enraged by the systemic oppression of African American communities, I also started reading more about its history and how it made its way into the system. How it all started the day Mayflower touched the shores of Virginia, to bloody Civil War, to police brutality, racial profiling during the traffic stops, and finally leading to the death of George Floyd, which led to marches and protests around the country. I started writing poems about it, donated money to the bail funds, and signed a petition. I also made and donated posters for the local protest march in Jersey City against police brutality along with my son, which I must say, has been one of the few things in these trying times that I'm really proud of. This pandemic has given a necessary pause in everybody's lives to introspect and realize the small things which really matter. Seeing myself in respect to the bigger world out there, I have also come to acknowledge our essential workers, our real heroes, and how privileged I'm to be sitting in my home and not risking my life to earn a living. It has taught me to be grateful for small things right from learning a small skill and to be patient when dealing with a string of meltdowns of my nine-year-old.

The Body of Memories

All these moments of pause have added a deep layer of introspection in our lives. We all have experienced this irrespective of what age group we belong to. I have observed appreciation of these moments even in my nine-year-old. When his school was about to close for the summer vacation, they were asked to share their experience of the pandemic as a one-liner to which my son responded: *"Everything comes to an end, Good times will come"*. This one-liner has stuck to me as my daily mantra. Something which shines like a bright light at the end of a dark tunnel. A flickering hope which never dies no matter how long we are confined indoors because of this invisible virus, and also holds a lien to our lives and keeps us away from our loved ones. I strongly believe that this temerity will end soon and we all soon be enjoying the warm company of our friends and families. This moment in my life also attests to the universal truth that children are the best teachers you ever get in your life.

I hope we all will come out of this stronger and kinder than before.

Bio:
Megha Sood is a Pushcart-nominated Poet, Editor, and Blogger from Jersey City, New Jersey. She is an Associate Poetry Editor at journals MookyChick(UK), Life and Legends (USA), and a Partner in the Literary project "Life in Quarantine" with CESTA, Stanford University, USA. Works featured in journals, including Poetry Society of New York, American Writers Review, Kissing Dynamite, Rising Phoenix Review, and many more. National Level Winner Spring Mahogany Lit Prize 2020 and Three-Time State-level winner of NJ Poetry Contest 2018/2019/2020. Co-Editor of anthologies ("The Medusa Project", Mookychick) and ("The Kali Project, Indie Blu(e) Press). Author of the forthcoming chapbook ("My Body is Not an Apology", Finishing line press, 2021) and Full-Length collection ("My Body Lives Like a Threat", FlowerSongPress,2021). Chosen twice as the panelist for the Jersey City Theater Center

Online Series "Voices Around the World". Blogs at
https://meghasworldsite.wordpress.com/ and tweets at
@meghasood16

Until We Meet Again

Meenakshi Mohan

'Should tomorrow appear in ghostly garbs
Of yesteryear, what shall we do
Where shall we go from the flooded Ark
Where shall we go.'

Tamam Shud, by Kshitij Mohan

Life is ephemeral; we all know that. But I often wondered how some people already get a hunch on how it will end for them! My mother and my husband, Kshitij Mohan, both had intimations about this. They both expressed their feelings in their poems much before their end. My husband wrote in his poem *Sanjh-Savera* (*Tamam Shud,* a collection of his poems, posthumously published in 2010):
Saanjh huey us paar mujhe
Jab kewat lene aayenge
mere lahoo ke do deepak
iss tut se disha dikhayengen. (1)

January 2nd, 2010 was a calamitous day for us. Kshitij took his last breath at the Sibley Hospital in Washington, D.C., due to complications following chemotherapy.

At the time of his demise, he was surrounded by his family and friends. My two children, Vivek and Kavita, were on both sides of his bed. I often wondered what he could be thinking. Was he able to hear us as we said our goodbyes? Perhaps he recalled the lines from his poem, "*mere lahoo ke do deepak*
iss tut se disha dikhayengen."

[Tamam Shudh; cover page]

Kshitij and I both enjoyed traveling and had traveled all over the world. The summer of 2009 was our last trip together to Europe. Soon after our journey, we planned our next holiday, and Kshitij, while looking at one of the catalogs, commented, "I will buy matching suitcases for us."

He often talked about early retirement. One day, as I was cooking, he came and put his arms around me and said, "I want to enjoy life as much as possible with you before I go." I laughingly disavowed his claim saying that it could be me who would go first.

[The author and her husband Kshitij]

Kshitij loved life, and he wanted to make the most of each experience – whether it was spending time with family and friends, traveling, or just enjoying good food. I remember one of the parties we planned for our friends -- we poured over the New York Times Cookbook to find recipes, looked for wines for wine-pairing, designed Menu Cards, made name tags for guests for a sit-down dinner -- such beautiful memories. He wrote to my daughter, Kavita,
'There is great beauty in this world – from the glisten of a snowflake to the shimmer of a cobweb – from the purity in a child's eye to the principles of mathematics. Explore it all, enjoy it all and revel in it.' (*Tamam Shud*. Letter to Kavita, 2010).

[Kshtij Mohan with daughter Kavita]

He took early retirement as a CEO and President of the Cytomedix Corporation, a medical device company, just a few months before his retirement. After his retirement, he wanted to spend the rest of his life pursuing his interests. He was a person with extraordinary breadth and depth of knowledge. He could discuss quantum theory with physicists and keep doctors on their toes to understand the latest medical research. According to Food and Drug Administration (FDA), Kshitij was one of the ten people who changed the Medtech Industry. He was passionate about literature and was an avid reader of English, Hindi, and Urdu texts. He could discuss poetry at length, whether it be by Dylan Thomas or Anna Akhmatova. He loved art and could appreciate the abstracts of Picasso as well as the modern paintings of India, Indonesia, and Argentina. He was a connoisseur of good food and could name his favorite restaurants in almost every country in the world. He had a desperate yearning for knowledge for knowledge's sake, and he believed in perfecting all things he did. He participated in a play, *Dara Shikoh*, produced by Global Performing Arts. It was a huge success. His performance, diction, clarity, and resonance of his voice enchanted the audience and drew many performing arts organizations' attention. He got himself involved with drama rehearsals and poetry/*Shayari* consortiums.

[Kshitij with President and Barbara Bush]

Kshitij believed in humanity, which for him was synonymous with harmony, empathy, and love. A scholar of world religions, Kshitij was very critical of organized religion. He believed religion should promote Godliness in individuals and felt that organized religion's ritualism frequently fed on weakness and nurtured fear and disharmony. He quoted Karl Marx, saying that "religion is the opiate of the masses." In his view, religion should promote social harmony and bring about an awareness of Creation's beauty, and it should be a unifying, not a dividing factor. In his letter to our daughter, Kavita, he wrote,
Godliness is more important than God because one is a metaphor for the other. This Godliness will be with you no matter where you go; it cannot be stolen from you. It will sustain and guide you – the more you use it, the more it will grow.

[Kshtij Mohan: 10 people who changed the medtech industry]

Many quoted him as a "renaissance man." Yet, with all his significant achievements, and a life that would be considered by anyone as successful on all counts, he had an unusual restlessness within him, as is evident in his writings. In his poem, *Storm in A Teacup,* he said, "I know I have swum too far ... beware ... the water is deep in this teacup." In his poem *Bheer,* he wrote, *"Kitni door aur is bheer mein jaana hogaa ..." (Tamam Shud,* 2010)

In the summer of 2009, soon after our Europe trip, he went for his routine colonoscopy. He was diagnosed with stage one lymphoma. As the doctor explained the treatment

The Body of Memories

protocol at the doctor's office, I clutched on to him. My mother's painful death with cancer a few years ago resurfaced before my eyes. How could life end so soon? He gave me a reassuring smile as if saying, "Don't worry; it is only stage one." We came home, he was behaving as if nothing happened, but my world had taken a topsy turvy turn.

[The author with her husband Kshtij and son Vivek many years back]

Four rounds of chemo went by smoothly. We would spend a lot of quality time together, watching movies, going to restaurants, meeting friends, but fifth and sixth rounds of chemo became tougher. He would often have fevers; his white blood cell counts were going down. He was losing weight, from hundred-sixty pounds to almost one-hundred-ten pounds.

We were still hopeful that this all would end soon. We talked about all the fun vacations we took, and we even planned for our future holidays. After the sixth chemo round, we practically lived in the hospital. His immune system was down; platelets, blood transfusions became the regular regime of his treatment. He was intubated and attached to a ventilator to assist with his breathing; heavily sedated, his organs had started failing. I was still surviving on hope. On January 2nd, 2010, this little driblet of hope also evaporated when the doctors gave up and said that it was just a matter of time for him.

****

We took his ashes to India to disperse in the Ganges. As the yellow and orange of the ascending sun peaked through the pinnacles of the Himalayas, my two children, Vivek and Kavita, my grandson, Anant, and I gathered on the banks of the Ganges to perform the last rites for my husband, Kshitij. The Ganges flowed with full force, piercing the hearts of the mountains. The misty-eyed clouds watched the old priest's religious performance; the only thing that broke the serenity of the occasion was the sound of the rain, the serenade of the Ganges, and the chanting of the *shlokas*. The transience of life stood naked before our eyes as my children dispersed his ashes in the Ganges. The lines from his poem, *Alaska ki Salmon* (*Tamam Shud*, 2010) kept ringing in my ears:
Har Jeevan path ka ant waheen
Janm jahan who paata hai
Jis shunya se hum aate hain
Usme hi kho jaate hain. (2)

Similarly, though Kshitij lived most of his life in America, his ashes traveled through the Ganges' holy water, passing through the place of his birth, finally merging with the Bay of Bengal.

After my husband's last rites, I stayed back with my son in Mumbai for a few months. My son was in Mumbai as an ex-pat with Abbott corporation. It was during that time when I compiled Kshitij's poems in a book, *Tamam Shud*. While

The Body of Memories

working on putting his works together, getting it published, and having a few launches, I felt as if I was filling in the empty crevices of my heart with his love; I was reliving him again.

Finally, it was time for me to get back home to Potomac, Maryland, a Washington DC suburb. Tears welled my eyes as I stepped into the empty house without him. His memory was there everywhere for me. This is the house we had decorated together – everything was as is – his well-arranged office, all the files labeled, his library with a reclining leather chair where he often sat to read his books with a glass of cognac. The book on the side-table had a bookmark where he had left it half-read next to his reading glasses. An empty hollowness filled my heart. I was contemplating what to do next when the doorbell rang. I ran to open the door; my neighbor was there with bags full of my mail and two large cardboard FedEx boxes. After my neighbor left, I put my mail aside to deal with them later, but I wondered what was in the boxes. I got a knife from the kitchen and opened the sealed containers – each box contained grey-colored matching Tumi suitcases with carry-ons inside each large one.

I sat there on the floor and cried. The matching suitcases had arrived, but this time my husband had left me far behind as he traversed on his eternal journey …. until we meet again! In *Saanjh-Savera* (*Tamam Shud*, 2010), he wrote:

Kal phir nai dharaa par priye
Ek nootan swarg banaunga
Tera maadak sneh saraa
Har baadal se barsaunga. (3)

[Kshitij's library]

[A collection of first edition rare books]

Reference:

Mohan, Meenakshi, Ed.D. (ed). *Tamam Shud: Poems in English and Hindi –*
   Kshitij Mohan. Bibliophile South Asia, 2010.

The Body of Memories

Translations (Roughly translated):
(1): At the dusk of my life, when my time comes to depart, and the ferryman arrives to
get me; my children will be the lights to guide me … to the other end of the world.
(2): Life ends from where it begins.
(3): Beloved, tomorrow, we will build new heaven on this earth with our love.

Saanjh-Savera: dusk-dawn

Bio:
Dr. Meenakshi Mohan is an educator, art critic, children's writer, painter, and poet. She has taught at universities in Chicago, Boston, and, more recently, for Towson University in Maryland. Her specialization is Early Childhood Leadership and Advocacy. She has published widely in this area and presented numerous papers and workshops. Her book reviews, art critics, interviews, and poems regularly appear in different journals. She has been listed twice in the *Who is Who Among American Teachers.* She authored two children's picture books, *The Rainbow in My Room* and *The Gift,* and edited *Tamam Shud, poems of Kshitij Mohan.* She recently had a solo exhibit of her paintings in Potomac, Maryland. Most of her paintings are in private collections. She is currently on the Advisory Committee of the Montgomery County Library System in its Potomac, Maryland branch. She is on the Editorial Team for *Inquiry in Education*, a peer-reviewed journal published by National Louis University, Chicago, Illinois.

Mother and Shiuli blossoms

Moinak Dutta

She had been a professional nurse. My mother. Sefali Ghosh was her maiden name before she got married to my dad and changed it to Sefali Dutta. Quite interestingly Sefali is the name of a flower found in this part of the world which blooms every autumn. So come autumn, I go into a different mind, a difficult mind too, if am I to say so, for it is like revisiting my childhood and having glimpses of my mother who happily went taking the stairs to heaven.

That year too, the autumn had been awesome. The festivity had been all around. I took her for a ride around the city. Being a person who knew how bodies work, how diseases spread, she perhaps guessed something about her illness. She had a heart which had erratic beats. I remember her telling me all the time while we were having a tour of the city, through its lanes and bylanes, watching people and the trees and cars and all that consist of the cityscape, that it might be her last tour with me. I laughed.

But then, she was a nurse. She knew it. Like she knew how my eyes had an inexpressible medical condition of being wet with salty water at that time when she said those words to me. She knew it that I was trying to be brave. Her brave boy.

And she climbed those stairs easily. Without even groaning. She just slept and woke not.

Next year, I planted a *sefali / shiuli* tree just on our small piece of land by the car shed, beside that patio. It was summer. A full grown horrid Indian summer. The sun blazed hot and cruel. But I had to save that *sefali* tree. Every morning, that summer, even before the sun would turn like a scorching red hot ball of fire, I would wake up and water the tree. And every time I did that, I just prayed with all my heart that it survived that summer, the sultry, boring, lifeless summer of that year. With all my heart, nerve and sinew, I took care of the *shiuli* tree. If I would find its leaves turning a bit yellowish, I would check the soil, rake it, apply manure and water. In the evening, I would go near the tree and touch its little branches and leaves. Perhaps, back then, I thought of myself as perfect gardener. Caressing it. Loving it. Not that I took no care of other trees. Of course, I did that. But that *shiuli* tree was always under my scanner. Once I found a worm crawling at its body. I took it and threw it far away. But before that I took a snapshot of it and searched the internet to find its genus and species. Once finding that, I, with a desperation like that of a medic, found out the measures to be taken to save the tree from onslaught of worms and pests like that.

That time I thought of myself as a nurse too. A nurse to a tree. The *shiuli* tree.

Then came the monsoon. It rained for hours each day that monsoon. I had to take a spade and create a nullah or a makeshift channel on the ground to prevent that particular spot from getting waterlogged, knowing accumulation of water could weaken the tree at its roots.

That time I felt like a construction worker. A sewage cleaner also.

And then, the monsoon also passed, giving way to autumn. The delightful autumn.

For the first few days of the season, all other trees bore flowers. But that *shiuli* tree had none. I was worried. I talked to my wife. She went with me to that small garden we had beside the car shed. Our son went there too. We checked for buds. The tree though had grown taller and greener, had no signs of buds.

Butterflies!
My son suddenly quipped.
Yes, we needed butterflies to carry pollens and to make the tree bloom.

So again, I searched for trees which attract butterflies the most. I found some, brought them and planted them.
That time I felt I was like a priest. Purifying the earth praying with all my heart for its beauty to arrive.
Praying those trees which attract birds and bees and butterflies to grow faster.
They did. Butterflies arrived. Bees too.
The smell of flowers wrought my senses with joy.
I felt that time I had become half of that garden.
Only that *shiuli* tree.
I waited.
We all waited.

Then one fine morning, as I went near the tree, I found them. Those white *shiuli* blossoms with an orange core waving to me from the branches of the tree. They had bloomed overnight!

I called my wife and son.
We three stood under the tree.
The air around it had that unmistakable fragrance of *shiuli* blossoms.
That time I felt perfect like a nurse.

Bio:
Moinak Dutta is a published fiction writer, poet and teacher from Kolkata, India. Many of his poems and stories are published in national and international anthologies and magazines and also dailies including 'Madras Courier', 'The Statesman' (Kolkata edition), ' World Peace Poetry anthology ' (United Nations), 'Spillwords', 'Setu', 'Riding and Writing' (as a featured poet twice, published from Ohio, USA), ' The Indian Periodical' ' Teesta Journal', ' Pangolin Review', ' Tuck Magazine', among numerous others.

He has also written reviews of books and fictions, among which notable ones are: on ' The Upanisads ' (translated by Valerie J. Roebuck) which can be found at and the review of ' The Ballad of Bapu' (written by Santosh Bakaya). His first full length English (genre: literary/romance) fiction *'Online@Offline'* had been published in 2014, by Lifi Publications. His second fiction (genre: literary/quest) titled 'In search of la radice' was published in 2017 by Xpress Publications. He has also worked as an editor of a poetry collection titled ' Whispering Poeisis', which had over one hundred poems from sixty poets from different parts of India and abroad, published in 2018 by Poeisis.

The Sounds and Sights of the Nineteen Forties

Monica Talukdar

The sounds and sights of the nineteen forties leave me nostalgic. It is a canvas of bright colours with areas of dark grey. I was born before the Indian Independence into a world rife with fear and uncertainty, while forging into the brave new world.

My childhood was spent in Allahabad (now Prayag Raj) at the confluence of the Ganga and Yamuna, with the Saraswati hidden out of sight. Boating on the Ganga was always thrilling. The splash of the boatman's oars; the cool breeze from the rivers brushing against our skin and the innumerable birds flying across the cobalt blue sky are some of the numerous images that are permanently etched in my mind.

Our home at 2, Canning road (now Mahatma Gandhi Marg) was near the crossing of Canning road and Kanpur road- a sprawling bungalow of early twentieth century, with orchards of mango and guava trees. The blazing hot summers of Allahabad were almost unbearable, with temperatures rising beyond 40 degrees centigrade; but the nights were cooler and more comfortable. Hence, during those soothing summer nights, we slept outside, in the open courtyard. Our stringed cots or *khatia* would be lined up in the open courtyard with mosquito nets tied to bamboo rods to protect us from mosquitoes. The uncemented courtyard would be well watered to cool the atmosphere. The mango and guava trees which overlooked our beds fanned us with their leafy branches, hushing us to sleep as the birds, bees, and insects were all sheltered in their branches that they dared not disturb.

But what fascinated me most was the starry sky, with the moon sailing across it. The twinkling stars of different hues

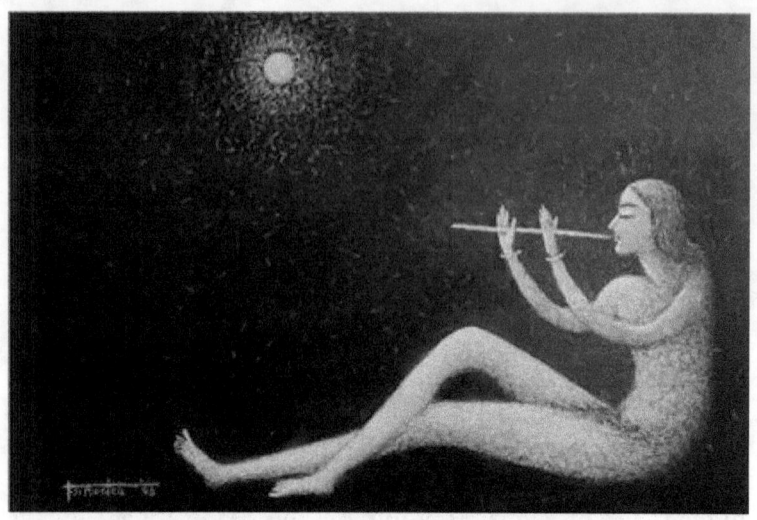

krishna's flute (oil) 36"x24" 2008

seemed to keep watch over us. The silent, unpolluted, boundless night sky would put me to sleep only to be awakened in the middle of the night by the lilting, full-throated song of the *Dalit* (untouchable) carrying the night soil of the town in his bullock cart. The songs of Radha and Krishna and their love would wake me up; the *Dalit*'s songs would carry my soul to his haunting music. The songs had no accompaniments, except for the creaking wheels of the bullock cart, and the tinkling bells that were tied around the bullock's neck. The *Dalit* had no companion and no audience except for the moon who accompanied him faithfully to his destination. Where did this heavenly being deposit our excretion? Where did he come from, and where did he go? I never saw him or met him. But his soulful songs convinced me that he was a complete and a happy being, one who was in rhythm with the universe- in eternal bliss! I forgot that he was carrying human excretion, our filth, which had kept us away from the *Dalit*! Krishna's flute could not have produced better music.

Early mornings meant waking up with the chatter of birds, then climbing the guava tree and throwing our washed clothes across the courtyard wall to the *dhobin* (washerwoman) who lived in our outhouse, to iron out our clothes. Our *dhobin* would promptly gather our clothes, greeting us with her toothless smile. Many an evening my younger brother and myself would visit the *dalit* washerwoman's little home coated with mud mixed with cow-dung to have bajra roti (flatbread made of millet) with *gur* (jaggery). *Dhobin*'s mud baked *chulah* (stove) lit with charcoal and wood would turn out delicious hot *rotis*.

After having our fill, we children along with her grandchildren would be huddled up in her decrepit old *khatia* to listen to her faraway village stories in Hindi, in the earthy Awadhi dialect. The little room lit up with a single oil lamp exuded warmth and unconditioned love. Love, without expectations. I am thankful to my parents who were known as high caste Brahmins for teaching us to respect all humanity irrespective of their caste, religion, or status.

Another favourite haunt of us children used to be the home of Mian Sahib, the *tongawallah* who lived in our outhouse. He owned an *ekka* and a *tonga* (wooden two-wheeled carriages drawn by horses), very popular in India those days. Whenever Mian Sahib was free, we would climb onto his *ekka* and take joyrides in Civil Lines where we lived. The steady swing of the *ekka* along with the clip-clop of the horse's hoofs thrilled us greatly. Sometimes we would take distant rides on his tonga. The rhythmic sound of the horse's trot, and the tinkle of bells tied round the horse's neck would remind me of all the nursery rhymes learned in Bengali from the age of three. I recited all the poems keeping in tune with the rhythm of the hoofs till I dozed off to sleep, only to be jerked out of my slumber on reaching our destination.

Nineteen-forties also remind me of my excruciating memories of war and famine. World War II had started, and there were grim repercussions of the war everywhere around us. There were days when droves of black, evil looking planes spitting dark grey smoke flooded the skies. The sounds of the planes were menacing and disturbing, and I would quickly hide under the divan in our veranda to escape from the horrors of being bombed that clouded my child mind. Luckily there was no bombing in Allahabad.

Grandma's tales- wash painting on paper 12"x18"

World War II and the great Bengal famine of 1943 were unnerving. Being exposed to the arts at an early age, we visited the art exhibition of the local artist Roma Mukherjee on the Bengal famine. The paintings were in oils and water colours of approximately 4'x7' in size. They depicted people dying of hunger. Their skinny, outstretched hands begging for a morsel of food was heartbreaking. Their hungry, open mouths and their sunken, stark, gaping eyes screaming out of the canvases left me overwhelmed, stunned and depressed. The man-made Bengal famine left me guilty. I felt guilty that I was living in comfort when thousands were dying of hunger and poverty. The ruthless British regime in our country had sucked us dry!

The *mali* (gardener) in our outhouse was very poor, but an amiable old man. Our sprawling garden housed all kinds of birds, bees and insects and also a host of dragon flies, and very often the two nephews-in-law of the late Prime Minister of India, Indira Gandhi would troop into our garden to catch the dragon flies with their nets. We wondered what they did with them. Somebody told us that their mother, the grand old Parsi lady, Mrs. Gandhi cooked them! She ran the Finaro Hotel in our neighbourhood. But it is still a mystery to us as to the fate of the dragon flies!

The old gardener would be digging in our garden, and what attracted me most were his bare feet. He was too poor to buy shoes or slippers and my father would often give his old shoes and clothes which did not fit him too well. His feet had deep cracks and when he lifted them, I could see innumerable holes under his feet made by ring worms. He wore patched clothes. I have fond memories of this friendly, unassuming old man. When I had matured into a painter, he inspired me to make a painting on him playing the *ektara*, a stringed instrument, which he never really played. The painting was sent to Australia to participate at a children's international art competition, but it never returned. I liked my old *mali* whose night blindness always distressed me.

I went to a British school where speaking in any language other than English was forbidden. At home we spoke in Bengali, our mother tongue. My elder sister Manju went to an English medium but an Indian school, where they had the privilege of communicating in any language of their choice. My sister one day defied me to shout '*Bande Mataram!*' in school- an act that would surely get me into trouble, as it was the slogan of our freedom fighters for India's independence.

But I wanted to prove myself patriotic and brave by defying the British government. So during lunch break, I rushed out of the dining hall, leaving my friends behind to the back of the school where there were clusters of tall, big trees. I fervently looked around, making sure that nobody was within hearing distance and then clutched onto a tree and shouted '*Bande Mataram!*' I had done it! At last I was set free from fear and inhibitions with this little act of defiance. I sought absolution from fear which reigned supreme in many of our minds during those days.

To speak of defiance against the British rule, let me add here that most of my uncles participated in the freedom struggle movement, and in a way, I was proud of my legacy. The doors of our house were always open to all the freedom fighters struggling to attain independence for our country. My mother Parul Debi would prepare quick meals which they would somehow consume and disappear, shouting '*Bande Mataram!*' and '*Allahu Akbar!*' My Father Dwijendranath Sanyal fought free cases for the freedom fighters and our home would be raided by the police quite often. We made bonfires of foreign goods in our courtyard along with some rare letters of the freedom fighters including the letters of M. N. Roy the eminent political philosopher. Our ancestral home in Varanasi was confiscated by the British government and our huge library completely destroyed, which included some rare manuscripts on the Rig Veda.

When the first radio entered our home, it was a day of celebration. It was one of the few radios in our locality. And the most exciting part of the programme was when we would shut all the doors and windows of our home to listen to the inspiring speeches of Netaji Subhash Chandra Bose. The volume of the radio would be reduced to the minimum, and our ears would be glued to the radio in an effort not to miss a single word of his. Netaji was our hero who spoke loud and clear from distant lands in the Far East, promising us freedom from the yoke of foreign rule. Later, the speeches of Netaji in India were not taken favorably by the British Government and anyone seen to be disobeying the law would be instantly arrested. As children, we did not understand the urgency of the situation, but the body language of our elders told us that we were not supposed to discuss or disclose these incidents outside our homes. Gradually, with the political onslaughts of the times, Netaji's speeches got far removed and we started missing his fiery and robust speeches.

In the milieu of events that followed, the demand for attaining freedom for our country was strengthened further. Some of our relatives who were in the British Indian army, as it was called then, had stopped saluting their British officers and began to defy them. On 15th August 1947, at the stroke of the midnight hour, India became free! Pandit Jawaharlal Nehru was sworn in as the first Prime Minister of Independent India. The tri-coloured Indian flag went up, bringing down the British flag. Our joy was boundless. So many Indians had sacrificed their lives for this beloved flag. We sang *'Jana Gana Mana...'* our National anthem written by Gurudev Rabindranath Tagore, and cried *'Jai Hind!'* loud and clear.

Unfortunately, this happiness was short lived. Rioting broke out in the country. People started killing and abusing each other as the country suffered the bitter onslaughts of the historic partition. Hindus and Muslims were now sworn enemies post-partition, carrying their bitterness towards each other for generations to come. Slogans that were honey to our ears were now obnoxious! We would be woken up in the middle of the night with menacing cries of *'Har! Har! Mahadev!'* and *'Allahu Akbar!'* They spewed hate and enmity. The Muslim leaders had chosen their country called Pakistan, carved out of the Indian sub-continent. West Punjab and East Bengal now became a separate nation- West Pakistan and East Pakistan (now Bangladesh) respectively. Like all sensitive souls, it appeared to me too that the Indian leaders were happy to accomplish a free, albeit a divided country. Did they care about the common people who became victims of their ruthless political deal?

I was confused as to what it meant to be free. Was it hate or love? Was it 1 and the other? I found no answers and my young, sensitive mind was disheartened. Gradually I saw a change of scene within my familiar surroundings. The good old *Mian Sahib* left for Pakistan with his three beautiful daughters. The *tonga* and *ekka* were gone. Many of my school friends left without a word. Many of my wealthy relatives fled from East Bengal in fear of being tortured and killed, leaving everything behind, hoping to return to their ancestral home someday.

Unfortunately, it never happened. My aunt's two families lived in a single room partitioned by a curtain for years, for the government had not given them any compensation. My brother-in- law and his family walked for days from Sylhet till they reached Kolkata. Many of my relatives who lived in East Bengal and fought bravely in the freedom struggle, found overnight with shock and dismay that the country which they loved and had fought for was no longer theirs!

I was confused as to how I should define myself, and my first reaction was that I stopped believing in God. I had no faith in human values.

Then gradually and surely, I gathered my strength from nature. From the trees, plants, rivers, mountains, birds, insects and the deep blue sky- that open space which taught me the first lessons of knowing the strength and bounty of the infinite!

My mind reverted back to my *dalit* hero carrying the night soil. I realized that it is he who had understood life, who fathomed the mysteries of the universe. He defined the meaning of acceptance and of happiness to me. He knew how to live in harmony with nature, and realized that his roots lay in nature. He understood that to serve mankind is the greatest service one can do to oneself. Good bye dear friend, I am still learning from you...

[Artwork by Monica Talukdar]

Bio:
Monica Talukdar was born and brought up in Allahabad (now Prayag Raj). An alumnus of Allahabad University, she studied English Literature and was exposed to the Art world at an early age. After her marriage she settled down in Dehradun where she pursued painting seriously which became her profession. She has exhibited her works nationally and internationally and has won several awards. In1999 she was awarded by the All India Fine Arts and Crafts Society, Delhi for her lifetime contribution to the Visual Arts. She organized several art exhibitions and workshops, and was founder president of the Doon Art Society, Dehradun.

Monica is also a writer who edited the book 'Footprints of Bengal on the Himalayas' which was inaugurated at the International Literature and Arts Festival at Dehradun in 2019.She lives and works in Dehradun in the backdrop of the beautiful Himalayas.

Email- tsmonica44@gmail.com

The Body of Memories

In a Gourmet of Memories

Nabanita Sengupta

Certain dishes carry whiffs of nostalgia, some stories hidden in the folds of memory, some gentle remembrances of dear faces. For me, most foods are stories. All that I cook generally have a face, a tale attached to them that blends with the spices and becomes a cuisine of its own. So cooking becomes for me an act of remembering. Each day a juggling of the memory, refreshingly sweet, at times even painful.

The black sandwich maker, my saviour during those very hectic mornings, that otherwise occupies a quiet corner in my kitchen, reminds me of the *bhaiya ji* in Delhi who used to serve homestyle mashed potato sandwiches with a yummy tomato sauce for just five rupees during my college days. He had a sandwich maker too, peeling off at various places, telling stories of overuse and slog. So many evening hunger pangs have been satiated by those crisp yet soft sandwiches and a bottle of aerated drink shared among friends. We used to stroll up to his stall in groups of five or six, chatting all the way about almost everything under the sun. There used to be two plastic stools wobbling on their four legs on which we generally kept our bags while we stood, our mouth engaged in the double action of talking and munching. A mere five rupees could get us a full tummy and an invigorating adda. One of the friends who used to be a part of the group often insisted on pastries after that, not caring a fig for the warnings of weight machines. When we meet up these days, which is very rare, I do not forget to remind him of his famous maxim - once I start earning, I shall ensure I always have good food to eat. Well, I have never seen him lacking it even in his pre-earning days!

Kulcha choley and master's classes share an intimate bond in my mind. So many M.A. classes have been sustained on the basis of those *choley kulchas* on three wheeled carts! Staying at a private hostel, most of the days we did not pack our lunches. The *chole kulcha bhaiya* used to wait for us just behind the Arts faculty gate and often we would rush to him for a quick and filling meal. Once I remember sitting under the tree and sharing bits of *kulcha* with a squirrel who had somehow lost its fear of humans and sat quite close to me. There was a *kulche wala* at law faculty too, but we always believed that the one who came to our Arts Faculty gate served tastier stuff. During these recent lockdown days, I mastered the art of making *kulchas*, but that's more in the traditional Amritsari style of North India. The *kulchas* I made did not resemble its white soft bun-like cousin from Delhi. Unfortunately, I have not yet come across a Google recipe to help me with that variety.

My roommate was an awesome cook. Even in the limited facilities of a private mess, she managed to tackle difficult dishes like raw jackfruit curry and stuffed *paranthas*. Oh yes, I did learn how to make a circular roti from her. Now, while I put the perfect round roti on the *tawa* each evening, I do remember her. Of course I do remember her for a thousand other reasons too. In our hostel days, whenever we would be in low spirits, our favourite refrain was, 'let's cook something delicious!' And that had never failed to cheer us up. How I wish cheering up could be so easy even now!

One good aspect of staying in a hostel is that it brings you in close contact with various cuisines. We had a Marwari friend whose fasting days were replete with short munching spells of dry fruits and normal fruits. She was an expert in *halwa* of all kinds. While our skill was limited to semolina, she made delightful *halwas* of wheat, potatoes, apples and much more. The other day when my *gajar ka halwa*, made with winter carrots turned blackish brown instead of red, I was so desperately thinking of her. How I wished she could be here to help me out and how relieved I was to realise that she wasn't a witness to that horror of a *halwa*!

Oh, fasting stories of hostels are so replete with food tales. *Saboo ka khichdi* used to be something we looked forward

The Body of Memories

to whenever another of my hostel friends, one from UP, decided to keep a fast. That *khichdi* tasted awesome. Till date, I have not managed to make it that way. But for me *saboo khichdi* had another meaning too. It was what my grandmother would also eat on her fasting days. Ma used to prepare it for her. I loved both the varieties, yet there was such a huge difference of taste between them. Never a believer in fasts, I however did always appreciate the various kinds of fares associated with fasting and happily participated in breaking the fast without even keeping it!

Talking about our cooking episodes in the hostel, there are a number of stories associated with it. Once I remember we wanted to watch one of the newly released Rajesh Kukunoor movies which was playing in one of the earliest multiplexes of Delhi. Delhi at that time had just two multiplexes, as far as I remember and the prices were exorbitant for our students' purses. The one which we wanted to visit was in the other part of the city and the only multiplex where a student I-card made us eligible for a seven-rupee ticket. Imagine paying just seven rupees for a ticket that would otherwise cost you a hundred! Those were the times when month ends also meant empty pockets as whatever cash came from home would be on the waning side by then. So, on an ambitious note, we woke up early in the morning, cooked and packed lunches for ourselves, jangling utensils much more than required to drive home the importance of the event, and headed towards the bus stand for a long ride from the North to the South of Delhi. Well, we reached there, got our tickets and watched the movie, but our packed lunches remained packed and waiting in our backpacks. We couldn't resist the temptations of the food stalls there; all our economic planning going down the drain! Thereafter we never packed lunches for outings.

Cosmopolitanism in food has been my good fortune since childhood. I remember George uncle and aunty, our first neighbours. They were from Kerala. Oh God, I can't even describe the variety of *dosas* they made. So in our last *dosa* party sometime back at my place, I too decided to add variety to the dish. It was almost thirty years later that I was suddenly reminded of them and inspired by this idea. So what we did was to make a menu card that included paneer *dosa*, egg *dosa*, chicken *dosa*, veg *dosa*, plain *dosa* and all these varieties available either plain, with cheese or with butter! It was such a hit with my family! I quietly thanked our first neighbours and sent some prayers for them in whichever part of the world they might be.

And noodles - a whole novel can be scripted in their serpentine strands! Noodles, chow, chow mein, so many names and so many types. In my childhood days, I remember those long bundles of Lycia noodles coming home and they would generally find place in our school lunch boxes or evening tiffin. Then I was introduced to the oil dripping, deep fried chow mein with cabbage leaves in the Delhi food stalls. Those became our friends in need - on the days when *dabbawalahs* failed to deliver food, chow mein from the nearby food joint satisfied our pangs. Nowadays in the times of YouTube, I love experimenting with various forms of noodles - Thai, Chinese, Singaporean, etc, all with an added trace of Indianness. My mom's harried face as she packed our lunch, the uncle from Delhi food stall, my friends with whom I shared a plate of those fried oily stuff - all merge into one loving memory as I browse the numerous Youtube channels in search of that perfect noodles recipe.

Rose cakes of Chako aunty, *thekuas* of Pandey aunty, *rasam* at a Tamil friends place, *sewai* from *Jiadali bhaiya*, a worker under my father, and much more had become a part of our everyday experience without much ado during my days at Gomia. That was why we celebrated *baisakhi, nababarsha,* Eid, Christmas, Durga Puja with equal elan. While growing up, we did not even realise the rich multiculturalism in our lives as that was the only way of life known to us. I have been fortunate in my childhood to have grown up among such a diverse but close-knit community which seems light years away now in this age of overt factionalism.

The Body of Memories

Such memories abound in my mindscape. The list goes on and on. My cooking becomes akin to visiting an old album, smiling faces peeking out from there. It becomes a chronicle of times gone by and a witness of a harmonious lifestyle. It also becomes a repertoire of lost stories - faces who now live just in memories. Sweets from New Market that my uncle used to keep for me or the small packs of fried nuts that an elder cousin brought home to share or long searches for a fish meal in Delhi, befitting our students' purse on the insistence of a dear friend. All these anecdotes have now become memories, never to be renewed. The key players in these memories have left this world long back. I cannot meet them ever, but they live through these moments. Each time I put a piece of fish in the *kadhai*, I think of my departed friend, the best buddy I ever had, snatched so early from all of us.

Each day my wok is filled with stories from the past as I try to whip up and recreate bits of nostalgia in my small kitchen. The past energises, fuels the present as I look optimistically towards a better tomorrow. And the tiredness just falls away….

Bio:

Nabanita Sengupta is presently working as assistant professor in English at Sarsuna College, affiliated to the University of Calcutta. A creative writer and translator, her area of doctoral research has been Translation Studies. She has participated in various translation workshops and presented papers in various national and international seminars in India and abroad. Her recent publication is *A Bengali Lady in England*, a translation of a nineteenth century travel writing by a woman from Bengal. A co-edited anthology on Displacement of women in South Asia is shortly to be published. Her creative writings have been published at various places like Muse India, Coldnoon, Café Dissensus, NewsMinute.in, etc. Currently she is writing a series of short stories under the title *Ghumi Stories* for the Borderless Journal.

Lovesong

Nandita De nee Chatterjee

[A family memoir, based on the author's personal experiences of elderly life and the bond of love in her filial setting.]

October 2000.

The dark, green leaves of the 'bokul' tree parted. The shiny black cuckoo perched on its favourite branch. Fresh after a night-long sleep, it let out its first morning song, full-throated and deep.

The early-morning golden rays from the east burnished the lady's hair into gold. Instinctively she looked up, eyes searching for the songbird, eager and expectant. The reverie broke through the 5 am stillness, and she turned her head to smile at the man in the armchair. The tiny balcony on the first-floor building had a few flowering plants with red and orange blooms shyly peeping through the silver grills.

A tiny table set with an immaculate, white and gold tea set in a tray was in the centre, flanked by two white nylon cane chairs.

A beautifully manicured hand poured out a cup of fresh Darjeeling tea and she leaned forward to give the cup to the gentleman. A trembling hand accepted it and over tea and toast the two sat back to savour the dawn concert.

The man's Grecian features under snowy, back-brushed hair had a forbidding line. His frame, even in rest, exuded command. Only his steely grey eyes had a serenity belying his trembling arm.

'Do you have to go anywhere today?" his wife asked.

He did not answer for some time. Then, 'yes, I have to go to the bank to furnish my 'Life Certificate'. Remember, you'll

The Body of Memories

have to do that every November to get the Air Force pension when I'm not there.'

'Someone will have to carry me', the plump lady in the chair next to him grinned. 'After all, my legs won't take me that far and the taxi stand is too far away. Also I can't get onto a rickshaw.'

'What about your younger daughter? She will surely take you.'

"Oh yes! surely. Only she won't be in time to pick up Babu from school. The poor little boy will have to stand, hungry and alone for hours while she runs helter-skelter trying to get through the Calcutta jams and road blockades to reach school. No, I don't think so. I won't be able to get your pension. But how much can one eat? Since I won't be able to do any shopping, I'll make do with 'dal' and eggs.'

The stern face breaks into merriment.

'What about electric bills, phone and milk bills, gas, corporation tax? How will you pay for those?'

'Why, what you have in the bank can settle that. The 'darwan' gives the bill for just Rs 20."

'And medical bills?'

'Oh, private clinics are too expensive. I'll tell my son-in-law to put me into Command Hospital,' she retorts.

'Have I explained to you all about my identity card and the other cards? That will take care of any heart problems or if you have any fancy disease. In Calcutta you'll be entitled to cashless treatment up to Rs.1 lakh at BM Birla.'

'Oh I know all about those! Haven't you told me that a hundred times? I won't need those. At 73, no new disease will attack me. This 20-year-old leg problem is my doom.'

'Nothing will happen to me,' he replies. 'I'll die like my mum, in one second over my lunch. Good people die that way. You'll have a harder time.'

'Oh no I won't, ' the old lady snaps. I have done my duties. I was an extremely loving child. I loved my father most in the world. I was the only one in 8 siblings who waited on him day and night. During his paralysis days he rested only on me when I was around.'

'What about your temper?'

'What temper? In school and college, I was the most helpful girl! My whole life I participated in sports, dance and music. All athletes and artistes have good dispositions. I'm warm, humorous, talkative. You don't even talk to your daughters much and never answer phones.'

'Three women in the house! Who will participate in your senseless banter? I liked talking to serious people in the Mess.'

'Oh Yes! Your Air Force friends! Where are they now? For the last 20 years you've refused to visit anyone, save your brothers and Kum Kum.'

'Didn't I go to Canada to be with Rangita for 3 months when she was pregnant?'

'Isn't she also your daughter?'

The elderly face becomes sad.

'I just cannot think what she will do - two sad marriages and now alone in California with a small child. Being her father, I can't do anything for her. She can't even have a normal life if she returns to India. This Parkinson has totally disabled my functions. I can't do anything for her.'

'Yes, you forget most things now. And your speech is getting slurred. But at 76 something has to happen. Look at it this

The Body of Memories

way, you don't have diabetes or heart disease. There is hardly any elderly person in our estate without serious problems.'

'Of course, I'm not pitying myself. After all, I need something to die. Haven't I been Military Fit for 72 years?'

'That's my main worry,' the lady replies. 'How will I die? I don't see anything happening to me in the near future. Nobody dies with arthritis legs. I'm agile, young at heart, I chat for hours on the phone, cook fancy dishes like I did 30 years ago and read every tit-bit news in papers and magazines.'

Suddenly she looks at the drawing room clock.

'My masseuse should be in soon. I'll wash this set. The help may break it. I've preserved it for 40 years now. You brought it from the UK, remember? '

'Yes, we were in Palam then. Andrew was with me. He is in a nursing home in Sydney now. I got a card from him yesterday.'

The doorbell rings. Mr. Mukherjee enters. 'Good morning Mr Chatterjee, *Boudi*. I see you are having your early morning tea.'

'Come in, come in. Can I make you some breakfast? ' Mrs. Chatterjee smiles.

'Of course! That's why I've come. Who feels like having tea alone every day?'

'I heard your son is joining the U.N. That's good,' Mr. Chatterjee says, settling down on a dull, blue velvet sofa.

'Yes, he'll be leaving for Africa. All my children are so far away. I have 7 grandchildren from 5 children and yet I'm so alone since Sumitra died.'

'Yes, I miss her too. We used to go for evening walks everyday,' Mrs. Chatterjee says.

'But anyway, they come once a year on holidays. Not everyone has that. See Roy - his wife never gets out of bed and no kids. Poor guy, he has to buy food most days.'

'Yes, these part-time helps and cooks are no good. Most days they are absent. They really take advantage of old people,' the lady replies. 'And there's no knowing what ills a full-timer may bring! Did you see the papers yesterday? An old couple stabbed by a resident help of 10 years!'

'Self-help is the best, I say,' Mr. Chatterjee responds. 'I never rely on anyone.'

'Except me, and Kum Kum and Tata. They took you to the ICU twice last month, didn't they?'

'Yes, poor things. He doesn't come home from office before dinner everyday. It's a shame putting so much burden on the kids. They have such a hectic life as it is.'

Mr. Mukherjee shakes his head. 'Why, didn't you nurse them when they were young? Now it's their turn to look after their parents. You think only of them!'

'Naturally, they are our family. If we won't think about the children, who will? Do they have anyone else?' Mrs. Chatterjee is now getting emotional.

'Don't inform them that the doctor called yesterday. I'm taking oxygen when I need it. That's good enough. I don't want to go to any hospital. I'll die here only,' Mr Chatterjee tells his wife. 'And you better learn to count money right and inform yourself of the different bank accounts.' He laughs, 'such a small amount in the bank. What does a serviceman have left? It won't pay for both our hospital bills. And you'll never be able to reach me to Command.'

The Body of Memories

He looks towards Mr. Mukherjee. 'Your *boudi* won't be able to visit me in Alipore. So I've told her to forget about Command Hospital.'

'What's more important, saving your life or visiting you at hospital?' she retorts. 'Haven't I been through several wars with you? Am I not a Defence wife? Have I not looked after your health for 42 years? Nothing will happen to you while I am here. Stop worrying about me.'

'What will you do when you are alone? Go off to Kumu. You are still like a baby. You have no knowledge about worldly matters. What will happen to you?'

'Why won't I be like a baby? You have treated me like a child all my life. You have never put any problems on me. So how can I learn now? In any case, one of us has to go first.'

She relaxed with the sweater she is knitting for her grandson. 'You'll be worse off if I go first. After all, I cook for you, dust the house, nurse you.'

' Oh, I'm fine,' Mr. Chatterjee laughs." I don't need you.'

'That's what he's said all his life,' Mrs. Chatterjee tells Mr. Mukherjee. 'If lunch is not ready by 12:30, you come and see his temper.'

They all laugh.

The faces are a little creased now. Mr. Chatterjee's hand shakes continuously. His once strong body is now slightly frail. But as he rests back on the sofa, he still looks infinitely handsome, stern brave.

Mr. Mukherjee leaves. He wanders around alone for a few hours every day before he enters an empty home.

Mrs. Chatterjee shuts the door. After a bath she wears a freshly ironed pink saree and puts a rose in her hair. The image looking back from her mirror is extremely lovely.

Taking the incense around the house after her Puja, she wakes up her napping husband.

'I'm bringing the 10 o'clock coffee.'

The birds keep singing outside. The cooing is now joined by sharper trills and the 'bokul' tree outside resplendent with different birds.

The steam disappears above the coffee mugs. This is always relaxing.

'I love this flat you've bought. The birds are a permanent joy. And there are new buds in the red hibiscus.'

'True. But Sapan didn't come to sell his fish for two days now. Do you have enough for today? My hand-shaking is not stopping even after the medicine. It doesn't have any effect anymore. I can't go to the bazaar.'

'So what? The vegetable man was here this week. I'm making your favourite '*musoor dal*' with 'dhania' leaves, paneer-capsicum, fried brinjal and egg curry. And your '*patali gurer payesh*' is also ready.'

'Remind me to buy more '*patali gur*' the next time I can make it to the market. Make large quantities. Guests drop in all the time.'

'Have I ever forgotten?' she returns.

The evening twilight creeps in. The tubelight is turned on and doors shut on the menacing mosquitos. TV is switched on. The elderly couple inside are laughing over their evening tea, remembering, joking, thinking back, thinking of tomorrow, thinking of the kids. The room is warm. The tray has to be removed.

She tries to get up from the sofa. But it will take her at least 10 minutes to stand. He rushes forward. His shaking hand picks up the tea tray. The clattering of the cups is loud.

The Body of Memories

'Leave it. Your hand is shaking too much. I'll take it in a few minutes.'

'No, I will. You can't walk.'

Bio:
Writer/freelance journalist/housewife. Formerly with Economic Times. Cover stories and Feature Writer with Statesman, Illustrated Weekly, Economic Times, Telegraph, Times of India, Femina, Filmfare, Germany Today, Voix Meets Mode, UK, Frontier Weekly, Namaste Ink. Co Author, Big Bang of Non-Fiction, Life in Reverse; 30 Best Poets; Sea; Coffee & Echos; Wrapped Up Feelings; Poetry Planet's Christmas in my Heart, Moonlight; Asian Literary Society's A Kaleidoscope of Asia & A Bilingual Anthology of Poems, Poetry Planet's Writers' Haven; Rewrite the Stars; Love Thy Mother; The Real Hero; Born to Dream Winners' Anthology; Heart of a Poet by Inner child press anthologies, USA; Ashes; Arise from the Stars; Striving for Survival & An Indian Summer by Plethora Blogazine.

Alternative Masculinity(?!)

Nandini Sahu

We surely were annoyed, rather uncomfortable, looking at the PDA of the middle-aged couple.

Dr.Harihar Panda and his wife Mrs.Savita Panda were my guests that evening, along with two other friends from Odisha—Dr. Manas and Dr.Shubhra. All of them except for Savita were in Delhi to attend a conference. Manas and Shubhra were my old friends, I invited them over dinner after the conference. Harihar and Savita came along; in fact, I had to invite them as well, because the four of them had come from Bhubaneswar as a team. I had booked three rooms in the university guest house for them—one for the couple and two for the other two.

Savita had nothing to do during the day when her husband and his friends were busy in the conference. She was rather restless and very worried about the food, medicines, etc. of her husband. She always remained worried about these trivial matters—starting with what he should wear any given day to how much tea he should consume in the evening. Should he apply oil on his hair today? What if he catches cold by a head bath? Should he eat chicken more than once a week? What if it upsets his stomach? Is he talking too much on the mobile? He may get a migraine, so the phone should be switched off now. And why is he taking such a long walk? It's windy today.

Their children were settled, grown up, and the fifty-plus wife's only concern, focus, topic of discussion, life, love, happiness, worry— just everything--was her sixty-plus husband.

Throughout the past couple of days, we were noticing Savita's overwhelming care and concern for Harihar. Initially, we found it cute.

My friend Manas was a writer, an emotionally charged, intelligent person, somewhat close to my heart. Shubhra was a chirpy, witty, pretty woman; she was most talkative.

That evening, my friends got introduced to my son Sonu, a humorous, intelligent and sober teen. They were happy to receive his hospitality. I had cooked quite a few dishes for them, and the guests thoroughly enjoyed the food. We chatted about Odisha; in between, Manas talked about his new stories. He knew I loved his stories, he wanted my complete attention, which I too was willingly giving. Shubhra was keen on knowing every detail of my friendship with Manas—when and how did we meet? How come we were so compatible with each other despite his happy married life in Odisha? Neither was I his lover or anything. She was trying to understand this special bonding.

Harihar was eager to get all the attention of me, his hostess; he tried to give his opinion about everything around, talked about his achievements, his admiration of the excellent life I had made for myself in Delhi. In between, he never forgot to praise each dish I had cooked; and I had to thank him politely every time he praised. Overall, it was a pleasant evening.

Beyond all of these, oblivious to us, Savita was in her usual fidgety disposition – checking and serving food on Harihar's plate, chiding him for eating more of one dish or less of one, restricting his intake of coffee after food. She even asked him if he washed his hands before food.

I said, "Madam, you please eat, Sir will help himself; if he needs any assistance, I'll look after." I guess as the hostess, that was my duty.

"No no!! How can he eat if I don't serve? I'll eat later; as such I had a lot of snacks in the guest house when you all were in the conference."

Shubhra has this crooked, uncontrollable sense of humour, which will make anyone laugh. She said, *"Arre* Savita madam, do you always take care of Sir like this? Is he a domestic animal?" (she actually said, '*gruhapalita pashu'!!*).

Unbelievable!! Incorrigible Shubhra!!

I couldn't control my laughter, nor could Manas and Sonu. I rushed to the kitchen to laugh in the plea of getting some pickles. In the kitchen I remembered Shakespeare's Lady Macbeth. Lady Macbeth said, "unsex me today". This statement paralleled negativity to manhood and power.

Was this over-consciousness Savita's reverse feminism? What a drama queen!

I joined them back with a desire to see a little more of domestic drama. I must confess.

Dr.Harihar, who was an Associate Professor, and was waiting for his CAS promotion to a Professor's position, of course did not like this 'domestic animal' adjective. He had to make his stand clear.

By then, Savita had started eating, and was relaxed, after feeding her husband to her satisfaction.

Harihar cleared his throat and said, looking at me, clearly avoiding Shubhra, "Madam, do you know, Savita is the most loving and caring wife I have ever seen. She takes care of everything. From morning to night, twenty-four into seven, she is there for me. She takes care of my home, my children, me. She cooks, cleans the house, arranges my shattered books, shabby study tables, irons my clothes, feeds me. I simply depend on her for every single thing. In fact, for every small thing I need her."

Savita had a beaming smile on her lips.

"I even make him wear his dress. Else this mindless man would go to his university in his underwear—he is so offhand." Announced Savita proudly.

"What the …!!!" Shubhra was unrelenting. She wanted more spice for the dinner table. "I mean, Savita Madam, do you actually make him sit on the chair semi-nude, and do his *shringaar* before he goes to the university? Every day?!"

"Oh yes! Definitely. I even give him a bath every morning. I have been doing that forever!"

I looked at Harihar covertly to see if he was feeling embarrassed. But he had a blank, nonchalant expression on his face. Like the Monalisa painting. I couldn't understand what exactly he was thinking at that moment of humiliation.

Savita got up, washed her hands quickly, and came back to her husband, wiped his mouth with her dupatta, arranged his scanty locks on the bald head, set his shirt collars right, and sat closely beside him, in the most 'lovey-dovey' position, making all of us uncomfortable.

Sonu is one more witty boy here. "Wow uncle and aunty! You both are young, like characters from a Bollywood film." He added. And then he left the dinner table, went to his study, to my utter relief. I didn't want him to watch this family drama of Savita-Harihar, neither I wanted him to give his expert opinions.

Seeing my awful discomfiture, Manas tried to change the topic. "Leave it Harihar bhai and Bhabhi. Let's plan something. Shall we all go to Agra, Mathura, Vrindaban over the weekend? We have our flight on Monday morning, so the weekend can be utilized with Madam and Sonu. All of us can fit in a bigger cab."

I thought, *thank God!*

But no! Savita and Shubhra didn't stop there.

"So, Savita Madam! It's most impressive that you help your husband so much! My husband will give me a divorce if he sees your example…haha!! What else do you do for Harihar Sir?"

That was quite an ego booster for Savita.

"I got married to *him* when he had just passed his Master's Degree and was newly appointed as a lecturer in a government college. He was lazy-number-one from the day one, I could see that. He did not have the training to pick his wet towel and put that in the washing machine, neither did he know how to make a cup of tea. I took over his complete charge. Ask him, I am the one who made him do his PhD, I am the one because of whom he wrote all these research papers and books. Because of me, he got his promotions. Tomorrow if he is promoted to a higher position in his workplace, it will also be because of me. Minus me, this man is a big zero."

"I see…". Shubhra was enjoying the conversation with a crooked smile.

At least now I expected Harihar to object to the discussions around him and his career. But he kept quiet. Nonchalantly he took two *rasagollas* in a small bowl. Savita quickly removed one from the bowl, and looked at him like a disciplinarian Principal of a primary school, chiding her naughty pupil.

Harihar pleaded for one more *rasagolla*, with a guilty smile. "No!! You cannot eat more."

Savita went on boasting about her contributions to Harihar's life, family and career. She took the credit for everything that he had been doing since their wedding some thirty-five years ago—he owed her his living and breathing.

I was feeling sick. I wished the evening to end there. Manas could see that. He finally got up, wishing me good night. Others too had to leave along with him.

Till late night I thought about this complex human behavior; to be precise, about this objectionable supremacy of a woman. It was surely a kind of male-harassment to me. The gender theorist inside me was concerned. The humanist in me was thinking, weighing the characters Harihar and Savita from Masculinity Studies standpoint. To me, it looked like poor Harihar was under a panoptical surveillance. Savita was inspecting him from all directions. I felt he was getting breathless with her attention, but he talked nicely about her love, dedication for him just to save his face before us elites. Maybe he didn't want us to judge him or Savita.

Poor thing. He earned my sympathies that night.

Next morning, I called Manas showing my inability to go to Agra with them as I had got some urgent work in the university. I also told him what I felt about Dr. Harihar. He didn't take much interest in their matter; rather he was upset that his evening with me was spoiled because of the couple. It could have been an evening of reading good literature, listening to good music, and a peaceful dinner with me and Sonu, had those stupid people not been there.

He had a point. Even I would have enjoyed that.

***

Time flew.

I almost forgot Harihar-Savita. Manas and Shubhra called me sometimes, but we made it a point not to discuss the couple. It was, we decided, none of our business. Because Harihar had apparently no objection to whatever was happening with him—though I had serious doubts about it. But Manas asked me to forget them.

So be it!

Yes, after five months of their visit to Delhi, I happened to visit Utkal University, Bhubaneswar, to deliver a lecture. Dr.

Harihar was eager to meet me; but I had no time, the kind of high-flyer that I have been. So I informed him over WhatsApp that I won't be able to meet him.

I mostly have morning-evening-round-trips. Padmashree poet Jayanta Mahapatra was in Bhubaneswar that day, and his car was scheduled to drop me in the airport in the evening. I always have never ending chats with Jayanta Sir, and I was elated, honoured, spending a couple of hours with him in the long drive and in the airport. And lo! Harihar was waiting for us in the Bhubaneswar airport! He had gathered this information from someone in the university, that Jayanta Sir would accompany me to the airport. I wasn't pleased to see him there; anyway, both Jayanta Sir and I exchanged pleasantries with him, maybe for a few seconds only, before I proceeded to the check in counter. Harihar requested us that he wanted to click us, and Jayanta Sir agreed. So he quickly handed over his mobile to some passerby, and got clicked with us, with a grin. I left Bhubaneswar after touching the feet of Jayanta Sir, and a casual 'namaste' to Harihar.

After a couple of days, I found Harihar had tagged me on Facebook, posted that picture with a long tag-line, "Wonderful time spent with Padmashree Jayanta Mahapatra and the unparalleled poet per excellence, Nandini Sahu, in Bhubaneswar. Had long dialogues with the poets on contemporary Indian literature, and possible future collaborations with both poets."

I felt pity rather than contempt—and laughed it off. All I remembered was, we spent maximum one minute with him in Bhubaneswar airport, that too, he was an uninvited presence.

Harihar sent me courtesy messages on festivals, functions, special occasions, to which I responded with a 'namaste' emoji. Technology sometimes makes life simpler.

After eight more months or so, once Harihar called me, with a request to book a room for him in our guest house. He had some work in North-East Delhi. I told him, we are in extreme South Delhi, so he'll have to travel long distance to reach his meeting venue. He said, it was ok, there were no rooms available elsewhere.

The moment he reached our guest house, he called me. In fact, he wanted to meet us the same morning. Anyway, I was busy; also, I was trying to avoid him. That day, at 5pm when I reached home, he was already seated comfortably, settled, in our living room. Sonu had offered him tea. He came to our place without an appointment, uninvited, and said he was getting bored in the guest house. I teased, "Dr. Harihar, people who get bored in their own company seem to be in danger." Maybe I wanted him to talk about himself, about his distressed life. He still had my sympathies. Of course, I did not respect him for being so meek and mild a man.

He took his sweet time, sipping his tea, savoring the snacks we offered. This time he looked relaxed, unlike last time when he was anxious even about a cup of tea or a *rasogolla*.

Poor thing.

He was relaxed till Savita called him after an hour (apparently, she called him every one hour!). I guessed, he lied to her about the network, and disconnected the phone. Perhaps put that on flight mode after talking to her for a minute.

"Sir, please call her from my phone. I too can wish her my regards."

"No no, Madam!! Let it be. I'll call her after an hour anyway."

He talked restlessly, stridently for an hour about his work, his university; poor Sonu had to sit with him nodding his head all the time, as I utilized the time in cooking our dinner, and pretending to be listening to his blabberings. I was clearly impolite. And I wanted him to leave. It was a wastage of time for me to have such meaningless talk.

He called his wife sharp at 7pm and told her that he was in the guest house, waiting for dinner, and then put the phone again on flight mode.

I understood. He didn't want his wife to know that he was sitting with us. Precisely, with me. A *single woman.*

Sonu asked, "but uncle, you are at our place!! Why did you lie?"

It was awkward.

Then I lied to him in order to throw him out. "Sir, you may have to please excuse us. Sonu has a lot of homework, and we'll study now."

"No mama! There is no homework today!"

I looked so stupid.

Harihar said, shamelessly, "Madam, can I have dinner before leaving? I didn't have a proper lunch in the guest house."

We had a silent, quick, early dinner. Then I offered to drop him back in the guest house in my car, though he had no mood to leave at 7.30pm.

He reluctantly said goodbye to Sonu and sat in my car, of course without forgetting to praise an independent, super-successful woman, driving a car all by herself. How disgusting was that!

Now that I was alone with him in the car, I had no reason to suppress my infuriation for an enslaved, spineless man. He owed me an explanation for lying to Savita that he was eating dinner in the guest house.

"Dr. Harihar, I do not teach any kind of lie and deception to my son; so what you did at my place was seriously objectionable. I do not know much about you or your family or the values that you people follow. You were introduced to me by common friends. I wanted to respect you, but unfortunately, I could not. I cannot. How can you allow a person to dominate, control you to such an extent? How can you lie to her in front of me, sitting at my place? You have humiliated us and our hospitality. I don't know for what all should I reprimand you, neither do I know if at all I should talk to you! You are so laid-back! You don't have the courage to tell Mrs.Savita that you are having dinner with a respectable family! And last time your behaviour was such shameful in front of all of us!! How can a man tolerate if a woman steals the entire credit of his life and career?? Have you no dignity? No shame? Are you not suffocated? How do you live such a life??"

I was gasping, angry. I stopped the car in front of the guest house and got down. He too got down and stood at a distance.

He said, quietly, considerately, "Madam, I thought you are an extremely intelligent person, and you can see the subtext behind this text behind this story of 'subjugation'. But to me, now you sound like Gandhari. To be born blind is not a crime, but to turn a blind eye? How can you not see the hidden depths of this story?"

Ahh…one more drama.

"Excuse me? I am still not getting what nonsense you are trying to explain. Come to the point." I was rude.

"Ok, let me come to the point. "

He scratched his head, searching for words, and then said, "My wife Savita is an empty-headed foolish woman; an erudite woman like you may not understand the mindset of such people. She is class three pass (or fail…haha), she cannot even sign in English. She puts her thumb impression on papers I ask her to. She is from a lavish, extravagant family where she had seen women being dominated by men. She got married to me when she was 18 and I was 25. Her parents offered me a fortune for dowry, and see the bonuses I have! A mansion and couple of nice cars. She can never understand what unproductive stuff she is engaged with. She has no time to think of anything except me and my needs. She cooks, cleans, takes care of all my wants and wishes— I get great food, clean, soft bed, clean tables to work, fresh towels, clean book shelves, healthy tea, health care, in fact everything for a good living. In return, I ignore her foolish talks, her self-styled *supremacy*. She feels emancipated, empowered by 'dominating' me. Can you believe--she signed her entire property in my name—I mean put her thumb impression—without an inkling of what she was doing. I told her that she had to sign the documents to secure her property."

I was amazed. My mouth agape, eyes wide open. What a revelation!!

"And Madam, which qualified person in my friend circle will believe that a class-three-fail woman, who looks like a dumb fool, who opens her mouth only to reveal her imprudence, her foolishness, has actually shaped my great academic career? Rather, some laugh at her foolishness, and some, like you, give me their sympathies!! Actually, it's a win-win situation for me."

I sat in my car without a goodbye or a good night. I reached home absent-minded, with a void in my cognizance, rethinking, swotting 'masculinity'.

Bio:
Prof. Nandini Sahu, Professor of English and Director, School of Foreign Languages, IGNOU, New Delhi, India, is an established Indian English poet, creative writer, theorist and folklorist. She is the author/editor of fourteen books; has

The Body of Memories

been widely published in India and outside. Prof. Sahu is a triple gold medalist in English Studies. Her areas of research interest cover New Literatures, Critical Theory, Folklore and Culture Studies, Children's Literature and American Literature.

Pickled

By Nishi Pulugurtha

May is hot. May is peak summer – scorching and sweltering. May is also pickle time for Telugus all over the world. It is also nostalgia time for Telugus living away from Andhra Pradesh and Telengana. Appagaru (that is how we addressed my father) mostly lived outside what used to be Andhra Pradesh, in Orissa and later in Bengal. Home, for him was always Calcutta. It was the same for my mother too. We did have very close links with folks back in Kakinada and Hyderabad and elsewhere, we still do. But, Calcutta/ Kolkata has always been home.

One of the troubles of living far away from home was finding the right ingredients and equipment needed for Telugu cuisine. A Telugu kitchen will always need coffee, and the grinding stone for making fluffy idlis and crisp dosas. When Amma set up home in Calcutta, her kitchen did not have the grinding stone and it was left to my uncle to get one for her, all the way from Kakinada in Andhra Pradesh. Things were much different in the Calcutta of the 70s. Coffee powder, not the instant kind, but the one needed for filter coffee, was available only in a few shops – in Metro Gali at Esplanade, a small shop tucked in Dacres Lane and in Lake Market. Today, of course, things are much different. Most of the things needed in a Telugu kitchen are available online.

Summer was the time when my parents got ready to make pickles. Hot, tangy, red mango pickles that would last a year. There were different kinds of such mango pickles that one could make. My parents made two types mostly – *avakai* and *magai*. Years of stay in Calcutta had taught Amma the right place to buy all the needed ingredients. The raw mangoes had to be of a particular kind and real sour, firm and green, with a perfectly formed seed. Not just that they had to be

The Body of Memories

chopped up into pieces of a particular size for *avakai*. I remember that in the 70s, 80s and well into the 90s, Amma used to travel to central Calcutta, to Burra Bazar to get them. Once they were home, the four of us - my parents, my sister and me would spread the pieces on an old, clean, cotton sari and then painstakingly wipe each mango piece clean and dry. Pickle making for Telugus, no matter where they are, has always been a family affair. Even before the raw mango pieces would be home, my parents would get all the spices needed for the pickle. They were not available in local shops. They had to be the best and it was either shops in Burra Bazar or Lake Market where one could get the best kind needed to make the perfect pickle.

After all the pieces would be wiped clean, a huge container would be dried and cleaned and readied for the mixing of the pickle. The spices, all in the correct proportions would be added by Amma, and Appagaru would be ready with the mixing spoon, all heated up, even a small amount of moisture would spoil the pickle. We used to be asked to leave the room, as all the spices might cause us to sneeze and then Appagaru would begin mixing the spices, mango pieces, salt and oil under the watchful eyes of Amma. I remember standing behind the door, peeping to see the mixing being done.

Huge ceramic containers, white and brown, cleaned, dried and kept ready at hand were kept close by. One of the most important ingredients in the pickle was fiery red chilly powder and mustard powder. It is this mustard powder added to the pickle that gives it its name – *avakai* (*avalu* is Telugu for mustard seeds). Fenugreek seeds were powdered and added too. All of the ingredients were then mixed and generous quantities of oil was be added. I remember my father struggling to mix them all, such was the quantity. The right amount of salt too. Oh yes, whole garlic was added to this. These garlic pods once they had soaked in all the spices and oil tasted heavenly in the pickle and added further flavour. All the mixing done, both of them transferred it all into jars to be stored. A layer of oil floating on the top could be seen acting as a preservative. The jars were covered with cloth that was tied securely at the neck and then the lids put on. A smaller quantity of the pickle would be kept in a container for consumption. The bigger jars were not be touched. Utmost care had to be taken so that the pickle remained good for a year.

The freshly prepared pickle soon reached our plates and tummies. However, Amma always had a rider – only a little of it was to be had, just to taste it. It could otherwise create havoc with our stomachs. Moreover, the mango pieces needed to take in all the spices and oil and get soft and be just the right taste and texture. The best way to have it, as with all such pickles is to mix them with hot rice and to be had with a raw onion, or maybe some curd or even some thick cream. *Avakai annam* – *avakai* with rice is comfort food.

Making *magai* was a bit more complicated. The spices are more or less the same only that mustard powder is not needed. Neither is the garlic too. The mango pieces had to be sun dried for this. The raw mangoes had to be peeled and this was once again a family affair – Amma cut the mangoes into thin, long pieces. They were put in a container and then salt and turmeric was added and mixed well. After about three days, the mango pieces were squeezed and put out to dry in the hot summer sun. The juices that oozed out due to the salt being added was put out to dry too. The raw and dried mango pieces tasted just delicious. We made it a point to eat them as they kept drying. The tangy, sour taste hit the palate – it sure was delightful. Once they were nice and dry, spices were mixed and it was stored away too to last for a year. There was often a problem though; summers in Calcutta saw frequent Norwesters and this disturbed the drying process. My sister and I joked about this often and when it would get too hot, we would tell Amma to ready mango pieces for drying – we were sure the rain gods would oblige us soon and it would get cooler.

These days, we do not make any pickle at home. Appagaru is not around anymore and Amma is not in state to make them. However, we do get our supply of pickles – not from shops were some of them are available. The readymade ones are a poor substitute. Aunts and cousins see to it that we do not miss all updates relating to the pickle season and pickles. They also ensure we get our pickle supply every year. This year (2019) *avakai* arrived a week ago by courier – my cousin, Valli, made sure we get it fresh. On a blazing summer morning, my aunt, Amma's sister, called up saying she had prepared *magai* and a couple of other types too *menthi avakai* and *thokkudu pachadi*, all made from raw mangoes. She said she is on the lookout on how to send it to us. The courier is way too expensive, she said. She is travelling to Vizag next week and she will see to it that the pickles, all packed wonderfully are handed over to my uncle at Kakinada. My uncle is planning a holiday to Shillong and enroute, he will stop at Kolkata to meet my mother and that is how the pickles are going to travel this time. They do find ways and means of reaching me and my sister each year.

2020 was a bit different. With the country in lockdown and life held in thrall by the pandemic, we were caught up in panic, learning to deal with things. Stuck at home, connected virtually, I realised that there was no way I could get my stock of fresh pickles. My cousin and aunts decided to give the year a miss, they were not making any pickles. They could not, even if they wanted to. Most of them were not venturing out, and markets were not stocking up on the necessary ingredients. My aunt said that they would try to make do with whatever little bit of last year's pickle they still had.

No one to give up, my sister managed to find an online seller. Our stock of pickles was over and we needed to get some. Of course, this was much after the summer months had gone by and the Unlock phase had begun in India. We did manage pickles delivered to us – to me in the East and to my sister in the North. They are just a substitute for what reached our tables every year. But the best we could manage in times such as this.

GLOSSARY
Telugu is the language spoken in the states of Andhra Pradesh and Telengana
Appagaru – an address for father
Amma – mother
Idli – a steamed snack made of fermented rice and lentil batter
Dosa – a pancake-like snack made of fermented rice and lentil batter
avakai – a mango pickle
magai – a mango pickle
annam – rice
menthi – fenugreek
thokkudu – coarsely ground
pachadi – chutney

Bio:
Nishi Pulugurtha is an academic and creative writer and writes on travel, film, short stories, poetry and on Alzheimer's Disease. Her work has been published in various journals and magazines. Her publications include a monograph on *Derozio* (2010), a collection of essays on travel, *Out in the Open* (2019), an edited volume of essays on travel, *Across and Beyond* (2020) and a volume of poems, *The Real and the Unreal and Other Poems* (2020).

A version of this essay was first published in *Café Dissensus*

It's not your fault!

Niharika Chibber Joe

Stephanie plonked an unusually large bottle of pink-hued wine on the scarred coffee table, and doubled over, as if to shield her scarred heart, as she shoved a wad of bunched up paper under the table's one wobbly leg. "Hey! That's Origami Yoda," I exclaimed. "My kid made it!"

"Yeah well, he'll have to do," she grunted drily, grabbing her battered laptop and folding her now grossly underweight 6'3" frame into an accordion. The clock in the kitchen indifferently chimed nine times. The spring sun had barely set, firing up, on its way down, millions of pollen spores that would savagely maul my mucous membranes in a matter of minutes. Friday night was only just beginning to take on a life of its own. But life, as Steph knew it, was circling the drain. "Sorry about this," she muttered, waving her newly-bony arms in a sweeping motion around the room. Her sweeping arms caught the dim lamp on their way back. "I am really truly sorry about all of this," she apologized, as if the world's every suffering was her fault.

I slid Portia a surreptitious look. "Oh stop it, Steph!" she snapped, as she dived and caught the lamp before it crashed to the ground. "The place is a mess, and so are you. It's over. It was over a long time ago. Get over it!" Stephanie blanched, and reached for the wine. Portia is thus named because she speaks her mind. She is a Portia. She could never be a Heather or a Betty.

But she could be a Jane. Or even a Jack. She is about my height with curly blonde hair, can prime a keg in a tight dress and heels and throw down with the best of them without tarnishing a single well-manicured nail. She's a Portia, and there's no known cure.

"Are you ready?" Stephanie hissed, pausing cautiously as her ears picked up the imperceptible sound of her youngest coughing in her sleep two floors above us. She had three cherubic children, ranging in age from nine to four. Born during the same 10-year span that he had viciously characterized in an angry Email as the "absolute worst" years of his life. The 10 years that had borne him three beautiful children were the years he had described as his worst.

"Allergies, Goddammit! It's always something with the kids." "Ok so are you ready for this?"

I had arrived ready a few minutes ago. Ready for *what*? I wondered. I only knew Stephanie through the elementary school birthday party circuit. We would swap sports practice logistics over Costco cake and pontificate about the state of the neighborhood. I had 'researched' her.

I have a desire to know. My research had told me she had graduated from law school at Ol' Miss. and was now part-time at a boutique law firm in downtown Washington, D.C. She had married Jason the Marine, her boyfriend of three years right before he deployed in the wake of 9-11, "and together they had three beautiful children." That was all I knew about Stephanie Smith. And that was quite enough.

That's also how I had met Portia. At a birthday party where the five-year-old Birthday Girl was tricked out like Batman. Portia and I had chuckled, and agreed we'd like to effing be Batman at our own effing party someday. I knew then we'd be friends. Not because she wanted to be Batman, too - but because she said her kids were "those little shits" who were going to eat too much cake and "eff up" her evening. I knew I would get along with Portia, and hoped she would be at the next birthday party. "No," she had said, "I have to go to church that day because I think the priest guy is pissed at me; but Mike will bring the kids if can ever get his ass off the couch." Portia didn't require research. What you saw was what you got. Like most people who live here, she worked for 'the government' and so did her husband Mike. They

The Body of Memories

spent their days, and sometimes nights in an acronym-ridden government agency inside a barbed wire compound, where they did acronym-ridden work in military time in corridors with unmarked doors that contained stacks of acronym riddled files marked "Top Secret." Whenever Portia mentioned her work, it was only to talk about the "freaks" who worked with her and made lewd comments about her derrière. As it turns out, the freaks are either longtime veterans of the acronym farm, and have sacrificed their final functioning brain cell to the bowels of the bunker inside which they run their algorithms, or they are recent college grads who think they are there to change the world one acronym at a time. 'murica! Portia hates them all, equally.

When it came to Portia and Mike, there were no online bios to be found, and definitely no flowery *New York Times* wedding announcements. They had met in college one night when they'd both been "shitfaced and ended up making out", and 15 years later, here they were. Happy as clams and annoyed as heck. Portia and I were destined to be friends. We had nothing in common. Yet, we had everything in common. She is of German-Dutch-African-Mizrahi Jewish ancestry, and I am, y'know, Indian. She grew up with a single mom and a much younger sibling in rural Ohio. I grew up with a single mom and a much younger sibling in urban India.

She is pale – translucent, almost. I am, not. I could be "tanned", "brown", "olive", "dusky" or "wheatish", depending on the company I keep. She is a harried, working mom, and so am I. She could stand to shed a few or more pounds, and so could I. But I didn't really know Stephanie beyond the polite platitudes. Not until a couple of months ago when she walked up to me at a school event and said, "Our boys are friends. I wanted you to hear from me that Jason has left us. We are getting a divorce."

"Ok, you guys! Are you ready or not?!" Stephanie regurgitated through clenched teeth. We were ready. We had dressed for the occasion. Sweatpants, college sweatshirts - UPenn for Portia, Georgetown for me, ponytails and comfy socks. Portia had graduated from Carnegie-Mellon, and I from 'Hopkins. We were traveling incognito. We'd put our kids to bed, stuck snacks and beer within arm's reach of our husbands, and fled. The Washington Nationals were playing. And so were the Washington Capitals. Baseball *and* hockey. They'd stay mesmerized for hours! Portia found three mugs, all chipped, and poured us all some wine. She handed us the mugs and plonked heavily down with a deep sigh before looking over disdainfully at me. "Shit!" she hissed. "Shit!" I whispered in unison, as I spied a wayward tear rolling merrily down Stephanie's right cheek. "Divorce sucks, doesn't it?!" "Who the hell said anything about divorce?" Portia hissed back. "I forgot you don't drink!! Seriously, who comes from complicated family situations and doesn't drink?! I mean, really! Aren't your parents divorced, too?!" I couldn't disregard her point.

Meanwhile, two decades and a lifetime ago in faraway India, Coke exhaled in a loud, wet belch, carefully extricated her oversized visage from her soda bottle-bottom glasses and gave me a cloudy cataract stare. "Divorce," she wheezed, "is genetic, you know!" She paused, as if considering carefully how to break the rest of the news to me gently. "And why do you think my eligible bachelor of a boy would marry you and your divorced family?" She spat the words to the side. In sheer contempt. I knew she was talking out of her you-know-what, yet my 23-year-old mind was relieved. I had blamed myself for so long, that never had I dared to imagine, that divorce resulted, unequivocally, from a petrified gene. A mortification of DNA that just slid along from one generation to another to another....and on and on and on. Did this mean it wasn't my fault? Did this mean my parents were blameless? The release of absolution washed over my guilt-ridden soul. And in its wake, it absolved me of any responsibility to marry Coke's Son, who had professed drunken love to me, and informed me that once we were married, I would have to leave my job because, "no wife of mine will ever work outside the home!"

Coke's Son was a rich, spoiled, entitled 28-year-old not very suitable 'Indian Boy.' He lived with his parents, rolled out of bed at noon, ate greasy food, smoked like a chimney, drank like a fish, stayed up late, and didn't really show up for work most days. Work was his dad's accounting business. Coke's Son did not like to work. So he didn't. Coke, on the other hand liked to make other people work. Like Jabba the Hutt she would lower her vastness gingerly into an enormous gilded sofa of red and gold brocade, and methodically holler instructions to an army of freaked out household staff as she sipped her hot water and lemon (no sugar). Every few hours a devoted minion would emerge with a black pouch, prick Coke's index finger and run her glucose levels. Then, another minion would appear with syringe in hand, go tap-tap to let out the air bubbles, and plunge the needle into the depths of Coke's belly fat. Insulin. Three times a day.

The minions were all diminutively-built boy-men with very light skin and high-pitched voices. They wore starched white uniforms and worked in two shifts. Morning, and evening.

The morning crew arrived promptly at six o'clock to supervise Coke's morning ablutions, and to get her affixed to her throne. The second shift rolled in at six o' clock in the evening to look after her nightly rituals. Each shift precise, robot-like, soundless – seen, not heard.

"So! Coke growled…squinting through her coke glasses. You have these divorced genes, but where are you *really* from? Are you a Bengali? Your surname is Punjabi, but you look like a Madrasi?" She looked like she had sniffed a bottle of vinegar. "Hai, so confusing! What will we tell people?! Madrasi *kahin ki! Kaali!* Broken home *waali!*"

This line of questioning wasn't new. For as long as I can remember, my mother and I - average-looking, highly educated, English-speaking, cosmopolitan Indians living in Delhi, have always been asked, *"Madam, aap kahan se hain? Madam, where are you from?"* We have been forced to re-examine our identity over, and over, and over again. We have answers. From the polite to the humorous to the confrontational. "Sir, we are from here – from this town.*"* *"Do we look like we are from England?"* *"How is it any of your business where the heck we are from?!"*

Yet, when Coke spat out her vitriol-laced question, cat got my tongue. "You are so...so...dark-skinned!" she admonished. "What exactly *are* you? Muslim? Hai! Hai!" She looked so green, I though she was going to throw up. I sat there. Politely. Saying something smart back to Coke would trigger an international incident of high magnitude, and I couldn't let my parents and our family friends down by telling her what I really thought of her lamentations, or her son.

Afterall, chances were high I'd be marrying Coke's son, in spite of my flawed gene, and my less than desirable skin color. Or the fact that I had a job. Suddenly, I couldn't see a way out.

"I am a military brat, I finally whispered. I am from everywhere. I am Indian." I had chosen to call myself "Indian", when as a five-year-old I was incessantly asked about my "mother-tongue." I had to have one. How could I not have one? Why was I so weird? Why did my mom pack sandwiches for me? That was so odd. Who ate sandwiches anyway? That, too, on brown bread! Yuck! *Kaali* bread! Black bread! No wonder my skin was black! My skin was black like the bread I ate, and I had no mother tongue. Who was I? Where was I from? Why did I look different? Why did my parents speak English to each other? How could I not have a mother tongue??!

But I have a mother, and we are of many tongues! My mother and I speak to each other in English, Hindi or Bangla. We

The Body of Memories

are polyglots. My father, my brother and I speak to each other in English and Hindi. And my stepfather and I speak to each other in English, Hindi and Nepali. When I am with friends, I speak in Japanese, Bangla, English and Hindi – or sometime Japanese and Nepali. Or even Korean and Japanese. We celebrated Christmas and Eid with as much fervor as we celebrated Diwali and everything else in between. My parents were military brats. And I am one too.

"I don't know," Coke flung her hands up in some sort of despair. She looked at me with as steady a cloudy gaze as she could muster. "I can't figure out what you are. And now my son says he wants to marry you. What am I supposed to do? Have dark-skinned Muslim grandchildren who have divorce genes?! I am truly cursed!" The clock in the dining room chimed six times. My insides felt rattled. My palms were sweaty. My heart was raw. I had been attacked, and somehow, this was my fault. I stood up, and smoothed out my *lucknavi* embroidered salwar kameez outfit, as the first minion padded in with the black pouch and began wordlessly fussing around Coke. "I'll take your leave now," I said. Not loudly. But I know my voice quivered.

I gathered my things, and let myself out of Coke's room. I had decided that was the last time I would ever see Coke. Sitting with my mom half an hour later, I found the courage to breathe the words, "I can't do this!" I did not have to say more. "You don't have to," my mom replied.

"You don't have to! This is not your fault!"

The following year, I moved to America. Here, I found no one cared about my mother tongue, or my divorce gene, or my black bread. They told me I was "Indian." No nuances available. They didn't need to ask me where I was from, because I looked Indian. Not long after arriving in what would become the Land of My Deeds, I married an American. And we have a son. Our son is named after a Greek warrior who fought my ancestor King Porus in the battle of the Hydaspes River in 326 BC, and eventually became his ally. Our son is also named after Swami Vivekananda -the first known Hindu Sage to come to the West in 1893, where he introduced Eastern Thought at the World's Parliament of Religions. Our boy's genetic heritage comes from unpronounceable parts of un-partitioned India, from unpronounceable parts of the United Kingdom and Germany and from even more unpronounceable parts of the Korean peninsula. Born in Washington, DC and boasting a cultural and genetic heritage as diverse as a trip around the world – he is an international child of the 21st century – he is post-racial – antiracist-- has more stamps on his passport than years in his life – and he may have just one identity. Human. "Where are you from?" is a question he can answer with alacrity. No matter how he chooses to answer it. Or whether he chooses to answer it at all.

I felt an arm on my shoulder as I was jolted out of my reverie by an irritated Portia. "You don't even drink, and you look like you're passed out! Get up! It's time to go! You've been asleep!" Meanwhile, Stephanie remained in her accordion fold on the couch. "I am so sorry. I am so, so sorry!" she muttered. Or perhaps mumbled – her empty wine glass by her side. It was nearly midnight. "It's all my fault!"

"No!" I hollered on my way out, as Portia shoved me out into the pollen-ridden night. "It was never your fault! And it was never mine, either!"

Bio:
Niharika Chibber Joe is a poet, and short story writer. Niharika writes in English, and sometimes in Japanese or in Hindi. Her work has been published in *In All the Spaces: Diverse Voices in Global Women's Poetry* (2020) and the *Setu Online Literary Journal* and in the upcoming anthology *Earth Fire Water Wind* (2021). Niharika is a United States civil servant. She is an anti-racist and is a racial equity, social justice and climate warrior. She holds a B.A and M.A. in Japanese Language and Literature from the Jawaharlal

The Body of Memories

Nehru University in India, and an M.A. in International Relations from the Johns Hopkins University's School of Advanced International Studies in Washington, D.C. She was born and raised in India, and "grew up" in the United States.

The Colour Story

Paromita Mukherjee Ojha

Growing up in the 90s, it was a childhood devoid of endless tuitions, no mad rush to get enrolled in varied summer camps offering to transform the happy-go-lucky into a newer version fit for the consumerist world. It was a childhood drenched in hopscotch, lazy picnics on terrace tops savouring simple mish-mash of boiled potatoes and chick peas, flying kites, gorging on date syrup fritters.

So, was everything hunky-dory in my childhood? The answer is NO. My childish mind was bogged down with my fate of having a dark skin tone. The barbs, from people, who called themselves 'relatives' was heart-searing. The onslaught of comments ranged from 'Oh! you must have been picked up from trashcan', 'A Bengali Brahmin girl cannot be this pitch dark' to the inane ones like 'no boy will marry a black girl', 'you are born under the wrong star', the outpouring was endless. My childish mind failed to connect the dots between my caste, the star I was born under and my complexion. The rejections and castigations were endless. I cursed myself for something that I was not responsible. On birthdays I was gifted with fairness creams, banal reminders of my dark skin tone. My mind was bogged down with the guilt of having been born dark –skinned. I readily identified with the anguish of the protagonist Pecola from Toni Morrison's *'The Bluest Eye'* who was pegged against the 'Shirley Temples' of this world. Fortunately for me, my parents did not attest such disgraceful notions of beauty. The pressure was immense and I searched ways to rationalize my 'skin colour' to people around me. I had unfortunately internalized the 'black sheep' tag. I was convinced of my inadequacy and the thought that 'I was never going to be good enough to be noticed by anyone'. My descent into self-pity and self-loathing was inevitable. My studies suffered; my self-esteem took a beating. I tried to distract people from noticing me or judging me by their parameters of beauty.

The insecurity strengthened its tentacles as I was growing up; I felt no one should notice me, so I hid my visage behind huge glasses. I refused to believe that anyone could speak to me without any ulterior motive. Sometimes my fear proved to be true as an adolescent girl who loathed herself was an easy prey for human carnivores. They attempted to feed upon my insecurity by pretending to be a well-meaning listener. I escaped every time and that's a blessing, else that would have been another vicious quagmire. It is not that my childhood suffered, confronting this colour bias, but as I grew up, I started believing that I should never marry anyone dark-skinned. If I did, my progeny would also would have to undergo this kind of mental abuse. I forgot the true meaning of beauty and subscribed readily to the problematic and disdainful notion that 'fair is beautiful'.

So, what turned the tide for me? It was a quote from Zora Neale Hurston that I read and imbibed:

I am not tragically coloured. There is no great sorrow dammed up in my soul, nor lurking behind my eyes......Even in the helter-skelter skirmish that is my life, I have seen that the world is to the strong regardless of a little pigmentation more or less. No, I don't weep at the world – I am too busy sharpening my oyster knife.

My perspective towards life changed, it did not hurt when someone complimented me by saying 'you are a black diamond' whatever that was supposed to mean.

I started focusing hard on my academics as I realized that 'success has many fathers, while failure remains an orphan'. All those years my studies had suffered due to my low self-esteem, failure to concentrate and then miraculously the tide turned when I literally burnt the midnight oil for my XII(ISC)examination, I stood third in my stream and my Alma Mater lauded my achievement on stage. Suddenly people were crowding around me hailing my parents, my efforts, no one that day noticed my skin colour. It was a life changing moment and I treasure that experience till date. That day gave me the necessary impetus to overhaul my outlook and the road was paved for further academic achievements, leading to my Doctorate.

In 1994, an 18-year-old dusky girl changed the misconception regarding beauty by overshadowing a fair, beautiful girl, a showstopper. Till date, she serves for me as a source of inspiration. She was our first Miss Universe title winner Miss. Sushmita Sen. She strengthened my belief that more than complexion or outward beauty, what matters is your wit, composure and holding your head high against all odds.

Fortunately, wheels of time are in motion and idealization of white standards of beauty is changing too. It is so heartening for me to notice that popular actors are refusing to endorse fairness creams, ebony and dusky models are ruling the fashion ramps and for me it is a welcome change.

We are slowly creeping out of our obsession of associating beauty with fair skin. Young people now are less haunted by the unrealistic standards of superficial beauty and coming out of their closet of insecurities and uncertainties.

Our society is slowly evolving and many are now no more subscribing to toxic standards of beauty. Dark-skinned people are now judged based more on their intelligence, educational qualification rather than on inane beauty standards. I have pledged not to ill-advise my two gorgeous dusky babies to apply turmeric, milk cream to become hypothetically fairer. Why should they need to change themselves by applying fairness creams and potions? I escaped from my insecurities after lots of internal struggle, and trust me, it was a tough fight. I am determined to celebrate my daughters' inner beauties and not let them tumble into a vortex of insecurities.

The Body of Memories

Society as a whole needs to overhaul its dubious standards. We should be more concerned about the mental trauma dark-skinned people undergo when they are compared, criticized, taunted for their skin tone. We should stop pushing people against miasmic walls. Beauty does not lie in skin tones, rather it lies in the acceptance of people with varied colour, preferences, caste, creed and religion. I am looking forward to the day when as a society, we will aim to be 'fair' in our deeds and behaviour towards people.

I am hopeful my daughters would live in a society '*where the clear stream of reason has not lost its way into the dreary desert sand of dead habit; Where the mind is led forward by thee into ever –widening thought and action* (Gitanjali, Rabindranath Tagore). I pray that into that heaven of freedom, my next generation would awake.

Bio:
Paromita Mukherjee Ojha lives in Delhi, India. After thirteen years of service in the aviation and teaching arena, after presenting 16 research papers to the academic fraternity, Paromita is now an ardent traveller in the world of fiction and poetry. She attempts to express her joys and sorrows through her writings and artworks. In her spare time, she loves to paint, sing, dream and laugh with her two precious daughters.

Lost in Time somewhere near Prague

Piku Chowdhury

Like a dream within a dream, the winding vistas to the old graveyard rose in front of my eyes. I walked along the narrow winding trail with a vast stretch of verdant fields on one side and a few brightly painted log cabins on the other. One or two roosters stood petrified like a rainbow-hued still life with strange dark pools of unfathomed depths quivering in circular eyes…like puddles of rain that had collected in tiny spaces on the sidewalks after the hasty mountain shower, and turned into bottomless mysteries with slices of mountain sky reflected in them. The oaks stood like grand high minarets of tranquil green and looked so fresh. The walk was not devoid of apprehensions.

The Body of Memories

I was clueless about my destination. I was lost. Majestic rain-soaked beech forests soon appeared on either way with the log cabins left far behind and with them vanished the last manifestation of human habitation. I wondered at myself. I should be very scared with the last rays of the mellow sun caressing the beech, but a strange vacant mood pervaded my heart. I walked on as if I had nothing to lose, nothing to fear. And suddenly I paused at a slope on the left-hand side, separated from the winding trail by a low stone wall. Something seemed vaguely familiar. Along the slope lay discoloured but sombre slabs with grey non-blatant, beautifully drowsy tombstones with engraved Christian names of a bygone era. The thickening mist and the evening hush greeted by the parting dim light of the day transformed the old graveyard into a sacred sanctum of frozen memories beyond the dictates of temporality and spatial limits. The swishing branches grew stronger in their strangely synchronized symphony as one or two diffident stars appeared in the tranquil stage of a dusky, mist-clad splendour. The distant slopes were coming alive with sparse twinkling lights, red, yellow and one or two white specs twinkling amidst ethereal darkness. I felt the piercing cold stab of evening mountain wind penetrating my flimsy shawl, partly moist with a hasty downpour.

Yes, I was drenched. Drenched and lost too, and yet strangely lightheaded and dazed. It seemed I had forgotten to panic. I stood still at the gate of the secluded sleepy space of silent memories, numbed and listless. The partially soaked map in hand was useless to the unaccustomed eye. A strange sedative lull pervaded my being as I shivered slightly, so near and yet so far from civilization. At this point, the listlessness was all-pervading and remained like the eternal stillness of the eye in the heart of a chaotic cyclonic storm. A stillness that inundates the mind as you kneel in front of the pulpit, lighting a candle in a silent desperate prayer carrying your meddled sensibilities, releasing your perplexity at turn of events in the whimsical world around.

But at the gates of the sanctum of eternal sleep, I uttered no prayer. Only like the flickering flame of a lone candle that burns at the foot of the Lord in a medieval church that I had visited in the earlier part of the day, strange flickers from the past evolved in the perceptual manifold.

The hope to get a hired vehicle on the way back to the city does not go well with extra hours spent in marvelling at the glass-paintings of an old forgotten church in central Europe that does not boast of tourist footfall. There I was, a day after an invited lecture at the Metropolitan University, Prague, venturing to a medieval, almost forgotten church in the outskirts on my own, with a map in hand and a naïve, inexperienced midlife view of facile urban navigation. I had ignored the dictates of the wrist watch as I breathed in the surreal beauty of the blackened stony walls and evocative glass etchings, only to discover that the locality had donned the appearance of a desolate dreamy landscape straight out of an old horror movie with a lone beautifully bizarre horse-drawn carriage clip-clopping to its evening shelter. To intensify the sense of desolation and absurdity, a hasty shower poured like a pre-planned conspiracy. I had forgotten to carry my umbrella as usual. It was then that I decided to walk. I could not spend the night out in an unfamiliar village with no sign of any decent hotel. There must be a gas station or tram stop nearby, just around some magical corner, was precisely the thought that urged me to trudge along. However, as I stood alone at the graveyard in a partly drenched shawl and twelve yards of *Murshidabadi* silk obstinately hugging my shivering frame with nagging icy stabs of consciousness, moments of some other mountain mist and silence swirled in strange vividness.

I could see us standing still on the steps of the desolate graveyard in Kurseong- just like it was yesterday, with the aroma of piping hot samosas bought from a wayside stall of an old wrinkled Nepali fellow, creating a strange concoction in the fern-scented shady corner. I remembered how the old

Nepali fellow had fondly bared his toothless gum with a smile like the fading twilight, as we called him *daddu* while buying the freshly fried cheap samosas. Peals of laughter echoed in my vacant mind; laughter that was congealed in whispering sound of rustling leaves or in the inaudible sigh of a falling dew in a magical evening of the past. We had raced down the slopes that day with childish competitiveness only to tumble into each other's eager anticipating embrace, and rolled with laughter like the free gurgling stream. The desolate slopes and sighing ferns had captured that laughter and frozen into eternity. In the twinkling gem like lights on the distant slopes remained congealed the smouldering breath of desire that pierced every dark chilly night in the hills during our sojourn. It's strange that those frozen memories were preserved only in the rustle of the obscure pines and ancient moss on the silent tombstones. You had forgotten your cheap Kodak camera in some park earlier in the day and we had returned hastily in a futile quest for the gadget that must have been picked up by some passer-by. But that moment knew no loss. It's strange how the buried moments return with such vividness and invade with incredible abruptness in the oddest of hours. It actually made me smile. The togetherness and unarticulated certitude of commitment had filled the sanctum of buried memories that day. We had no money to venture into the city to the fine dining joints with crystal chandeliers sparkling with dazzling splendour and gentle tinkle of silver cutlery creating a symphony with mild sizzling sound and aroma of piping hot sizzlers or a faint melody crooned by some live artist in the hall, and yet as your cold hand clasped a newspaper packet of hot cheap samosas, the moment knew no loss. The moment returned with strange vividness - the moment on the pavement outside the glass-walled eatery where we, hopelessly naive and young, had stopped with wistful eyes but smiling lips. The rich vermillion on the forehead and the tinkle of the *sankh* with gold bangles on the hand exuded the warmth of the sacred fire that had witnessed the holy union of two souls sans feeling of wealth or loss. In the silent sigh of the towering pines remained congealed the contentment of the beginners who were to prosper but travel thousands of miles around the world alone with filmstrips of memories to return in the oddest of hours.

How the vortex of time revolves. I was here with limited euros in purse, trudging in the same chilly mist, albeit in a distant shore, towards a destination craved yet unclear. You had been in oblivion for years, each of us comfortably snuggling into our newly carved nooks of familial bliss, millions of miles away from midnight dreams of ethereal hush of a forgotten graveyard in the mountains. We thought that moments had been buried and yet now they flashed with clarity of a breathing life. The moments returned in a distant graveyard like ethereal beings from their peaceful oblivion. Memories of stupendous failures in form of miserable deflated *puris* fried together on Sunday mornings or the collaborative fiasco of donning twelve yards around an inexperienced eager frame in a one-room flat emerged in the silent graveyard. We had travelled miles away from a hundred dreams of the luxury of a two-room flat and hours spent in planning interior decorations to be achieved with cheap clay pots or self-made paintings on the wall. I smiled. Memories are but strange shadow lines that elude and emerge in a grand play of time. Like magic lanterns unfolding magical figures of the walls of a silent bedroom of a wondering child, they return to challenge our maturity and complacent certitude, catching us off-guard. It felt like the slithering red Molly fish you used to hold in your palm with sparkling eyes, hauled from a small tank of water maintained by your uncle in a mossy old courtyard. Dreams and dreams of a grand aquarium in some fantastic future living room …the molly fish swam in the hidden crevices of a mellowed heart. The moments swim too, slithering past the grand narratives of willful oblivion and successful moving on. And I moved on again. Started walking slowly like a person taking a leisurely stroll in a volatile surreal realm, lost in myriad mazes of cavorting memories.

The Body of Memories

A gas station emerged from the mist like a spec of light in the tangible opacity of the dark evening after walking for quite some time. The listless girl at the counter stared incomprehensibly as I asked for a cup of coffee in English. There perished our pride in communicative efficacy of English as her visage reflected tremendous boredom and impatience at a tongue she failed to comprehend. Five euros for a tiny cup of black bitter brew was gained through relentless exercise of nonverbal gestures. The two free cookies seemed heavenly to the famished traveller lost in time. Cheap things can bring such satisfaction. What is wealth in this supreme absurdity called life? The psychedelic moments defying time and space flirt relentlessly with feelings of deep satiation irrespective of the change in our material condition. The cheap samosas and the free cookies blended in a supreme collage. The journey must continue still, along the road stretching with a lure of destination and I got up. The map shown to the lady at the counter elicited no enthusiasm and calls to the hotel reception were futile. In limited english the receptionist advised to stick to the map and I was in no position to specify my location. I walked on, energized by the bitter coffee and the cookies. Disturbing the organisers at that hour was not a good option. Passers-by, few in number, reflected the same courteous incomprehensibility as I tried to communicate in English. That was reason enough to panic but I smiled. Specks of stardust are we, so eternally lost and separated by Babel, by desires, by vested interests- lost in a magnificent mist where love, lust, vows all swirl elusive in the imaginative forays of the mind. We carry our lives in our fantasy, our memories in our abrupt dreams and they play strange games as we trudge on to find our way. One or two lonely shops were closing. As I approached one, an old Chinese gentleman was pulling down the shutter. Amidst the unfamiliar tall and lovely Caucasian people around, the shrivelled up, stooping Chinese man seemed so familiar. He was poorly versed in English too and yet like the Nepali *daddu* smiling at us in

Kurseong, a twilight toothless smile lit his wizened face as I stood bewildered at the surreal similarity.

Like some magical play of frivolous moments in time, *daddu* seemed to have reappeared in the dark misty night, to flash his assuring indulgent smile. He walked with me with a comforting silence absorbing the uncertainty of the moment, like the silent certitude that had wrapped us in the graveyard, only to disappear like a chimera in the near future. It seemed it was *daddu*, from the long-lost moment, now walked with me, silently guiding me to a distant tram stop and waited till the tram arrived like a dreamy vessel through the yellow fog. His parting words spelled the name of the station where I should get off to reach my hotel safely and just then I remembered with a stabbing pang, you had not mentioned the name of my destination when you threw the bag of rainbow moments overboard and took the train alone to your distant alluring destination forever.

Bio:
Piku Chowdhury is the Assistant Professor of Satyapriya Roy College of Education a Govt. aided Post Graduate

College. She is also an author of 9 books and many articles in international journals, a translator, editor, poet, state curriculum revision core committee member, project director, non-clinical mental health worker and research guide.

Three Days of Turmoil

Pranab Ghosh

Mind lost its way. Moved restlessly in the labyrinth of time. Layer by layer, memories spilled on the street. Dust-clad, they lay homeless by the roadside. I expected you to pick those up and return those to me, but you lay asleep in my dream and I decided to bid you a final adieu.

I picked up one memory from the dust and it smiled at me. I saw my dead grandmother walking into a gorge. The train that I was travelling stood stationary beside it. And I felt like disembarking the train and dive into the gorge to dissolve from this earth forever. I could not do it. Instead, I sat quietly, staring out of the window and she in her white widow dress, slowly dissolved into the gorge. The train began to move and I left her behind in that gorge, carrying her memory with me down the train tracks into the nowhere land. The nowhere land where I reside now with known and unknown faces.

This was years ago. Today, I think of that evening and clear the dust that accumulated on that picture. And as my brush makes the dust float, I sneeze. I have caught cold. Allergic or viral fever? I do not know, nor do I want to check; but sit firm on my decision to bid you all a final goodbye. He came and then he came and then he. They all came in succession and stood in solidarity to death and I looked out of the window into the morning sky and swore in the name of life to escape it.

The river, still, reflecting the morning sun flowed. And I walked into it slowly; the water flowed above me and I sank. With tears in my eyes, as I sat in front of the window, I saw my body resting in peace on the river bed. And then she came. She told me that my bloated body will shore up at a distant land with my eyes eaten away by fishes. The flesh

The Body of Memories

rotting and body denied a decent burial, I looked outside the widow and decided to do away with the river.

I thought about morphine. I thought about prostitutes. I thought about rich people bored with life and embracing death. I thought of the migrant labors sleeping to death on the train tracks. I thought of you. I thought of her. Her voice overpowered my soul. I want to live, I say, but my soul, tired and torn, my dreams scattered on the roadside of life wants me to run away from it, beyond life and beyond death, into the void where glowing light alone will keep company of my soul. I will bury my pain in her bosom to bloom again in a distant land away from you all. Away from all pain and sufferings. Away from all tears and heartbreaks. Away from this dreary, desolate living. Away from you and me. But with her, I wanted to live – with her alone. But… I set the deadline. The countdown has begun.

She came in the evening. I watched from a distance. I did not see her disembark from her car. But I saw the car stop. Then I found my dream walking. She walked the street I walk day and night. I saw her from a distance. My soul left me. Ran down the stairs. Opened the gates and ran after the dream. I sat quietly contemplating. I found excuses. My fear taking sway on my limbs. Making them numb, inactive, but my rebel soul left me and I sat a lump of flesh. My soul walked with her, to my favorite roadside joint. Ignominy heaped on love. Passion cried for help and my soul rebuked the abusers of love, as my lump of flesh watched.

The decision to bid the world a farewell was already weakening.

Love. Sighs. Pangs. Passion.

She stood there waiting for me with my soul keeping her company. She was all over my senses. My life flow that left me in the morning started to return. Slowly it became a deluge. And I sank in it. Then she left. With a renewed mission, I looked at the semi-lit street where her car stood.

Where she walked. Walked away from me, but into my life, my being and my existence. I kept on sitting. Working. And waiting for her to return!

II

The morphine injection was ready, as we six sat quietly in the room. She was supposed to come to inject freedom into our blood. But her voice floated in and implored me of reviewing the mission and gave an impression of a journey with her, beyond life. With the sense of togetherness overpowering my lonely self, I sat idly watching her vanishing footsteps. And then I looked for the other five. They too were gone!

Was she real? Or was she a fantasy as committed as death? Is life a mission not to be terminated? Or is life a dream that we can desert midway in search of that escape from which no one returns? She vowed to pick up the pieces of dream lying scattered on the roadside. She vowed to repair my broken mind and recreate the dreams that life can go on, dreaming ages after ages, without boredom, without the heart sinking and without the malice that one feels against the world, up in arms to destroy you and your dream!

III

This is day 2. I slept through the night before, thinking of the six of us with morphine injection ready. But she did not come to inject us and we shelved the idea for a week. I was asleep. But I was wide awake too. In a faraway place, farmers stayed awake under the night sky. Some slept, while others were on the vigil. They were all looking towards a new dawn. They wanted all anti-farmer bills scrapped. They had new life, new times to usher in. Here, as I dreamt of the determined faces of the farmers, I dreamt of syringes too. Of a woman clad in a white saree, pushing death into our being.

And as we went numb, we thought of our lives, our times, our goals, and our desires. We thought of you and I together.

And I thought of the other five sitting idly, waiting for death with me. What had gone wrong? What had gone amiss? I thought of the pandemic situation; I thought of the dead bodies on railway tracks; I thought of the trucks carrying migrant labors colliding with death. Isn't death the only escape route left for those routed by the sinking Covid-19-struck economy? It's no midlife crisis. It's not a tale of any man or any woman. It's not a tale of a man denied love. It's not a tale of a woman going for revenge when her love got stabbed. It's not anything of that sort. It's about life getting derailed midway. It's about life jumping to a halt all of a sudden and then trying to limp back to desired normality.

It's about time testing the mettle of Man. It's about a failing and falling economy, crushing Man out of existence. I had a job then. I had… I had… I had… But a sense of discomfort haunted me. Haunted me… Haunted me… Haunted me… For how many days? For how many months? There was no certainty. Uncertain times had seeped into the soul with its vitality giving way. What if? What if? What if? What if everything turns to dust one fine morning? What if dreams come crashing down one fine night? What if? What if? What if?

The serenity of life is gone. Its pristine exuberance cannot be felt. Morbid time crawls in our veins and make the blood turn cold and in cold perspiration you think of bidding your times a good-bye. A final adieu to save yourself from all uncertainties, all pangs, all sufferings and all ignominy of unemployment. And then it happened. In the morning mail I found the letter. Termination of my job. "Thank you for your services rendered. We no longer are in a position to continue with your services. Your last month's pay has been deposited. We will get in touch with you in future if we find a place for you…" bla…bla….bla… .

You are not surprised. You are not baffled. You are not pained. It is not that the unthinkable has happened. It is what had been expected. What had to happen had taken place. You begin to chew your saliva and remorse and wait for the sun to come out. Wait for the new day to dawn on you. Will there be new hope? You do not know. Yet you wait for the sun to rise. Yet you wait for the new day!

Is there a new resolve? Is there any call to attend that will change the course of your life? Pleasantly I did not remember morphine. I did not remember her as I bid her a farewell. I remembered the farmers, the migrant labors, the homeless and the jobless millions. I remembered that to fight to finish is the requirement of the time; it is survival for the fittest. To quit is to succumb to the designs of the 'outlawed', who make laws in the nation! To die is to surrender! Then who did inject the idea of death into my head? Was it you? You? You? The nation? It's leaders? Your enemies? Your opposition? Who? Who? Who?

I look for an answer as I prepare to live for another day and fight for my life and my times. Jobs eaten away, dreams stolen, I wait for her return. I wait for her to pick up the pieces of my dream from the roadside and wipe the dust off it. I wait…I wait…I wait… as I prepare for a new day!

IV

This is day 3. Breaking the news of job loss to an aging mother, a disillusioned wife and expectant daughter was like solving a jigsaw puzzle. This was the second such disheartening news in the span of six months. Memories began to unfold. Dissolving granny in the gorge, the slow chugging train, her vanishing footsteps – all jostled for space in the brain and tried to push out the ignominy of unemployment. Hungry faces stared at me. Mad, bad times have sealed a deal once again, more severe than death. Life was on the back foot. The resolve to wait for a new day clashed with the madness of the uncertain times.

Mind seemed to give way to unforeseen images of life cracking up and refusing to rejuvenate. But I had to hold on to life, expecting the sad times to change. I had to stick to

The Body of Memories

the resolve of ushering in a new dawn, a new day, a new chapter. Frozen times would have to be broken into bits and warmth of life is to be injected into the dead dreams. Morphine overdose is not the answer. Life's renewed mission has to be the key. The pep talk to self over, I dialed my wife. She wasn't taken aback. She did not shout. She did not shudder, but listened stoically! Was there a sigh of relief that escaped me unobserved or was I too engrossed in my resolve of ushering in a new dawn to notice the unheard sigh escaping me?

The relief... The relief... The relief.... . From what?... From what?....From what?...

I dare not question. I dare not think. Only I try to cling on to a non-existent dream, a love unrequited or requited I do not remember, but I manage to cling on to life, with the resolve of settling in for a new dawn; what if she never came to rescue me? ... What if a passing dream disappeared like a dissolving fragrance of a withering flower? What if she was unreal? What if the six men waiting to be injected with morphine, a desire of a lost soul? What if the dream that rescued me from death a vivid imagery drawn from forgotten times?

What if? ... What if? ... What if?...

Bio:
Pranab Ghosh is a journalist, writer and poet. He runs a blog "Existential Problems" (pranabomkar.wordpress.com).His poems and prose piece have been published in various international journals including Dissident Voice, Spillwords, The Piker Press, Memoryhouse etc. His first solo book of poems "Soul Searching and Other Poems" has been published by Scarlet Leaf Publishing, Toronto, in 2017. His second collection of poems "Vision of the World and Other Poems" has been published by Impspired.com in 2020.

My Baby is My Home

Ramaa Sonti

If at all there are memories, if at all there's something to be grateful in life and where I had made a perfect decision, this is it.

When I was 14-15, I overheard my *chachi* saying about her neighbour in Berhampur: "That woman is a social type, she is interested in adopting and all such things".

Exact words. At that time, I could not comprehend the word social or the adoption. But it made me think. I knew the word before. I read in textbooks and storybooks about orphans, meaning individuals who don't have a mom or dad and who live in an *ashram,* and mostly live by alms.

See, don't blame me, this is the perception of a cloistered orthodox South Indian girl. I read a lot. The thought grew on me. I wanted to become that 'social type' who can adopt.

Further education, job happened and at the age of 27, I got married. Not an arranged one, but my brother's friend, someone from our community happened to fall in love with me.

My husband Aditya was an Ex-Airforce. So he had a comparatively broader outlook than many. Two months after my marriage I tentatively expressed my wish. And then, we shifted to Bhubaneswar. The idea took a solid shape.

We planned to adopt after I pass my departmental. By mid of 2000, the goals we set for ourselves were reached and we were ready for the big step. Coincidence or whatever, one day the son of my College principal came to my department on some personal work. Though quite senior to me, he knew me personally, and we started talking.

When he asked me about kids, I replied that I plan to adopt. Till that moment we had done nothing to further this plan. There was a vague notion somewhere that there are some clinics that sell unwanted kids.

When he heard this, he immediately said that he can give me a list of orphanages in Bhubaneshwar and Cuttack from where I can adopt.

Next day I got the full list of NGOs and adoption centres. I showed it to a colleague from Cuttack who immediately said that the NGO 'Sanjog' in there is run by his *Mausi*. A day after was Saturday. Aditya arranged for a day off and we started towards Cuttack.

The NGO people interviewed us. I told them my specifications. A girl, more than 6 months old. They made some calls, and then we were taken to 'Basundhara', a state-run orphanage at Bidanasi, Cuttack.

A girl was brought to us, exactly to my specifications. I didn't feel anything. Not even an inclination to hold her. They denied having any other girl child for us. And then the *aaya* in there reminded them of that two-month-old baby who weighed approximately 2.5 kilos.

They looked at each other and then said you may not want her, she is an infant. But Aditya insisted on seeing her once.

'No sir, she is having her milk now, it will be late.' They said.

We decided to wait.

25 minutes gone by, they tried to dissuade us from waiting, but we stayed put. She was brought to us at last, a tiny dark-coloured bundle. I was scared to hold her. Aditya did. She was two-and-a-half-month-old. Born on a rainy night in a good hospital. These were the details given to us.

'How do you know?' I asked them.

The hospital informed us of an abandoned baby. We went in our jeep in the rain and brought her. Aditya looked at her face for a minute and then announced:

"This is my Sona".

They gave us a week to get ready with the documents required, while they would look into the legal things.

While returning, I asked Aditya 'What made him take the decision?'

'I felt bonded,' he replied.

The following Sunday we went home and told our respective parents. Mine as usual termed me crazy. My in-laws said clearly that they won't approve of this nonsense.

Typical of me, I told both: 'I came to inform, not to take permission...'

We had a week to prepare ourselves for parenthood, which was spent running for documents required, from people endorsing our character and integrity. I sewed mattresses with old bedsheets. We bought everything that a child will need—bed, towels, bibs, feeding bottles, all in pink, and a lot of baby clothes. In my office, some appreciated, some snickered and some attempted to advice. As usual, I never listened to anything.

The date dawned. 9th November 2000. We booked a car. Dressed and spruced, armed with the pink layette, a small feeding bottle for water and a blanket, we started for Cuttack. My colleague-cum-friend who helped us get to Basundhara was waiting there before us.

The documents shown, money given, and I wanted my baby. The *aaya* brought her, took me to the other room with her to put in the diaper and change the clothes. She wanted to say something, I could sense that, but she didn't. She put on the new clothes, the diaper and gave me my child. Laddus were distributed throughout the orphanage, photos were taken and we set off as three, with the infant in tow.

The whole distance, Sona was in my lap, but was looking intently at Aditya. It was love at first sight for both of them. Nobody was there at home to welcome us. Shanti, my domestic help waited for me near the door. Tanu came running, mandatory snaps were taken. The baby started howling.

'She's hungry, Shanti,' I said.

The cow milk which was kept in fridge was carefully heated, due water was added and the baby was fed. It pooped immediately. Shanti, while wiping her butt, noticed something raw in there.

We immediately rushed to the pediatrician who said, it might be some infection as she is from orphanage and gave an ointment.

The whole evening, she howled, was fed & pooped. It was a continuous process. Neighbours who came to see her, remarked about her frail body and dark colour. The whole night the stool was watery and she was crying. All the carefully cut & stitched baby sheets I stored up got exhausted, like me. In the morning, I washed a mountain, and she continued to poop.

When we went to the doctor he said: 'New climate, new milk, don't worry.'

The next day was a Friday. I gave the medicines prescribed, held her while she cried. It was the same situation on Saturday. But I guessed she wasn't passing that much of stool. I was glad.

My parents and in-laws visited us that day. Sunday morning, my sister-in-law who was a pharmacist came. The moment she held the girl, she told us to go and get an auto. 'We have to admit her in hospital, she stopped responding.'

We three hurried to the waiting auto, much to the curiosity of the building people (I used to live in the colony).

It was a reputed hospital in Bhubaneswar, but the receptionist refused consultation saying that it's a Sunday and no doctor is available. I marched to the owner of the hospital, a medicine specialist's chamber. Someone in there stopped me, saying that the doctor is in a meeting with other doctors.

With the child in my arms, I ran to the meeting room, yanked open the door, and literally threw my daughter on the table. Shocked, the doctors stood up.

Now it was my turn to howl.

'I adopted this girl on Thursday, today she is half dead. Just save her.' I commanded.

The owner doctor took charge of everything immediately, ordering the pediatrician present at the meeting to have a look, and if its serious, to get her admitted right away.

The moment he started examining her, a fountain of watery poop came out, drenching me and him. He immediately ordered admission and an ICU. My brothers also came running to the hospital.

She was admitted, put in a room, drip was given. 'Now she will be hydrated.' The doctor said.

The nurse came and told me: 'You need not give her milk anymore.'

10 minutes later, we heard a small whimper and then she starting crying loudly.

'What kind of a mother you are, the baby needs milk, can't you see?' The patient's caretaker from the next room came and asked me. We called the nurse, who gave one look at the crying, reddened baby and said: 'Give her formula'.

While Aditya ran to get the formula, my brother went for the hot water.

Formula in stock now, it continued the same for every two hours. The whole night me and my sister-in-law remained with the girl, holding her hand so that the needle wont slip. The poop formed bits of crusts on my dress. I didn't care.

She was there in hospital for 3 days and then I went to my *Mausi*'s home in Bhubaneswar as she has to be given regular injections & monitored carefully. I was scared to be alone with her (My parents along with brothers and my in-laws stay a good distance away at Jatni, a small town 30 kms from Bhubaneswar).

Two days of medications later, she was perfectly fine, but had not yet passed stool. Nights were spent holding her and moving around.

The third night, suddenly her face got squeezed, she stopped breathing and out came a very thin strand of poop. Till then, we have not given much thought to her raw butt, except for putting the ointment. For the first time, I felt something is wrong with her. Exhausted from the marathon of passing the stool, my daughter slept.

The next day, I rang up the orphanage. The madam, Ms. Jena- Director of Basundhara picked the phone, listened to me and said: "Yaa yaa, that girl had some problem. Why don't you bring her back and take a new one? We have two new entrees."

"If you bring a dress from the market, you will think twice before replacing it, and this is a human being we were talking about. And she has been with me for one whole week. How can you even say that?" I shouted at her.

It worked on her, I guess. She asked me to wait, went through her files, returned and announced that the girl had a surgery at the anus region.

'She was in Sisubhawan for two days. If you want to, you can go and ask the doctor there about her condition'. She added.

I called my sister-in-law, and again we three went to Cuttack. I went straight to the orphanage, and demanded to be given the medical reports.

Outside the gate, the *aaya* who dressed Sona told me: 'That girl you took had her anus stitched. She used to cry the whole day and night. We all thought she won't live long. Besides, these people here ordered us to feed all the infants flattened rice (*chuda*) powder alternately with milk.'

I looked at my baby. In the red frock, a kilo more (from 2.5 -3.5), she looked like a doll. We went to the Sisubhawan. The doctor looked at the reports and remembered of a newborn being admitted in hospital on a rainy day and a newly appointed surgeon botching up the operation.

'There was no opening to pass the stool. So when they brought her, the surgeon, made a large opening and in order to cover it up, stitched it more. So now, Sona was left with a tiny opening to pass the waste.' He explained.

'What can be done?' I asked him.

He showed me thin rods. He instructed me to apply xylocan jelly and insert it for 1 minute twice a day every day. Slowly, as the rod's width increases, the opening will also be (I did it for 2 years, still have the rods with me).

Confused and satisfied, I returned. Now I knew the problem at least.

The Body of Memories

The next day I shifted to my parent's home. On Sunday, Aditya came to visit us. He brought a bag load of clothes for the girl, cuddled her and while returning, got hit by a running vehicle and fractured his leg.

Everyone said, it's the girl's bad luck that he got hit. Some colleagues even advised me to return her so that my husband would become healthy again.

'It's her luck that he survived a near fatal accident.' We replied to them.

Thrice operated, Aditya stayed at home for a better part of the first year. And he took complete care of her. I sometimes used to think that if the child is adopted, my husband may not give her the complete affection she deserves. But with him at home, that problem got solved and there grew that special bond between the father and daughter, which I can never break into.

Ps. 1. One incident stands out in my mind. Aditya was in Cuttack for operation and one day after the surgery, I went to see him leaving the daughter with my mom and another sister-in-law. A few hours later, when I called them, they asked me to return immediately. Sona was neither drinking milk, nor had she stopped crying/screaming.

I took the first available bus, reached home. By that time, it was evening. I went to the home to a harassed mom and sister-in-law. I could hear whimpers from the bedroom. I went in, switched off the light, took her in my arms and started talking. My mom handed me the feeding bottle. Sona drank the entire milk, held my little finger and slept in my arms. She was tired of waiting for me. And more than that, she recognized me as her mother. How much fancier it can get?

Ps. 2. A month later, Tanu & Kavita, two of my friends came to visit her. She was sleeping and was secured under a yellow-coloured basket net. They couldn't recognize the ball she became.

Ps. 3 On the advice of a surgeon at Vizag, we made her join swimming classes and later, the 7 years of dancing had set her muscles. She is completely fine now.

Ps 4. In June last year, after a particularly huge fight between the father and daughter, I started crying and behind the closed doors of her room, I told her the history of her birth.

No. she never rejected me. She cried for a while, thanked and hugged me, went to her dad who was cooking, hugged and kissed him.

My baby is my home now. In every which way.

Bio:
Ramaa Sonti is an Income tax officer by default. Would have loved to be Historian or something fancy which didn't involve figures. An introvert by choice, her passions include reading, and writing. Friends call her Ramaa, non-friends don't call anything. She is presently residing in Bhubaneswar with husband Aditya & daughter Sona.

Sundori

Rhiti Chatterjee Bose

There was an enormous four track railway lines, a huge pond teaming with fishes, and right by the pond was our garden. The messy overflowing garden with wild flowers and fruit trees surrounded our house; it was home to many birds, frogs and a very naughty mongoose. I lived there with my Baba, Ma and my Ammu, my grandmother. The house was big, sprawling over two floors, opening up to a second-floor terrace. On clear nights, you could see numerous stars from the terrace, and we didn't even know their names. To us, they were a splatter of tiny lights across the ink blue sky, with the North Star shining the brightest. Baba would often take Ma and me upstairs and told us stories that were born out of the stars. Our house in the little sleepy town of Barrackpore was truly what they call as bliss. The days I lived there could be counted not in years, but in love and happiness.

Although all these are a memory now, but it is still fresh as yesterday in my mind's canvas. The thrum of the tracks when the trains passed by throughout the night became the throb of my heartbeats. The water rippled in the pond every now and then whenever a big Goods carriage train would pass. On stormy nights the shuddering, quivering trees would dance in a rhythm matching the pulsation from the tracks. A lot of people who came to visit us hated it, couldn't sleep at night from all the vibrating noises and creaks from doors and windows, but I loved it. The strumming of the tracks when the trains passed by still tugs at my heartstrings.

Many animals would get hurt at the tracks, some even died from the trains that passed by in full speed. When a bigger animal like a goat or a cow died, Vultures gathered, feasting on the carcasses. Sounds morbid I know, but to an eleven-year-old me, it was just fascinating. I watched them, dancing in circles, tugging on the flesh and eating their fill, through our upstairs windows. I have grown up seeing vultures roaming about our terrace, they had terrifying eyes and sharp beaks, yet such enigmatic presence. I was strictly told by my parents not to disturb them when they were there. I obeyed.

It was the summer holidays. The days were hot and the nights humid, filled with the thick, sweet aroma that came from our Jasmine bushes. One morning, parents were having their morning tea; I sat nearby with my Grandma, both of us reading our own books. As we were all lazing about, we heard a shriek coming from the neighbours' courtyard, quite out of place on a bright sunny morning like that. The four of us ran to our back garden following the stream of screams. Minati *Kakima* was screaming at the top of her voice, looking disheveled, and pointing her fingers towards places where we could see nothing. My mom approached the boundary wall that divided the two houses and asked her in a calming manner, '*Boudi ki hoyeche*? What happened?'

'*Shakun!*' she panted, 'In my kitchen, walked right in…' She couldn't finish her sentence and broke into sobs, 'brings bad luck for the family, you know,' her husband completed for her.

She gathered her breath and said, 'I told him before not to build a house by the railway tracks, such ominous things keep happening, no one listens to me…' and once again, her voice trailed off behind her sobs.

The little me was pretty dumbfounded as to how a bird like a vulture could bring bad luck. So I looked at my Baba for a better explanation, he lowered his voice down to a whisper and said, 'Some grownups believe a lot of rubbish, it's nothing.' Then he raised his voice a little more and asked our neighbour, 'Where is it now?'

Manab *Kaku* nodded his head and pointed nowhere really, '*Jaani na dada*, it ran away somewhere, we didn't see.'

The Body of Memories

Baba said, 'Strange, a walking vulture!' he asked again, 'Are you sure, it didn't fly off?'

'Who cares where it is!!! Now I have to go arrange for a *Satya Narayan Puja* to ward off the evil it brought along.' He huffed. Baba chuckled softly.

Slowly, the few people who had gathered dispersed, talking about the walking vulture and the bad omen. Ma and Ammu went indoors to get back to their tea and books. Baba stood there curiously, in silence. I stayed by his side hoping to catch a glimpse of the walking vulture. He looked at me and said, 'Vulture's won't walk around, unless it's hurt. Maybe it has hurt her wings, that's why was looking for a place to rest.' I nodded; this theory made a lot more sense than a walking vulture trying to bring bad luck for a family.

'Come' he said, 'Let's look in the garden, maybe she is still here.'
I followed.

The back garden was clear, no signs of the so-called ill-luck bearing bird. We tiptoed towards the front garden and there she was. Right at the corner of the boundary wall which joined the two houses, behind the Jasmine bushes. I stepped forward, and Baba put his hand in front of me, 'Stop' he said, 'We don't want to scare the poor thing off, do we?'

It felt like the bird looked straight at me with her eyes full of terror and anger, piercing my little body. I shuddered a little.

'Let's go', Baba said softly.
'Why?' I asked.
'She is scared, she needs to rest, and we better not disturb her. Also it's wise not to tell the neighbours she is hiding here or else they will pounce on us with more theories of omens and bad lucks.'

He took my hand and we left the way we came.

He walked indoors and told my ma, 'We found her.'

Ma looked up from her book and asked 'Is she hurt?'

Baba said 'yes, we will put out some water and food later for her, for now let her rest.'

'So you don't believe in the omen then, Ma?' I asked.

She smiled, 'No *beta,* animals are fine, it's the humans which scare me more.'

Looking at my bewildered face, she said, 'Go upstairs now, finish your shower before breakfast, someday I will explain what I said, for now just remember, animals and birds don't carry bad luck.' I nodded and left.

Later in the afternoon, as I watched from my upstairs window, I saw the bird sleeping, and my father gently stepping forward and setting a bowl of water in front of her and a piece of raw fish and walking away quietly.

Baba named her 'Sundori' meaning beautiful.

She stayed for four days, not touching any food that we gave, just drinking the water from time to time. On the fifth morning when I looked out of my window, my heart sank, she was gone.

I had hoped that she would stay a few more days.

Baba seemed a little sad too.

So I told him, 'Don't worry Baba, she will come back one day to visit us.' He smiled.

But Sundori never returned.

One day I asked Baba, 'Why didn't Sundori return to us? We were nice to her, weren't we?'

He kindly placed a hand on my head and said, 'Some of us are a bit too wild, our souls are not meant to be tamed by the lure of food or water, we need to fly, we need to fly away so far that no one can bind us with earthy offerings.'

I didn't understand much of what he said then.

But now, when I look back at that memory, it all makes sense. Not all of us are to be tamed; it is okay to remain wild and reject all mundane offerings of this world and its domesticated people. A life lesson from a father to his little girl, which she would remember all her life long.

Sundori, I am glad you remained to your sky, unbound.

Bio:
Rhiti is an Artist and Art Therapist. She has a teacher's degree from Manchester Metropolitan University, UK and Post graduate diploma in Psychotherapy and Child Psychology from School of Natural Health and Science, London, UK.

She is the founder of the art company ArtIsana, focusing on art Counselling, art classes and art exhibitions, providing a platform to new and emerging artists. Co-Founder of a community library called Kitaabshaala, which not only provides a reading space to book lovers, but free classes to underprivileged children, and also a safe space for LGBTQIA community. Founder of Incredible Women of India, which is now under Readomania.

She is also a published writer and poet. She is a mother of two kids and based in Bhubaneswar.

The Wind Still Whispers in the Willows

Dr. Santosh Bakaya

In the stillness of the bedroom, when the cicadas start chirping, the owls confer with loud hoots and the dwindling noises of a retiring household drop off one by one into some sort of a disciplined silence, I quietly lie on the bed, dutifully scrolling Facebook.

Yesterday night as I lay down on the bed, I came across a meme of a cute little kitten all set to leave her house, a briefcase by her side and the caption: *Eight year old ready to move out of my parents' house cause they yelled at me* .My daughter, has tagged me in the meme, with the comment "You are this kitten," suffixed with a winking Smiley.

Well, therein lies a story of my childhood escapades which she has heard from me time and again. I was a universally acknowledged imp and would disappear from the house when scolded, either heading for the attic which was in my granny's room or towards the neem tree in our verdant garden in our university quarters in Jaipur, where my father was a professor of English.

"Don't scold Baby, she will run away." Everyone was asked to treat me with kid's gloves, but how long? I was forever devising devious plans and hatching conspiracies; some of my pranks deserved punitive action, so I was punished and I ran away, as predicted.

I close my eyes and see! Yes, I very clearly see a ten-year-old girl, [a brat actually], climbing up to the attic. Eyes gleaming, hands itching, she heads towards an ancient looking trunk, a relic from her granny's Kashmir days, and flings it open. The trunk has nothing but books heaped one

The Body of Memories

upon another. Books which take her to different worlds. Books which she loves touching, feeling, smelling.... books which she carries to her bedside and sleeps, surrounded by the tantalizing smell of the carefully book- marked bibliophilic treasure, both hands lying possessively on two books. *The Wind in the Willows* by Kenneth Grahame and My *Family and other Animals* by Gerald Durrell, her constant bedside companions.

Many were the times her dad and mum would tiptoe to her bedside and gingerly disentangle the books from her firm grasp. She would play possum as they patted her on the head and tiptoed out of the room, fingers on their lips.

When I had got tired of the attic, my fertile mind had started hunting for new and more exciting hideouts. After one such parental reprimand in which my elder brother had also chipped in, I had stealthily crept out of the house with a baggage strung on a stick and the stick on my ten-year-old shoulder. You know what the baggage held? A copy of *The Wind in the Willows,* my floral night suit, an apple and a toothbrush. The pilgrim had progressed towards the neem tree in the garden, and in three giant leaps had slithered up the tree, settled herself on a fragile branch and pulled out the book and the apple from the baggage. The moment I had sunk my teeth into the luscious fruit, there was a huge bellow from down below.

"Where is Baby now?"

An apple a day was known to have kept doctors at bay, but definitely not an indignant dad, who was shouting at the top of his baritone. In the frenzy of the moment, instead of sinking my teeth into the apple, I almost swallowed the Adam's apple!

In my haste to set right my folly, I fell down on to the lawn, my limbs flailing, and my pathetic little baggage open, for all to see. What followed was a cascade of sibling jeers, sniggers and jibes. To this day, my siblings don't tire of asking me how I had intended to brush my teeth, since I was not carrying any water bottle with me, and how I planned to change into my night- suit ensconced on a fragile branch of a tree?

When all my hideouts were found out, I started heading towards the hills, nay hillocks. Just a little away from the boundary wall of the campus, which adjoined our house, hillocks, big and small, made a perfect picture postcard scene. What absolute pleasure it used to be standing on one hillock, a triumphant glint in my eyes, drums of victory echoing in the ears. My joy was no different from the joy one mountaineer would feel after having climbed the Mount Everest.

I recalled; my juvenile mind had then believed that they were waves which had been put under a spell by some mischievous wizard.

Every night is my tryst with this lost world of mine, where I read meanings in the polyglot silence, whispering and mumbling, stammering and stuttering, lisping and purring notes from a long-forgotten song.

In this multi layered eloquence of the nights, I fumble and scavenge for some notes of sanity in the rampant insanity around. Somewhere a door shuts, a window opens, the curtains are drawn, a lost cat purrs, a stray whines, the trees rustle and the night yaks on.

Is it some surreal dreamscape? As the silence becomes a glib talker, sounds from the past, also become confident and stride into the present, galloping fast – faster – faster…

A lost universe suddenly finds its moorings- there is a sudden profusion of all those moments which had long dwindled into mere pinpoints in the whole wide world. All these lost moments suddenly start shining with a dazzling radiance.

In this lost universe, it is books that hold sway, as I see myself lovingly fingering dad's huge collection of books, and a lost moment sparks in memory, "this Santosh will someday write a novel, she has a very fertile imagination, is always reading books and cooking up stories." This was Sr. Theodora beaming at me in Sophia School, Jaipur. I was looking at her, misty eyed, when I heard a voice:

"How many times will you read *The Bell jar*? Oh, I see this is my copy of the book! I was wondering where it had disappeared. And you have filched *Not that kind of Girl* too! Honestly, this book is not your cup of tea, this cup will cheer you better." This was my daughter removing the books from under my hands and handing me a steaming hot cup of tea.

Life seemed to have come full circle, and I sat happily perched on the circle still basking in all the love, while sounds from the past continued to serenade me with their soothing strains.

Bio:
Internationally acclaimed for her book 'Ballad of Bapu' [Vitasta Publishers, 2015, a poetic biography of Mahatma Gandhi], Santosh Bakaya is an academic, poet, essayist, novelist and TEDX speaker whose poems have been translated into many languages and received laurels worldwide.

A die-hard believer in Martin Luther King's dream and John Lenon's Imagine, dreaming a day 'when there is nothing to kill or die for', and 'all the people sharing all the world', she is the recipient of the Reuel International Prize for Writing and Literature [2014] for her long poem 'Oh Hark! And has been conferred with the Universal Inspirational Poet Award [2016] by Pentasi B Friendship Poetry group and Ghana

Government; and The Setu Award (USA] 'in recognition of a stellar contribution to world literature' (Individual category, 2018). She has received the first Keshav Malik award 2019 for her entirely "staggeringly prolific and quality conscious oeuvre" in fiction, prose and poetry.

There is a way if there is a drive

Satadeepa Gupta Mallick

We all have a story to tell about ourselves. Whoever we are, wherever we come from, we all hope to prosper in life in our own way. Hope and prosperity are all very relative terms, but whatever be the account of our life, we desire to touch the pinnacle of success someday. This is because we humans have a powerful gadget called the brain which somehow pushes us to challenge our intelligence. But what is the force that leads us to achieve what we want? Is it our passion or hard work? A good connection or just luck? Maybe a bit of each.

As a Bengali kid born to a mother who was a proficient, soulful singer, I had the privilege of attending a music school and dreamt of becoming a professional singer. Although I regularly sang at school concerts, my traditional and educated family background forbade me to set singing as my priority. So, studying and getting a good University degree became more important and singing became a pastime. When I was sixteen, I had a vocal degree in hand, but was engaged in thinking about a career in science. This seemed justified during that time as that was what my parents had expected from me and also my school friends were pursuing the same. I have always been very flexible in nature. My parents were incredibly good people with exceptional virtues and going against their wish was not something which even arched my mind. Gradually, with time I was dissolved in their hopes about me and nearly forgot what my own dream was. My mother was typically beautiful and I was very simple looking, in fact everyone said I wasn't blessed with Ma's beauty and looked like my father and grandmother who were ordinary looking people. Interestingly, my parents didn't forget that once I was serious about my singing. So, in social gatherings and friendly meetups I was asked to sing. In my early twenties, I suddenly discovered I didn't want to sing in front of any relatives or friends anymore. I couldn't fathom the reason why I felt cocooned within myself when it came to singing publicly. Eventually, the seal of me being "too shy to sing' was imprinted on me. Some thought I was self-conscious, others thought I lacked confidence. Some even thought I was a snob. Strangely enough, I just didn't want to sing, although I hadn't forgotten my childhood dream of becoming a singer.

My singing in front of others made a dramatic return after my arranged marriage. Some of you may be acquainted with the common Bengali saying that an ideal Bengali bride is one who can sing Rabindra Sangeet in front of their prospective in-laws. Rabindra Sangeet is a genre of music written by the Bard of Bengal, the Nobel Prize winner Rabindranath Tagore. My parents must have praised my music degree to the groom's family already. So in keeping with the custom, I was expected to sing in front of them during their first visit to get acquainted with me. But I had to be firm in my "too shy to sing' stance, so I showed my unsureness at first. I asked them 'Do I have to sing today?' My would-be mother-in-law had said something which dispersed the ice of my 'hesitation-to-sing' syndrome, a block which I was carrying deep inside me since my early youth.

"Look dear, you don't have to sing for us, sing for your own happiness, we will just listen." She said to me very affectionately. I was very much influenced by her simple words, coming from someone who was no less than a stranger to me during our first interaction. I had sensed a good connection with her. The expression 'own happiness' came across with a different meaning and deeper impact. Yes, I know they say, 'dance as if no one is watching and sing as if no one is listening'. But to seek it became easier with the simple phrase 'own happiness'. I realised that I should sing for my own delight. I never had regrets that I didn't do it for so many years. An urge which had taken back seat got promoted in the pilot seat once again. It never overtook my dedication towards PhD, but my inhibition of

The Body of Memories

singing in front of others was gone. Years have passed since then and now I not only sing, but have also been taking guidance from Pandits. I have a YouTube channel which is like my second kid and am active on social media with my songs. I also enjoy teaching music methodically to people of all age groups and motivate people to sing as I truly believe that singing can have an amazing positive effect on one's mood, health and well-being. I have no regrets for not becoming a professional singer anymore. Having lived in the UK since the last two decades, I have proudly served the sick in the National Health Service for over sixteen years. For this I can only thank my parents who were assertive to propel me to the exciting world of studying science. At present, I spend most of my time with music, poetry and other creative forms. This only makes me think that good things happen only when the time is right. Cherry on the top, my physician husband is very much inclined to drama and is very much together in my creative journey.

As I look back, I feel my acceptance without any regrets throughout my life helped me to remain positive and optimistic in whatever little I have achieved, and I would attribute this to none other than my grandmother's genes.

My grandmother's name is Ashapurna Debi (8th Jan 1909 - 13th July 1995). My elder sister Satarupa and I used to call her by the name Ashapurna, which at first glance could be considered quite ill-mannered. When we were young, eminent poets, authors and people from famous publishing houses used to visit our house. All of them would refer to my grandmother either as Ashapurna Di (sister), Ashapurna *Mashima* or *Jethima* (aunts) or using other appropriate extensions. So my elder sister and I thought we would do something similar and decided to call her lovingly as Ashapurna! That audacious act of calling my grandmother by name continued forever. Ashapurna took this as a symbol of pure innocence and acknowledged the love beneath it. After that whenever she gave us something in writing like a birthday greeting or blessings in the Bengali new year, she would always sign it as Ashapurna. No wonder Ashapurna understood the child's mind so well and was famous as a child writer throughout her writing career.

She was a very well-known author who spoke about women's freedom in simple words. She is known in India as a great novelist who wrote powerful, uniquely crafted short stories on feministic consciousness. She never had the opportunity to read literature in any language other than our vernacular Bengali. Her only means of knowing the world was through the characters she had met in her own life, brushed with her imagination. She won the Jnanpith Award, the highest literary award in India and has four Honorary D.Litt degrees from renowned Universities. Unfortunately, she never had the opportunity of receiving any formal education when she was young, which was a reality of girls in her time and age. Girls in her family were forbidden from attending schools under the strict instructions of her orthodox-minded grandmother Nistarini Debi.

The discrimination between boys and girls triggered the revolting question: why shouldn't girls be treated equally as boys? This protest came out through her pen in the form of a plethora of stories where the focal point was women, their problems, their unfulfilled desires. Ashapurna was a person with clear and unbiased thinking, she never portrayed men as villains, her protest was against societal regulations and not against men. Her writings reveal a deep understanding of child psychology as well. When I was ten years old, I clearly remember occasions where she understood me better than Ma. No wonder that her writing career started when she was herself thirteen years old with a poem and then a children's story. She wrote over 240 novels, over 2000 stories, and 62 books for children. When people asked: how do you manage to write so much? She would simply reply 'I am Ma Saraswati's (Hindu Goddess of knowledge, wisdom and learning) disciple. She only makes me write'.

The Body of Memories

In absence of schooling, it is hard to believe how she siphoned the motivation to read and write. Here is how. Desperate to study, she would sit opposite to her brothers when they were studying and memorise the looks of the Bengali alphabets (*Borno Porichoy*) upside down only to correct them mentally as quickly as she could. She self-educated herself, a mind-boggling example of will power beyond my imagination. Her mother Sarala Sundari was a keen reader of Bengali literature and their home was always overflowing with library books. Indeed, such an irony that her daughters were not allowed to go to schools! But this was a blessing in disguise. Sarala Sundari knew how much Ashapurna loved to read, so if she was acting too bubbly, she would often make Ashapurna sit with books as a punishment.

What we see here is a perfect example of the proverb "If life gives you lemon, make lemonade". The misfortune of not getting an education didn't stop Ashapurna from educating herself. The fact that she couldn't attend school led to endless readings of literary greats including Rabindranath, Saratchandra and Bankimchandra, which made her gain a strong grasp on the Bengali language. From an early age, she learnt how to turn an adverse circumstance into a hopeful situation and achieve what she wanted.

Throughout her life she was always determined to fulfill her wish, although I cannot remember a single instance when she ever disappointed or ignored anyone. She never showed any negligence towards her family chores. My mother Nupur was a Professor of English at a college, and Ashapurna was a busy writer, but there was not a single day when they would not be involved in deciding what we will have for lunch or dinner. We had two separate kitchens, one was vegetarian and the other was for non-vegetarian cooking. Ashapurna was a strict vegetarian along with my *Dadu* (grandfather), Kalidas Gupta. He was a gem of a person and always expressed his pride in Ashapurna's achievements. *Dadu* was very generous in nature. There is a reason why I used the adjective generous for him. Poet couple Narendra Deb and Radharani Debi were the people who had helped Ashapurna to step out of her house and get acquainted with the stalwarts of the literary world. *Dadu* always accompanied her in all literary meetings and never showed any narrow-mindedness and put restrictions on her. When I was in college, I used to have long hours of chatting with Ashapurna. I remember she once said, in life we meet many good and honest people, but with only good luck our lives will criss-cross with generous people who support us in a bountiful way. And *Dadu* was one such soul. I myself have come across very few people who can be totally open-handed with little expectations, maybe because the modern world is all about give and take.

Having said that, I would be failing in my moral duty if I didn't mention how caring and alert Ashapurna was towards the everyday needs of *Dadu* and all of us. She was very strong-willed and at times was impulsive too. I remember an occasion when she wanted to change the curtains of her room just two days before her birthday. As she didn't go outside much; her son Susanta, my Baba, had to get the cloth samples from a shop for Ashapurna to choose from. My elder sister Satarupa and myself loved the pandemonium centered around Ashapurna's impulsive ventures. It was like an emergency in the house, the curtain-maker came to take measurements and delivered and fitted them the day before 8 Jan, just as she had desired. This was a big example of Baba's dedication towards fulfilling his mother's wish. Ma was an extraordinary woman and like Baba, equally dutiful towards Ashapurna. Ma's dictionary impatience was not a virtue, and for Ashapurna, waiting did not exist. It was interesting how both the ladies with very strong personalities and opposite outlooks lived peacefully with little or no clashes. Maybe they knew the importance of each other. The successful life that Ashapurna had when her writing career started to flourish wouldn't have been the same if *Dadu*, Baba and Ma did not cooperate. I have witnessed in them a

The Body of Memories

great deal of understanding and respect for each other. From my family, I have learnt that to be successful in family life or career, one does not need to blame or ignore the needs of others. Besides being a successful author, at the end of the day she was a responsible wife, a loving mother and mother-in-law and of course my grandmother. I have tried to follow her footsteps in my life, made myself available to all my family needs first and then followed my other pursuits.

My nickname Phuljhuri was coined by her, a name I was very embarrassed about when I was small. Her affection was beautifully expressed in her exchanges with me. I was the youngest of all her grandkids and I had unlimited freedom to do anything that I wanted to do at any time. Whenever I wanted to have a quick chat, I would rush into her room. People commonly say that for writers, isolation from all distractions is essential for good creation but I cannot recall a single occasion when she had prevented me from interrupting her work even if there was a close deadline. She never disappointed me. She never upset anyone.

She lovingly gave me pocket money of Rs 200/- which was a very big sum for a teenager. I used to help her to buy the stationeries from shops. It would be wrong not to mention that she used to spread her open-handedness to all the people around her. She had distributed the gift money of Jnanpith award to all her near and dear ones, including some close publisher friends. She was very charitable towards our helpers at home and I have observed this quality in my parents too. She maintained a diary and there is a regular mention of our helpers, especially our driver Akhtar Mandal who is now the caretaker of our Garia home in Kolkata, India. Her generosity was towards everyone and not just the favourite few, a virtue which not all of us always apply.

Apparently we were a small family. But our extended family was huge, consisting of all the people connected to Ashapurna for her literary work. We never thought they were separate from us. They would arrive anytime uninvited and would get the best possible hospitality. On Ashapurna's birthday, a lot of people, including publishers and near and dear ones came to wish her in the morning before going to work. My beloved mother was the pillar of our household and she used to prepare food for all the guests. Her fish chop and peas *kochuri* were the famous ones. Ashapurna and Ma shared a very close relationship. Both were dominating in nature, but the traditionally controversial relationship of mother-in-law and daughter-in-law was never a problem as both were mutually understanding towards each other. Both of them had a great degree of flexibility in their characters and this made their relationship successful.

Ashapurna was a religious-minded person. At home, both *Dadu* and she used to worship two times a day, but never exaggerated it in front of others. When I was small, I used to accompany her to our prayer room and tried to pick up the customs for doing the daily veneration. I tried to imitate her activities and learnt the proper *aarti* procedure. She had beautiful Sanskrit pronunciation which my grandfather had taught her, which still rings in my ears. For somebody like her who had such strong religious beliefs, it was very exceptional that she had no reservation towards other castes or people of other religions. Her mind was free of any superstitious beliefs.

Besides being a successful author, at the end of the day she was a responsible wife, a loving mother and mother-in-law and of course my grandmother. I learnt the greatest lesson of life that if one wants to achieve something, it can always be done with love as long as we do not hurt others.

Sharing a loving note written to me by Ashapurna. She had given me some money as a token of appreciation for good results in academics and this beautiful poem.

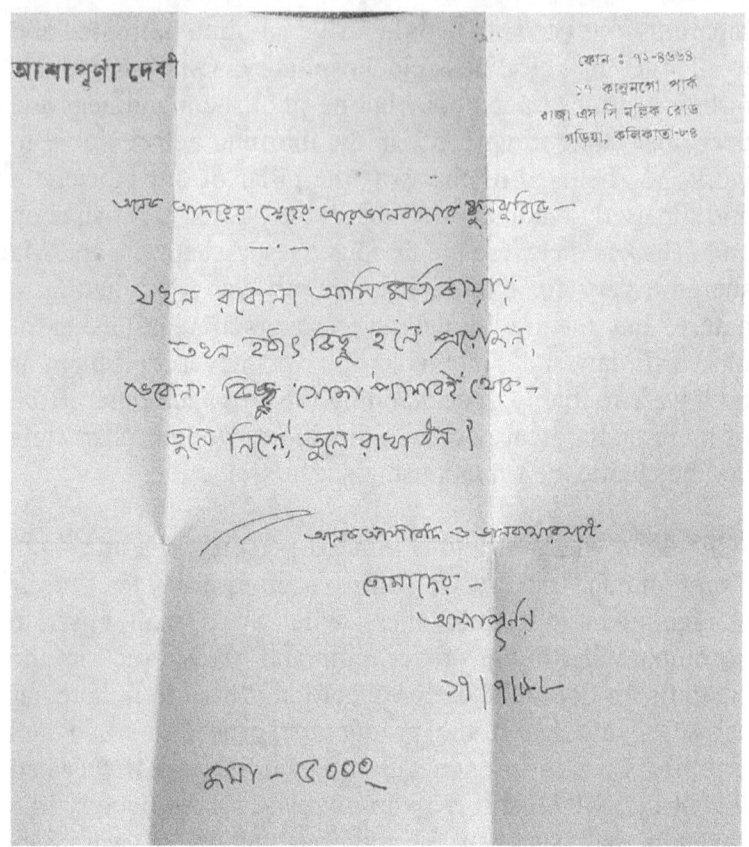

Ashapurna left us on 13th July, 1995. She lived a rewarding life of 86 years. A long life always means experiencing harsh grievances of losing many near and dear ones including much younger people. Although heart-broken from inside, I cannot remember if she was ever inconsolable. Her tremendous mental strength and a positive attitude towards life helped her to sail smoothly through all adversities.

Her perseverance and hard work were exemplary. She enjoyed a life of affluence and luxury. Her life was an extraordinary story of an ordinary person. Our lives revolved around hers. Because her life had started with self-education, she always said without hesitation that she learns every day. Even before a few days of her sad demise, she continued to read others' writings and newspapers. Such was her ardent passion for reading. The yawning gulf between aspiration and reality can be reduced, it is in our hands. Living twenty-six years with my grandmother taught me the biggest lesson of life: if there is a will, there is a way. I call it: there is a way if there is a drive.

Bio:

Satadeepa Gupta was born to parents Susanta and Nupur in a traditional Bengali family in Kolkata. She studied Biochemistry and did PhD (Science) from Calcutta University. From an early age she was trained in Rabindra Sangeet vocals and completed her Gitabharati degree from Gitabitan music school in Kolkata. She got married to Srikumar Mallick, with whom she later migrated to UK where she has served the NHS as a Scientist in Pathology Services for over 16 years. Having lived over 20 years away from home, she is deep rooted to her culture and is dedicated to music. She started to get trained in Indian Classical Music later in life. She performs regularly and has collaborative work with other groups of singers and dancers and believes her religion is Indian music. She is a music teacher and also takes interest in drama and elocution. Her family has a home production series of drama and has also performed drama in England at national level. The person who had the greatest impact on the philosophy of her life is her grandmother Ashapurna Debi, the one of the doyennes of Bengali literature in India.

Memories of a Pilgrim

Satbir Chadha

A pilgrimage always makes you feel that you're close to God, that you can feel Him better and He will hear you, and Sikhism being a young religion, we can fortunately visit the historical Gurudwaras, where the most important events of our history took place, and they are well chronicled too. My earliest memory is of a visit to 'Nankana Sahib' which is the birthplace of our first guru, Guru Nanak, which is now in Pakistan.

I was barely eight years old and Mom and I were visiting my aunt in Jammu when a group of people were travelling to Nankana Sahib to celebrate His birthday, so we managed to get a temporary passport and visa and joined them along with my aunt and uncle. We changed trains at Lahore and all along it felt like a divine journey with everyone praying and sharing episodes of our history, but when we reached there it was unbelievable, that we were at the place where Guruji was born, we were touching things He may have touched, walking where He must have walked. We saw the place where Guruji had spent all the capital given Him by His father to start a business, to distribute food to hungry sadhus and poor people, sowing the seeds of 'Langar' as it is done all over the world today. We were shown the place where His father then slapped Him, and the field where he then quietly lay Himself to rest and where a cobra spread its hood across His face to shade it, and we burst into tears, such was the feeling of 'bairag'. The next day we took part in a long memorial procession, and when we returned, we experienced a miracle. A small child less than a year old, slipped from his mother's arms and fell from the third-floor terrace where she was leaning to see the procession, and fell in the main veranda. The mother ran screaming down the stairs, to find the baby sit up unharmed. All of us fell to the ground in devotion and thanking Guruji, whose abode we were visiting.

Another Gurudwara we visit often is at Nanded in Maharashtra, 'Sri Huzoor Sahib' where our tenth guru, Furu Gobind Singh breathed His last after appointing the 'Guru Granth Sahib' as our eternal guru. The main complex has a glorious and peaceful ambience, and we get to see Guruji's own arms and weapons, leaving us in awe. Each arrow has on its tip twelve grams of gold, for those hurt to be able to get treated, and in case of the adversary's death, it would be useful to his widow or mother to survive, a sight of these arrows is so moving. There is also the enormous gun used by Mai Bhago, the famous lady warrior in Guruji's army, which is about four feet in length and weighs over thirty kilograms. We admire it lovingly as it hangs on the wall as a relic of the battle, and marvel at the courage and strength of Mai Bhago as she is said to have been six feet tall.

We explored other places of historical significance, like 'Maltekri Sahib' where Guruji paid the salary to his soldiers retiring to Punjab after the battles, measuring out gold coins by shieldfuls. He filled His own shield that He wore to war with them, and we can still have a 'darshan' of that shield, eyes brimming with tears, touched by Guruji's grandeur and nobility.

We also paid a visit to 'Hira Ghat' on the banks of the Godavary river. It so happened at this place that Bahadur Shah Zafar gifted Guruji a rare and large sparkling gem. Guruji thanked him and then threw the gem into the river. The king felt annoyed and doubted Guruji's discerning eye, then Guruji told Him to look into the river and get it back and now He would accept it, but when Zafar looked into the river, he found the bed full of gems, bigger and brighter than any. Guruji was teaching him a lesson in humility, and the pain a big 'ego' causes to man. While Maltekri Sahib gave me a lesson of 'contentment', 'Hira Ghat' made me pray that I be free of my ego.

Another unforgettable site is the gurudwara 'Sangat Sahib', where I realised what it means to be in a 'sangat'. It means being one with the 'sangat', being one with everyone, being one with every one grows further into being one with the Almighty. So simply said, but so difficult to achieve.

The most inspiring and empowering part of my pilgrimage that I recollect, is my visit to the gurudwara 'Banda Ghat'. There dwelt a *faqir* named Madho Das who had acquired some powers after doing *bhakti*, and he used them to topple unsuspecting folks who came to his hut and sat on the bed; he would use his powers to turn the bed upside down, leaving his guest confounded. But when Guruji sat on the bed, Madho Das's powers failed, so Guruji told him to stop being a mischievous faqir and become a 'banda' that is a good human being. Thereafter, he became a devout Sikh and remains one of the most valiant warriors, who went to Punjab after Guruji's demise and avenged the martyrdom of the Guruji's younger two sons. He also established the first Sikh kingdom where the rule was fair and just and the land belonged to the tillers, and under whose mighty armies, every subject was secure and safe.

The gurudwara where I get the most solace is 'Paonta Sahib' on the banks of the Yamuna in the district of Nahan in Himachal. This is where Guru Gobind Singh, the tenth guru spent His most peaceful years, writing volumes of poetry and having poets compose and recite every day, to the extent that the mighty roaring Yamuna also is silent and still while it flows by that place, as requested by Guruji, as his darling poets were being disturbed. That is the loving peaceful guru, teaching us to find peace in rhyme and verse and in singing pious hymns.

And how can I not talk about the trip to the wonderful 'Hemkunt Sahib' ten thousand feet up the lofty Himalayas, past Joshimath and past the famous Valley of Flowers, where Guru Gobind Singh meditated for thousands of years before the Almighty commanded Him to come down to earth to uplift the human race, and give new vigour to the weakened gentry? This is on the side of a deep lake surrounded by seven remarkable peaks in a most picturesque valley. The peace felt here after a trek of nineteen kilometres is so pervasive, it has to be felt if one wants to know the true essence of the place.

I could go on and on and such profound experiences would enrich me endlessly, but the guru has also taught us that running around in pilgrimage does not give you a 'moksha', that comes only by following your religion and practising kindness and the path of truth, by reciting the Almighty's name, by earning an honest living and sharing generously, by performing 'sewa' that is service, by shunning greed and avarice, by being fair and just.

It is remarkable that Guru Nanak travelled so many continents more than five centuries ago, leaving His footprints in Tibet, where He is called Nanak Llama. There is a historical Gurudwara at Dangmar Lake, one of the highest in the world, in Assam on the banks of the Brahmaputra where He was when the news of His son's birth came, far west in Samarkand, Baku and Afghanistan, where some Sikhs still survive and practise Sikhism, to the south in Sri Lanka where there still exists the gurudwara He made, then called a *dharamsaal*.

Bio:
Satbir Chadha was born in Nainital to a prosperous business family. She is the author of the highly acclaimed memoir FOR GOD LOVES FOOLISH PEOPLE, for which she won the Reuel International Prize for Literature in 2017. Her next novel was BETRAYED, a medical thriller, both published by Vitasta, again much applauded by readers. Her poems and short stories find place in several national and international anthologies including SILHOUETTE 1&2 by Authorspress. BREEZE was her first solo collection of poems, by Authorspress. Her second collection of poems, "Glass Doors" is in print. Satbir Chadha was awarded the Litpreneur award instituted by Authorspress in 2019 for her

contribution to literature. Satbir has instituted the NISSIM International Award for Literature which is awarded to upcoming writers in English prose and poetry. She lives in Delhi, India with her four sons and six grandchildren.

Of Homes in Winter Heartlands

Sonia Dogra

Peeling layers of life, travelling backwards to open windows once again has often given me a perspective I may have overlooked at a point in time, but one that has forever resided in the subconscious mind, only to emerge in a moment of revisiting.

The year was 1989. It was a rare occasion when my father had planned a visit to the home of his maternal grandparents, which was nestled in the alluring Dhauladhar Ranges of the Himalayas. It was not often that we travelled to the tiny village in Tehsil Palampur. On the contrary, this was my first ever visit. I was a chatty ten-year-old with an almost perceptible excitement, the kind that makes children cross the sacrosanct line of the "code of conduct" drawn by their vigilant parents. My actions were harmless, but a running commentary on almost everything easily annoyed unsuspecting adults.

There was another person whose near identical escapades attracted exasperated looks. *Ammaji.* My grandmother with her child-like exuberance had always been a perfect accomplice. Her over-enthusiasm was not new but this time its strangeness was palpable. I saw her stuff slices of orange in a cotton drawstring bag along with other titbits which together made their way into a bigger tote bag.

'The *mithai* and *sewaiyan* are for your cousins. The *paranthas* for the journey…and the orange candy is for the both of us,' she said bringing her face close to mine. 'Travelling in the hills can make one feel giddy and the orange candy will come to our rescue!'

I smiled. *Ammaji* returned to the bag, her dangling *chamba balis* (earrings) doing a happy dance.

'Who are my cousins? I don't know them!' I asked, my eyes fixed on the *balis*.

'Oh, you will know them soon. I haven't seen them in a long time now, so I've forgotten their names,' she stated in a matter-of-fact way. The revelation did not surprise me. For me, *Ammaji* was solely a grandmother and that was the only way I had always known her.

The ten-hour-long journey on the next day did not turn out to be as exciting as I had anticipated. *Ammaji* and I shared a seat in the rattly bus, swinging back and forth at every sharp turn. The orange candies could only partially save me from throwing up. As for *Ammaji*, she did not need them at all!

'A *pahadan* who needs pills to travel in the hills. Tch, tch. Such a disgrace that would be!' she chuckled.

My parents sat right behind us, asking for their share of the candy only to prevent me from gobbling it all up. Or so, I thought.

That day, despite tall claims about its relativity, time followed the same ticktock rhythm for both *Ammaji* and me, even though for different reasons.

For me, it was like being forever on those winding roads, my impatience marked by the repetitive "how far are we" question. For *Ammaji*, it was more of an eternal longing, knowing very well "how far we were".

By the time we reached the village, the daylight was already fading away. The bus swished past silhouettes of pine trees standing in rows. The wind was bitter cold but it did not deter me from leaving the window open. I could hear the flutter of *Ammaji*'s dupatta as she struggled to keep it over her head. But not once did she ask me to shut the window, even though my mother shot me several warnings.

The bus dropped us off almost at the doorstep of *Ammaji*'s parental home. She scuttered up a little track lit up by the night sky without waiting for any of us.

'Watch out, *Ammaji*,' my father called out after her.

'Don't you worry,' she shouted right back. 'I know this place like the back of my hand!'

For the next three days, *Ammaji* metamorphosed from my grandmother into a young girl who spent the afternoons stashing away *ber* (jujube) which she gathered in her dupatta from a tree in the courtyard. Some made their way into the tote bag while others she nibbled with her nearly toothless mouth. In the mornings, she could be seen inspecting the terrace farms right outside the house, a humble two-room abode with blue walls and slate roof tiles.

'How do you know so much about farming, *Ammaji*?' I asked.

'Why!' she exclaimed. 'I've done it all my life.'

One of the most treasured things I saw in *Ammaji*'s parental home was a black and white picture of hers in a silver frame when she was all of thirteen.

'This was just before my marriage,' she sighed, looking at her younger self.

'That would be just before you quit farming, you mean!' my father added, laughing heartily.

I passed my days in the place where my grandmother had spent her childhood running up and down the slopes with my cousins who I would never meet again. I experimented with the hand pump, climbing trees and literally playing in dirt– all of the things that were near impossible in city apartments.

The evening meals near the *chullah* were accompanied with warm reminiscences of *Ammaji*'s parents, her siblings, some

The Body of Memories

of whom had moved to the cities and some whom she had lost forever. Her only brother who lived in the blue-walled house with his wife and children, now suffered from total loss of memory.

That was my only trip to my grandmother's parental home ever. As for her, I think she may have visited the place only once or twice again, but never with me.

Years passed by and I added another twenty to my ten. I lost my grandfather in those years and in the days that followed, *Ammaji* lost a part of her memory. It was probably an onset of Alzheimer's. But on days when she could recall, she often spoke of her home in the beautiful Dhauladhar Ranges, which she longed to visit just one more time. Often, she asked us to take her there. It was difficult to make her understand that the place had now been abandoned and those who were left behind did not know her. Neither did she know or at least remember any of them. Concerns over her health, winter and the bitter cold of the mountains was another reason that kept us from undertaking the journey.

Ammaji left for her heavenly abode with this unfulfilled desire. Whenever I remember her, she reminds me of all the people, men and women who leave their childhood homes, sometimes never to return, and on other times, only to go back occasionally. She reminds me of homes in winter heartlands that are often cold on the outside, but are enough to fill migrant hearts with an everlasting warmth.

Bio:
Sonia Dogra hails from Shimla and is currently located at Delhi. Having worked as an educator for ten years, she continues to provide voluntary teaching services to the lesser privileged. She works as an editor with AuthorsUpFront.

Writing is the manna that nourishes her soul and helps her to connect with her inner self. Her words have found a home in several published (and upcoming) anthologies such as 'Poems from 30 Best Poets'; 'You, Me & the Universe' and 'The Kali Project'. She has blogged for platforms such as 'Momspresso' and 'Women's Web'. Her rants and soulful poetry may be read on her blog 'A Hundred Quills'.

She can be followed at https://soniadogra.com/ and https://twitter.com/SoniaDogra16 . A collection of her poems is available on Juggernaut (https://www.juggernaut.in/books/52454518356a4e9d).

The Body of Memories

Do you cook at midnight?

Soumyanetra Chattopadhyay

It took exactly thirteen minutes by the 9:19am NJ Transit train from Princeton Junction to New Brunswick, which I used to avail every weekday in the morning to attend my graduate classes at Rutgers' College Ave campus. It used to be a bit crowded, though the NY peak hours rush used to be over by then. It was on one such ride that I met another Bengali woman like me. After some exchanges of pleasantries, we discovered a bit more about each other - she had married a person settled here and found herself adjusted to this new land, not new to her anymore. I however, had arrived a few months earlier and hoped to return to India after my studies were over, I said. How do you find it here? she asked me. I smiled and said that a lot of things were so startling and new. She immediately said that I should write them down, since after a while they will not seem that startling and new anymore. Now, that I look back, I couldn't agree more with her. With passing days and years in the US, the newness and startling factors definitely started withering off, ever more so with increasing pressure of comprehensive examinations and field examinations, integral parts of the doctoral studies there. Yet there were some apparently trivial incidences that have etched themselves in memory, and have always wanted themselves written. Here's one such.

My husband happened to be a graduate student at Princeton and for the first year of my graduate study, we used to stay at the graduate family housing of Princeton, 207 Lawrence Apartments, to be precise. When pressure in the graduate school was a bit light for both of us, it used to be a ritual to drive over to Edison, that was lovingly known as a little India, packed with Indian (often actually Pakistani and Bangladeshi) grocery stores, apparel and garment stores, restaurants, beauty parlours, and so on. In fact, one of the restaurant boards listing the menu said "Kolkata-style Chinese food". Our main interest though was in frozen fish

(Rohu mostly) that we got in some of the shops selling fish and meat. Such trips however, were not often, given there used to be work to be done during the weekends or we just felt too lazy to make the trip. So when we did make it, it meant that culinary misgivings of missing sumptuous and mouth-watering Bengali delicacies were quite at a peak.

On this particular occasion, we had planned on preparing *doi maachh* with our Edison catch. Returning from Edison, we had probably fallen asleep, and then after our evening studies, it usually was quite late by the time we got up to cook our dinner. This time too it was quite late when the fish has finally defrosted and I had started cooking the fish. Needless to say, that mustard oil, bay leaves, *garam masala,* onions, chilly, curd, turmeric powder and of course, fish, created that unforgettable odour that would have aroused hunger pangs even in the uninitiated, and we were absolute loyalists of Bengali cuisine. Thereafter we had relished our rice and *doi maachh,* reliving our Bengali sentiments, pampering our very Bengali taste buds and all the time missing our homes.

The next day was a Monday and after a usual workday, we were probably studying in the evening, when the bell rang. Just to emphasise here, socialising among the residents of our apartment was extremely rare. For example, we lived in one of the apartments in a floor that housed about seven others, but other than closed identical seven other doors, we hardly knew anything more about them. In case of any other delivery or arrival, it would be wholly expected or conveyed to us via the intercom from the main gate below the building. In other words, a calling bell meant someone with access to the building had wanted to come over, which was completely unexpected and unlikely, given our total lack of acquaintance with others in the building.

We opened the door and found a Chinese man trying to explain something in his extremely unintelligible English.

Like all graduate schools, Princeton too was extremely cosmopolitan with students from all over the globe flocking together with their varied cultures, languages, and tastes. Students from China were not known for their proficiency in English, so we really had a hard time trying to figure out what he said. All we could decipher really from the Chinese was, "Do you cook at midnight?" We looked at each other, surprised! Yes, we did! But how on earth does this man know about it? And how is it his business whether we did or not? A whole lot of questions troubled us. What kind of a question which sounded more like an allegation, was this?

Our most sincere efforts at understanding him continued for a while and what we were able to gather at the end of it all was this - he stays in the apartment right above us, his wife is pregnant and is unable to stand strong odours. It seemed there must be some leakage in the chimney ducts so that the smell of our cooking (*doi maachh of course!*) reached them yesterday around midnight, causing the wife to feel nauseated. He has complained about it to the maintenance staff but still wishes to request us to refrain from cooking stuff that had very strong odours. Of course, we would! I apologised to the husband for the unintentional trouble caused to his wife and really felt sorry for her.

In the days to come, the incident has remained with me, not only as a funny instance of how seemingly innocuous things like cooking in your own house at your own convenience, can actually cause inconvenience to others, but also as a remembrance of several other things. That how even the most advanced technology in the most advanced nation can sometimes go wrong, causing suffering. And of course, the famous saying that one man's nectar can be another man's poison - the Chinese woman couldn't stand our yummy *doi maach* (and Chinese are fish-eating)!

Looking back now, it was an episode like a beautiful pattern in an attire that is held in place by several other strings attached to it - days of hectic studies interspersed by little pleasures of cooking and having Bengali food, an incessant attempt of numbing a continuous pain of missing near ones, of an exposure to myriad people and their ways and more importantly an invisible bonding with their cultures and lives, of an unparalleled academic ambience that forced us to put studies on the top of our priority lists, of youthful aspirations and longings that seemed so immature then but so invaluable now. We have returned to our country now and have settled in Kolkata. Needless to say, we often have *doi maachh* here, but it seldom tastes that good.

Bio:

Soumyanetra is an associate professor of Economics at the Indian Statistical Institute, Kolkata. Though she is trained in Economics, she is an ardent lover of English and is very passionate about writing. She regularly contributes to The Statesman and has recently published her debut collection of poems titled "You're the Mecca I Never Want to Visit".

An Immigrant's Journey

Sutapa Chattopadhyay

I was born in Patna in 1957, 8 years after the Indian Constitution was signed on Jan 26, 1949. The writing of the Indian Constitution was an effort that could not have been completed without the participation of women in the Indian Lower House of the Parliament, the Lok Sabha. It was a time of great patriotism, of hope and a sense of sacrifice for the country. It was a time for optimism. India had managed to stitch together a national identity by bringing together disparate people speaking many languages and different cultural identities and doing it with justice and equity for all.

My grandfather was the Director of Public Health in the state of Bihar. I got a very warm welcome when I arrived, being the first child of both sides of my family and having the status of being the granddaughter of my distinguished grandfather. The hospital suite was reserved just for my mother and both she and my dad were elated on having me.

Life as a young child growing up in the industrial city of Jamshedpur was ideal, and being a ruminative soul indulging in nostalgia, I loved to get immersed in those memories sometimes. We lived in company quarters, so my dad did not have to pay exorbitant rent for a genuinely comfortable house that accommodated the needs of my family. My dad was an electrical engineer and was an officer of the Tube Company (later Tata Steel) and so we were well off financially. In fact, my parents' home was visited by a lot of relatives during the summer. They were there to recuperate from illnesses or to take a break from difficult circumstances in their own lives. This gave me a unique perspective on how to view the larger society I grew up in and how to be a caretaker of people.

However, it was not as if Jamshedpur was peaceful all the time. There were always factional riots between the Muslims and the Hindus. I personally witnessed the killing of a Muslim by a Hindu who used to deliver milk to our house during the Hindu-Muslim riots of 1967. My parents immediately fired him from the job. However, when it came to having me testify against him, they protected me thinking I was too young to get involved in such gruesome business.

The reason I brought up the writing of the Indian Constitution is that despite the law of the land saying women are equal, there is no denying that I grew up in a society where women were second class citizens. In my nuclear family, this was not obvious to me at first. But when I became a teenager, it was made painfully clear to me that my time to crave my own niche and my own identity, solidify it with education and grooming was just restricted to my college years, and beyond that, an uncertain future embedded in the values of a patriarchal society loomed large. After that, I was supposed to get married, have children and support my husband in all he did. I found this totally unjust, but didn't have much clue on how to fight back the system.

I saw myself as an intelligent young woman who wanted to explore the world and to go to college where I would pursue a scientific education with rigor. I also wanted to pursue graduate education. After a bit of a struggle and some serendipity, I was able to go to Birla Institute of Technology and Science in Pilani, an Institute of excellence in Rajasthan close to the Haryana border. I studied Electronics Engineering. After the 5-year coursework, I enrolled in graduate studies at IIT Kharagpur.

This is when I came in conflict with my parents who wanted me to get married. They had it in their minds that my biological clock would run out. That was a pretty ridiculous notion for someone who was 23, but one cannot argue much with age-old, established precedents in a patriarchal society. I got married on July 27, 1980.

The Body of Memories

My husband, Ashesh, on the other hand, had graduated in the early 70s from Jadavpur University with a degree in Pharmacy. Those were hard economic times and getting his first job was a feat of ingenuity and perseverance. It was also an era when Communists, especially Naxals had managed to disrupt education in West Bengal. Many students lost a year or more sitting at home because of strikes and violence. While Ashesh did not experience this disruption, he and his older siblings were threatened with violence and police brutality. Young men suspected of Naxal affiliation disappeared from his neighborhood, never to come back.

His primary reason for immigration to the United States was this police brutality, corruption and economic hardship that he experienced firsthand while working in India. He had a job as an inspector of Pharmaceutical Industries, and he inspected their process control in making drugs to see if those processes adhered to standards. But the job involved navigating layers of bureaucracy where corruption reigned supreme. Often, people would bribe him, and he could not refuse because that meant he would brush up against superiors who also took bribes on purpose to enrich themselves. Bribery and corruption were rife in the Government bureaucracies at that time in India.

He had landed in New York in December 1977. Jimmy Carter was the President at that time. The country was going through economic hardship as well. Oil prices had skyrocketed due to huge demand and a supply squeeze by OPEC nations led by Saudi Arabia. There were no jobs. Even a McDonald's job or a job as a bank teller was not available.

His navigation through this difficult landscape was harder than mine. He managed to get a job as a waiter in a restaurant in Manhattan. After about a year, he enrolled in graduate school at the City University of New York. He often took night courses to complete his degree. He lived with four of his friends in a rat-infested apartment in Sunnyside, Queens.

1979 was a particularly difficult year in the annals of US history. There was a more severe oil shortage brought on by the Iran hostage situation. In March 1979, the Three Mile Island nuclear disaster happened. A nuclear power plant near Three Mile Island breached and had a partial meltdown. Things could not have been worse especially for new immigrants, many who had to look for temporary work to support themselves.

My husband persevered through all this and thrived. Perhaps the optimism of the new immigrant kept him going. Most new immigrants are too busy in their jobs and careers to pay attention to the news. And in the late 70s, the news cycle was not a 24-hour cycle as it is today. There were no cable channels.

In 1980, his parents had set up my marriage with him. I met him only once before getting married. On October 17th, 1980, I got up on an airplane for the first time to come to America. My husband and my uncle and aunt gave me a warm welcome at the airport, and I arrived at the same rat-infested apartment in Queens. I was not really disappointed at the apartment. I had not expected anything, and I knew from my friends in India that the immigrant experience is hard. Also, a 23-year-old has a lot of courage, some of it the reckless courage of youth. The courage expresses itself in taking risks which now would horrify me.

For me, emigrating to the West was not assumed as my birthright and I was not trained to emigrate. I could have stayed in India. The choice of marriage partner was also not mine. But I certainly was excited to come to the United States to make a life for myself and my husband. I had not paid much attention either to whether US society would be more egalitarian or more accommodative of immigrants and women. I sailed along, like a small boat tugged along by larger currents in life, the predominant patriarchal mindset that as a woman, I needed to get married and settle down with a husband. But soon, I realized after starting my life in

The Body of Memories

a foreign land with my husband that he sincerely wanted me to pursue my own dreams. Such mindset seemed more possible in the United States than in India.

I started attending graduate school at the City University of New York. Both of us were now students making a meager but satisfactory living, working and studying in the United States. We knew we were on our way to achieving our goals.

The joy of living in New York city, coupled with occasional visits to the countryside in a beaten-up old car kept us happy and contented. I remember with incredible wonder watching the first snowfall of the winter of 1980. Subway tokens were seventy-five cents in 1981! I rode the subway to different parts of the sprawling metropolis. One special treat for me was the New York City Public library's main branch at Bryant Park which housed millions of historical records and newspaper cuttings from significant periods in history. I sat in the shaded and beautiful reading rooms thinking of the millions who had passed through this grand library and what they were thinking. The most delightful fact about the library was that it was free to everyone, an amazing portal of knowledge and enrichment, regardless of status or money.

In 1982, the economy was as bad if not worse than in 1977. It was difficult but I landed my first job at AT&T Bell Labs in Lincroft, New Jersey. I started my long life as a corporate citizen of many companies. Life at Bell Labs offered me the first glimpse of elite American citizens. Most of the people I worked with graduated from top universities and were white males. Some were Indians who were children of immigrants and therefore a lot more assimilated than I was.

I started having difficulties with this process of integration. My difficulties were all in my head. People did not know that I had problems. But most people had not worked with an Indian woman in 1982. We were ridiculously small in number at AT&T: brown Asian women. I was paired up with mentors who were senior to me who came from the Indian diaspora. It was difficult. I did not know how to behave with white men. I did not know their customs or their turns of phrase. Even though I was very fluent in English, I still had difficulty with the language and customs. I even had difficulty with the dress code at work because prior to coming to the US, I had always worn a saree and I could not do that at work.

I remember that AT&T would hold discussions with all its employees to make people aware of issues with minorities. Unlike the social milieu today, in the early 80s, those discussions were painful for us minorities. We were met with hostility by the mainstream Americans – the non-immigrants. Most were resentful that they had to attend these meetings. They felt it was not their problem that the minorities feel left out. "The onus is on them to assimilate with us". They argued. I did not disagree. I just did not think a path existed for me to assimilate with my white male colleagues. For example, was I supposed to go play golf with them? Would I be going fishing with them? How would I engage in those activities that were totally alien to me? And when would I find the time?

In a few months' times, I won over their confidence with my professional competence, but the overall process of assimilation with my colleagues at all my places of work was still a work-in-progress. Today, my colleagues are less white and more Indian and Chinese. Workplace integration has happened in leaps and bounds in the US. However, I am still overwhelmingly the only woman in my group, or one of only a few women in a larger group. Being a woman also presents difficulties that men do not understand. And talking about leadership positions in the corporate world, women do not get those as easily as men because we cannot establish ourselves as natural leaders. Especially for women from South Asia, we are taught to "fit in" in society and serve others but not to lead, right from the time we are in elementary school.

In 1986, I had a child, a boy. Having a child growing in this country as an American also contributes to the process of assimilation for the parents. A child learns to dissociate from his or her parents in order to become a unique person. That process teaches the parents a lot of hard lessons about life in America.

My son Ayan was a delightful child and teenager. He did brilliantly in school and left for college. Then, 3 years into his college life, he revealed to me that he was gay. This was another struggle for me. Not only was I supposed to navigate my son's passage through adulthood without any difficulties, deconstructing my old ideas about his future life, but I was also supposed to learn about the LGBTQ struggle for identity in America in order to understand what he was going through.

In 2007, gay marriage was not legal anywhere except in the state of Massachusetts and "Don't Ask, don't tell" was a policy practiced by the military. It was unjust because "Don't ask, don't tell" implies that as a gay person, you hide your identity – who you really are at the core of your being – in order to stay in the military. And because of a Clinton era law "Defense of Marriage Act", gay partners had no rights as partners of people they loved. For example, if their partners were ill or dying, they had no visitation rights. If the partners died, they could not inherit property.

There was also the issue of violence against LGBTQ people even in the cosmopolitan New York City. In 2008, there was this incident of violent beating of a gay man in Spanish Harlem. All this left me terrified of my son being the victim of violence. He too was a young man brimming with passion and ideas, unable to see how imperiled he was. The very fact that he tested for AIDS every 4 months left me panicked and anxious for him, unable to sleep at night. By this time, testing for AIDS was done for free by the LGBTQ community in Manhattan; it is still carried out for free, and considered a safe practice. Moreover, by 2008, there were medications that made AIDS a chronic disease like diabetes. Still, I wondered if keeping silent about him and not sharing my burden with anyone I knew was the best thing to do.

At home, I was sure my husband would not approve of my son being gay, thinking it was a choice one made. Having grown up in India, we did not know all those who were different hid from society. For example, homosexuals were known to marry and lead a heterosexual life even if it was painful for them to reconcile to the life they were forced to lead. And transgender people had the most difficult time because they were normally exiled from society in a very cruel way. He was not aware of gay people even in our microcosm of a Bengali community in the US. He would not have accepted this facet of his son and would have challenged him at every turn. That was another burden on me: to keep this a secret from him until Ayan was independent of us. I played the waiting game for another five years, determined to see him financially independent and then take the plunge. It was exceedingly difficult to keep this secret and be at peace with myself.

Finally, in the spring of 2013, I told my husband about my son. He simply could not believe it in the initial days. But eventually he made peace with it, simply because of the bond of love between father and son was incredibly strong. For him, the process of coming to peace with my son's homosexuality was also a process of assimilation with the American mainstream that has come to accept its gay citizens as equal partners and citizens in society. Today, through a variety of Supreme Court cases that struck down existing unjust laws passed in State Legislatures, most states in the US protect its gay citizens, allow them to be partners, marry and live like other citizens, inheriting each other's property, getting benefits like health insurance and social security. Moreover, all the states of these United States – Red and Blue, Republican or Democratically controlled— have made these changes, which makes me ecstatic, after years of an uphill battle. It is a triumph for the LGBTQ cause.

In 2011, gay marriage was legalized in the state of New York. This allowed my son to marry the love of his life in 2016 in New York City. It was a ceremony which none of my immediate relatives except my mother attended. If this were a normal wedding of a heterosexual couple, we would have a lavish wedding in New York and back in India. None of that happened. Still, I was not sad. I was simply happy that I was able to navigate my son's life to the best of my abilities and it all turned out well in the end.

My first change of heart about where "home" was when I started going to India and thought of "going back home". Despite all the struggles here, America was and is my home now. This first happened during my brother's wedding in 1994 in Calcutta. The wedding was an enjoyable experience but at the end of it, I was homesick for New York City, my workplace and my home in New Jersey. I saw it as a sign that I had finally assimilated in America.

Last year, and in 2018, I actively participated in the political process and talked to many hundreds of people over the phone convincing people to vote, exercise their democratic rights and defeat the Republicans and President Trump, who is against immigration, legal or otherwise. I have met thousands of immigrants from many counties even before that. My own experience allows me to understand their experience and establish an emotional connection with them. Together, we make up the fabric of this society that we are all so proud of. A society that rejoices in its differences, but comes together as Americans.

When we go to Washington DC and walk at the National Mall, we often see a lot of large quilts on display as part of some demonstration or national protest. I remember the first quilt in the 1980s and it was for victims of AIDs. It was a mournful sight to see the victim's loved ones crying over their portion of the quilt. I see a large American quilt built joyfully for every person here in the United States, every unique story stitched on each portion of the quilt. I am part of a quilt, the national quilt. My story is one of many millions, but it holds significance for me and my family. However, as a chronicler of events and people that I hope to be and also as a writer, I see the need to look at other's quilts and to write about them to make a wholesome, coherent story of immigrant experiences in America.

Bio:
Sutapa Chattopadhyay is a lifelong technologist, having worked for more than 38 years in various industries, the last 27 years in financial technology at Wall Street banks. In her spare time, she loves reading and writing. Her favorite genres are biography, history, literature of the nineteenth century. Authors like Jane Austen, the Bronte Sisters, Louisa May Alcott, Dickens and Victor Hugo inspire her to look closely for inspiration at the history of mankind's progress – especially those of women in various countries. She also loves realistic science fiction as written by twentieth century and contemporary authors such as Margaret Atwood, AC Clarke, Isaac Asimov. She also gets inspiration from writers of Indian origin, including Jhumpa Lahiri.

In most of her endeavors, she sees herself as a craftsman, whether it is in writing software or in writing short stories or memoirs.

In Search of Lost Treasure

Sura Charlier

When I was six, we moved from our tract neighborhood in S.B. up to The Ranch. I felt sad. When we lived in the neighborhood, we were friends with the family two houses up, who put in a pool while we were there. My brother, John, and I spent a million hours playing and swimming with the two children, Heidi and Paul. Their mom was an artist and their dad an aerospace engineer, and I thought their home was heaven. Once in a while, we were invited to eat dinner with them, and they had luscious food like artichokes and Cornish game hens. I thought this exotic food was the best I had ever tasted. (My mom was a great cook, but never used garlic as my dad hated it, so the food at "Aunt Thea's" house tasted fantastic to me.) I loved being there. Once when I lost my favorite stuffed animal (my oldest brother, David's worn-out zebra which I called "ZeeBee"), I found it again outside, all wet and Aunt Thea washed and dried it for me and made it "all better." That was nice. A funny thing about the zebra toy, was that it was so worn out that there was only one place where the synthetic fur was not rubbed away: between its sets of legs. We loved looking there to get an idea of what the zebra had originally looked like (black & white, with FUR!) After we moved, I lost all sense of community, friendship, recreation and familiness outside my own. We rarely spent time with others after that.

When I was about twelve, I cleaned the trailer of one of my parent's tenants for money. The woman was really messy, and I was a bit disgusted. There were dirty plates with stinky cheese on them that had been left soaking in the sink for days, etc. I really had to overcome my repulsion in order to get started. One of the other tenants on the property was a woman who was dating a man with a teen son. The son was nice-looking, black-haired and blue-eyed, and I liked him. On rare occasions I was allowed to go to the cottage they rented on my parents' property and play. I'm saying "rare" because I had no social life other than school for years. Once in a while when a new family moved in, I would try to get to know the kids and spend time with them, but my father was the surveillance police and just as we started to play, would call me home. Utterly paranoid. I could never relax, and developed hyper-vigilance.

One day when I was cleaning the lady's trailer, the other tenant's son and the son of her man friend came over. I liked them, but I was working. Then, the tenant's son said he had to go for a minute, and I thought he had left. The other boy, whom I liked, began chatting me up, and then kissed me. I really liked it and kissed him back. I thought that this meant he liked me and that he wanted to be my boyfriend (I always equated sexual interest from a boy/man as indicative of interest in relationship; where on earth did I get that?!) After a few minutes, the boy said he had to go. He always had a laugh on his face and a twinkle in those blue eyes! I hoped he would be my boyfriend, but was wondering why out of all the girls he must know that he would like me (I felt not-that-great about myself.) I would have liked to have done some social stuff with him, but I knew my father would never allow it, so told myself to "just forgeddaboudit." Then I heard my dad call me and went over to talk to him. He said he didn't want those boys over while I was working. I was like, "Dad, I'm working, what do you think is going to happen?" Hmm.

I think the other tenant broke up with the boy's father because he wasn't over anymore. I thought of him sometimes but realized that the boyfriend/girlfriend thing wasn't realistic for me anyway with an overly-surveillant father. A few months later, the tenant's son was over at my house and he told me that the reason the boy had kissed me was because they had made a bet that he could do it. The tenant's son had hid in the closet and watched. I felt cheap and humiliated. The event had been something special and enjoyable to me and finding out that it was just an insincere bet felt horrible and humiliating. Especially knowing that

The Body of Memories

someone had watched: yuck! I was really angry at the other boy and felt used.

When I was in the sixth grade at elementary school, I was attending band rehearsals at the middle school with seventh and eighth graders. There was a special assembly, so I was to stay later at the school in order to play for that, instead of going back on the bus to my elementary school as usual. My mom had bought me a little orange culotte jumper and blouse to wear. The shorts-skirt was quite short. I decided I would wear it. My dad said, "Isn't that a bit short?" My mom said, "No, it's okay: she can wear it with pantyhose." I wore it; it was the first time I had worn pantyhose. As soon as I got to the middle school, all the boys began hanging around like flies, staring at me and teasing me for wearing pantyhose. I was awakened to my sexual attractiveness in that moment, but I also felt ashamed and humiliated, because what my mom had bought for me was for a little girl, and I had worn it in that spirit, but I was no longer a little girl; I was a young woman and that cute, little-girl outfit became very sexy to the older boys. I wished I could hide.

Then we were told that the assembly was cancelled. I didn't want to go back to school; I wanted to stay with the older kids. One of the boys liked me and invited me to see his class and then stay for lunch. I asked if that would be okay, and he said he would ask his teacher. His teacher said that I could not attend without a pass. I didn't want to ask the office for a pass because I was pretty sure they would make me go back to my school. The boy skipped his class and we went out to the field for lunch, the boy talking to me and acting to his friends like he was my boyfriend. He gave me his jacket to tie around my waist so I wouldn't feel so bare. I liked this and thought he was nice. I was trying to look like I fit in, but then the lady vice-principal came up and said, "Who are you; why are you here?" The boy explained truthfully, but the vice-principal didn't like it, took me to her office and called my parents who were really angry. They all asked, "If the assembly was cancelled, why didn't you just go back to school?" I didn't know how to explain it.

I left to catch the bus and the young man said he would walk me there. He said his house was on the way and asked if I wanted to see it. I wasn't sure if it was okay without his parents being home, but said, "Okay." We stopped by. He showed me his house and room. He wanted to kiss me, but I said that wasn't okay and that I had to go. Instead of taking the bus, I walked all the way back to my school (a long way)! I was angry and confused about why everyone was making such a big deal and putting such shame on me for being curious. When I got home, my parents were horrible to me and said that I was jeopardizing my arrangement to be able to attend the 7/8th grade band.

The next day, the middle school band director was also angry and yelled at me in front of the whole band: what was I doing and was I trying to get him fired, etc. I felt shamed and terrible and a little rebellious. I felt vindicated by my decision to walk back to my elementary school and not take the bus. This was because it gave me a margin of freedom and choice which I didn't possess in my circumstances. I felt strong that I could walk that far, that my parents didn't know where I was for two seconds, and that I could make my own decision about something. I gave away the outfit and never wore it again.

When we were fourteen, my school friend and I were taking the school bus up the mountain and were excited that we would be attending a neighbor's Halloween party, so we showed the notes from our parents and got off the bus several stops early. After the bus departed, two older neighbor boys grabbed us, pulled down our tank tops and groped us. I was afraid it was going to get worse. We screamed and twisted away, hoping there would be someone nearby who would help us, but there wasn't any. We ran towards the neighbor's house, but quickly realized that it was a long way, and that the boys could quickly catch up to us. Finally another boy

The Body of Memories

said, "Guys, leave them alone; they're too young anyway." We straightened our clothing, our hearts beating wildly, and hiked the rest of the way to the party. We rode the bus everyday with the boys, pretended that nothing had happened and never even thought of telling anyone.

I remember being called out of my peaceful room so many times to help my dad do some senseless-to-me "make-work" on the ranch. I hated that. I also hated that our father made us work on the ranch all summer instead of being able to work for others, or do something in terms of participation with the community. He justified this by saying, "Well, I'm paying you." Being paid for a job you think is meaningless and that you are impressed into doing doesn't make it okay. I remember when I suggested that I could work making sandwiches for the fire-fighters at the tiny C. Store, one of the few potential employers within walking distance; he suggested that being around all those male fire-fighters would be dangerous for me. After arguing with them about this, my mom finally agreed that I could work as a house-cleaner for her friend who lived nearby. Her friend repeatedly left me alone with her repulsive husband who molested me. I dreaded when she told us that she was "going downtown for a while." I finally had the guts to quit, in order to escape this lecher, and my mom condemned me for leaving her friend's service without respectful notice. I couldn't tell her. I was only fifteen or sixteen and my dad had already molested me.

Later, after I had married J., this all came up after watching a video I had borrowed from the library in hopes of teaching our children how to protect themselves: "The Terrible Secret". My terrible secret came up and out. J. was really nice about hearing me: his father had raped his sister for years. All of this had come out at our wedding the year before. I called my mom and dad and told them about my having been molested while house-cleaning. They thought it was terrible and my mom told me that her friend's husband had even tried to molest her! She said she was sorry and that she should have known that he would try it with me. My father's abuse was still hiding, to be looked at later.

Our children went off to school for the first time. I was very burned out from twelve years of intensive, committed parenting. I slept a lot. I wondered what to do with my life after years of wanting to write music, constantly being interrupted in it, not being able to focus on it, and mostly giving up doing something with it career-wise. I thought about taking an office job working for the S.O. My spirit leapt up and shouted, "I never want to be a secretary again; I am a frustrated composer!" I didn't take the job that had been offered.

I had recovered my love of dancing, and began spending quite a bit of time at the neighborhood dance school, where I was able to barter for ballet lessons for my children and myself by serving as a dance accompanist. It was fun and I composed a lot of music while there. I loved dancing, and wanted to do it more and more. My husband didn't like my being away so much and having more care of the children in the evenings, or when I went to my leadership training for the S.O. Plus, I was getting in really great shape, and I think he found this threatening. In the evenings I always left dinner, but he became resentful and distancing. Every several years I took a longer retreat away from home and finally became certified as a retreat guide. He bought a sailboat.

I took a fifteen-day retreat. I slept a lot on this retreat. Slept a lot and cried a lot. I learned how to be a friend to myself through excruciatingly painful states I had not the wherewithal to explore before. My retreat guide was not only a retreat guide, but a clinical psychologist. She asked me a lot of questions about my wounded teenage woman, and about my husband's lack of support for developing my talents away from the family as more than a "hobby." She asked about sexual abuse and about my father. I told her my father had abused me. She said she thought I had minimized the effect it had had upon me. I was ready to look at it. So much pain. Wings cruelly clipped. Treasure of Self stolen. A mother who was oblivious. How can a mother be oblivious to such a thing? Wouldn't a woman know if her husband were abusing her daughters? Can't understand this. I would know. No locks or guards on the Treasure remaining. Throwing away the Tainted Treasure. Horrible anger, horrible grief. It wasn't my fault. Clarity and consciousness born of courage to confront, courage to feel. Freedom from shame. The teenager is brought home. Home to a house where I am the adult in charge now. Astute retreat guide; I love her. She becomes my mentor.

I went home, but first I visited my parents. I told them about the robbery of my treasure of Self. It is one of the hardest things I have had to find the courage to do. My father tells me he knew it was wrong and apologizes. I forgive him. My mother takes him to task privately. My father said he was so afraid I would tell the court the time I ran away and was sent back home, as no reason could be found to keep me in a foster home. Everyone else had kept telling me how wrong I was to run away from such a good home: even the family counselor we were sent to. I had even begun to question my own sanity. How could I tell such a thing when I had hidden it from myself to survive?

I told my husband I had been robbed. I told him I had recovered the Treasure. He was compassionate. I told him I had recovered my passion and realized that had I been supported properly and had healthy boundaries, I would have gone to an arts academy and sung, and danced, studied and written music: taken private lessons. He said, "Yes, that is a tragedy: you are probably one of those women who would have chosen not to have children if you hadn't been abused, and your career in the arts would have been your whole focus." I said, "Yes, possibly, but I am so happy that I have the children; I love them and now that I have recovered my vision, I can go to music school." He said, "No, now that you've chosen motherhood, you can't just go off and leave your family to follow your teenage dream, it's not realistic. Things got messed up for you and that was crummy, but now you have other responsibilities." He couldn't see any middle ground. I was awakening from the dream and could not go back to sleep.

I danced in the Snowflakes in the "Nutcracker" for the first time. My husband and I were growing further and further apart. We discussed divorce. Neither of us wanted it. I asked why he didn't cherish me. He said he didn't respect me. He thought any mature woman would give up her teenage desires for the reality of motherhood she had chosen and would follow her outside interests in moderation as hobbies. In addition, he thought my behavior around other men flirtatious and immodest. I had a hard time discerning this. I couldn't see it. It was left-over scar tissue and I didn't have enough distance from it to understand the difference between my behavior and myself. Neither did he.

At the rehearsals for the Nutcracker, I met a fellow dancer and developed a friendship. One of my hidden desires was to do ballet partnering and our teacher had told us that if we wanted a partner to work with, we would have to find our own. I asked him. He was interested. I appreciated his warm encouragement of my interests and found my heart becoming torn. I engaged our teacher to choreograph a pas de deux for me and my dance partner set to a piece of music I had written on retreat the year before. I was afraid to tell my husband. I was afraid he would act like my father. He overheard a phone conversation about it. He felt threatened and was furious that I had not discussed it with him. I was bitter and brazen, feeling that if he loved me, he should encourage, support, cherish and trust me, not suspect me of disloyalty after ten years of marriage.

The next month, I left to take a twenty-one-day retreat in New Hampshire to sort out my interior mess. Heaven and Hell were so mixed up together, and I couldn't seem to separate the wounded parts of my psyche from the healthy ones. I was suffering a healing crisis in the midst of a breakdown. The vision of a life lived in pursuing my passion and further developing my talents and career was appearing on the horizon, and I could see no room for it in the scope of my marriage with J. Near the end of the retreat, I told my retreat guide that I wasn't sure I wanted to be married anymore. She said she thought marriage was mostly about endurance. I realized that I valued fulfilling one's vision more than I valued sacrificing something that one does not yet possess for the sake of enduring. I went home pledging myself toward nothing but being truthful.

I told my husband how awful I felt about having romantic thoughts about my dance partner, and that I did not know what to do. He said he had already divided up our property. I told him that I loved him and that I did not want a divorce. I said that maybe if I went to music school, I could dance in the daytime and be home with the family in the evenings. He said I just had too many things I wanted to do in my life, and that loyalty was not the issue, but differences in interests and values.

My soul called out that it was time to make the spiritual journey to the Original Home, and I signed up, never knowing that you would stay onshore in the cozy little home we made together. You called, "Come back – let's just go back to the way we were and everything will be okay," but I couldn't: the ship had already left the harbor and I couldn't fit in that tiny place anymore. That tiny cozy place that contained our familiness, our home for ourselves and our children: all gone from sight. My heart was wretched when I saw this, but it was too late to go back. I wish you had hired the first boat and come after us, bringing the children with you, but you didn't. You just watched the ship getting smaller and smaller and waved.

Sometimes I think the Universe will surprise me with a new and greater love, but there's no getting this back for any of us. So sorry, children, wish we could have taken a different way. This is the only thing my heart bothers crying about anymore. I don't even cry for myself; I cry for Us.

Bio:
Sura Charlier is the Founder/Director of the Kalyan Center (kalyancenter.org), a Sufi Universalist center in Bradenton, Florida, USA, dedicated toward the awakening of humanity to the divinity of the soul. She serves as a spiritual guide, minister of the Universal Worship Service, and offers retreats and seminars for personal and spiritual growth (sacredhealingsacredretreat.com). Sura is also an accomplished professional composer and musician, who seeks to use music as a means of collective healing, connection, inspiration, and embodied Joy. Sura dances, writes and is an advocate for living in harmony with ourselves, one another, and All Our Relations, sustainably with this beautiful wondrous planet, Earth.

Surajit Saha

The sound of the wind plays different tunes, depending on where you are at the moment. It feels good. For me the wind is like a soothing song whenever my eyes gaze towards the night sky.

Though I am penniless these days like a lot of people, I'm grateful to the supreme energy that has kept my loved ones safe. Jobs are vanishing, and soon more people will eventually die due to the pandemic or other reasons. But life is beyond the horizon; it's about hope and the forthcoming revelations that will overwhelm all of us in every way possible, and this story is about that undying pursuit of HOPE.

3rd September 2017

I was humming the tune of one of my songs which was ready to be recorded soon. Wisdom explores the idea that 'the process of art is way more important and fun than the masterpiece itself'. On the day of recording, the first scratch was completed by 10:30 in the night. I had successfully executed two concerts professionally as an organizer on that very day; and two of my latest acting projects had just released. It was evident, I was super happy that night, feeling as if my struggle was finally over, and I had finally found a way to balance job, music and acting.

However, destiny had other plans for me in the coming days.

As I was almost dancing my way towards home, a sudden breeze changed something inside me, a new seed of an idea had been planted in my mind, the idea of a new song. Within a few days me and my journey-mates finally gave the song a structure and called it, "The UFO song" inspired by the work of Erich von Däniken.

17th September 2017

It was like a dream, I was literally sitting in the middle of a beach, surrounded by my loved ones, the moon was shining her grace on us, the water of the mighty sea was taking the sand away from beneath my feet. I had just finished a couple of more music videos, so there were other reasons for me to celebrate as well. That was one of the happiest moments in my life, when my phone rang. Within moments I could hear nothing, but the voice of my father merged with the gurgling sound of waves and wind from the sea. I remained absolutely still when he informed me that a ball of lightning had struck the front of my house, and then it radically started spinning, travelling through our neighborhood and then spiraling its way towards the main road, leaving a lot of damaged electrical equipment behind, including a few of my own. A lightning strike was not the reason for my astonishment, but the fact that it acted like a living thing did, since in a strange way it was like a premonition for me, because it was the exact situation that I had just finished writing in my notebook as a song!

How can that exact thing happen in real life?

27th December 2017

Zuluk, The Himalayas

My body and mind were tingling due to the immense cold of Sikkim. We had just reached the resting place for the night. I thought let's absorb the place, since we'll not be there again, and I didn't want to waste the experience. I left the warmth of the homestay and marched on the hilly slope for a better view of the place. There I stood, looking at the horizon, listening to the breeze of the Himalayas, smelling the pure Himalayan air. Soon I became lightheaded since oxygen was not enough at that altitude.

The Body of Memories

I closed my eyes and tried to lower my excitement and breathed slowly. Feeling better, I opened my eyes and saw a star moving and blinking gently like a firefly. It came out from a mountain near the horizon, changed its course and kept flying right towards me; as if it was talking to me using the science of telepathy! But perhaps the speed of speech was so fast that I couldn't make out what it was saying. As the thing kept flying towards me, it was adjusting its direction as if it could see me. At this point, my brain felt like it was on fire.

The fictitious song I made on Daniken's theory, all the conspiracy theories on the multimedia platforms that I have seen, and my belief system about everything was suspended as I kept staring at the ever so majestic blinking star, which was getting bigger at an alarming rate. As a fighter fights, no matter what, suddenly my logical brain kicked in. I grabbed my camera and boom... it disappeared. At this point my knees were demanding for a chair or even better, a bed right then and there, which I negotiated with a cigarette instead. I was shocked, confused and curious. This incident and the latter ones led me to a research which was going to change my life and belief patterns about life forever.

January 2018,

I started my own research on UFOs to avoid any kinds of misinformation through my art. As I delved deep into the research gradually, I realized that it's not new at all, every missing link went back to the pages of mythology rather than the unknown.

'The Book of Enoch' uncovered an unseen side of our own past which connects *Sanatan* (ancient Indian) mythology with the biblical story of Genesis. As slowly the research traded places from official CIA disclosed documents to the witnesses, to Bob Lazar, the Roswell fiasco to SETI, and from Phobos to finally Mansarovar, The Himalayas.

Early February, 2018

The Pentagon officially released 3 real military footages which confirm the existence of the phenomena of UFO/UAP. This incident acted like fuel for my initiative. It was then, when I delved into real stories where people either turned spiritual after witnessing an UFO or spiritual people found their masters coming out from one of those living light balls. Deep down, I knew it had something to do with ancient science and something deadly. These entities were multidimensional and spiritual in nature. They would show up from nowhere before catastrophic incidents which usually changed the world as per the historic reports and vanished into thin air. Generally, people who came in contact with these entities either went mad or started practicing various religious or cult rituals. I, on the other hand, became more stubborn about the logical side as a scientific mind would do.

22nd April, 2018

I was in my room, editing a wedding project which was dangerously close to missing its deadline!

Suddenly I felt like a voice was talking in my head. I immediately recognized the voice because I had heard it earlier, back in Zuluk, the only difference was that I could understand the voice at that moment; it was asking me to go out and look at a certain part of the night sky. I was overwhelmed as I saw another UFO again; but this time not in the Himalayas but right above my house...

To make sure that it was real and not some hallucination, I called my mom out and showed her. It was beautiful and my logical-questioning mind was destroyed at this point. The

UFO slowed down, then sped up and disappeared after a few seconds.

It was almost the morning of 23rd April, 2018.
I was lying on my bed sleepless when suddenly I felt a million volts of electricity running through my body, and I literally couldn't move or close my eyes. I was trying to scream, but couldn't. The joints of my arm and feet started feeling like they're on fire. I saw the Past, Present and felt a deadly possibility of the near Future which I simply couldn't believe. I saw mass deaths, which were about to happen, and it felt like someone wanted me to know what was about to happen.

Within moments I was changed forever.

The next morning, I ran to a renowned spiritual place called 'BELUR MATH' to tell the spiritual gurus about my experience. I was crying like a madman, I thought I had gone completely mad and delusional, but somehow my heart knew that the message was loud and clear. Maharaj of Veda University couldn't help me in any way and asked me to take a break. I came back home helpless, and questioning my own sanity, the nature of reality and my own existence.

Since then, a lot has changed - I lost my job, my laptop, and even friends.
People around me had started calling me insane and useless. My confidence crumbled day by day as I kept questioning the visions I had. For two long years, I had kept myself locked in a room thinking that an event of mass death could be impossible and silly to think about, but now…
Everything has changed.
If you are reading this, then you already know what I saw that night. I also saw how after darkness, new life prospers in a new light of hope, love and eventually peace.

Bio:

Surajit Saha is a singer-songwriter, actor & content writer from Kolkata. He has been working in movies since 2012 with names like *Mahapurush o kapurush, Room number 103, Maach Mishti & More, Kancher Dewal* etc. under his portfolio. He has also been featured in several serials, short films and music videos along the years. Meanwhile, as a Singer-songwriter, he has released songs like "*Bodhir Hoye Probhu*" & "*Ek Poshla Brishtir Gondho*" on online content platforms while performing his songs in more than 100 concerts. He has represented independent singer-songwriters of West Bengal in Live in Youth in association with The British Council and at Gorky Sadan in association with The Russian Embassy. He has used his musical curation and graphic designing skills to make a music movement (LIVE IN SERIES) relevant in Kolkata and the world(CALCUTTA CLASSICAL GUITAR SOCIETY) from 2014 until December, 2017. During his journey of LIVE IN SERIES & CALCUTTA CLASSICAL GUITAR SOCIETY, Surajit has worked with the embassies & artists of several countries of the world. Since then he has been writing quite a few scripts and stories along with poetry in the shape of songs and offers his writing, video editing & graphic designing services to the clients with passion for art.

The Ferris Wheel

Vandita Dharni

Life was a ferris-wheel of highs and lows for me. The highs were always uplifting but the lows always badgered me with an existential crisis. Deep in the recesses of my mind, I was battling an avalanche of depression. I had lost my mother to cancer in the October of 2017 and I could fathom my entire world collapsing after her demise. Two years hence, a profound interest in the macrocosm had sprouted within my being. It dawned on me that somewhere the connect with nature and people had diminished with my hectic work schedules and the invasion of social media that made me addicted and unsociable. Yet I knew I wasn't going to succumb to the vermin. I began retracing pathways of life, unravelling the ones I hadn't traversed before, surging on towards the ones I wanted to and chartering my own paths too. I was on a quest, searching for answers to questions that plagued me, leaving me in a conundrum.

I had fallen in love all over again. The 'City Green' just captured my heart and I let it grow veins and arteries into my flesh that craved for pure oxygen. Parks were the hub of creative impulses and the ideal place to introspect about life, delving into its mysterious facets and myriad hues. Sometimes, life would snowball into dimensions unfathomable, creeping over Hibiscus hedges that skirted along the lawns and on other occasions it lay entangled in Bougainvillea creepers espaliered to walls of houses overlooking the parks. There were parks in every sector, each with their own distinctive features and aesthetic layout. The muse within always inspired me to explore these serpentine pathways where the dew of nature's bounteous gifts would douse my restless spirit.

Often, I'd undertake long, arduous walks through picturesque landscapes of the garden city of Chandigarh, now my permanent home, trying to reminiscence and capture snatches that could enliven my foggy spirits or pulse an adrenaline rush in my veins, but to no avail. Memories of Mumbai would still haunt me like dead echoes from the blighted past. We had moved to Mumbai for two years in 2008 on account of my husband's transfer and the concrete jungle had stifled my free spirit. I was never enamored by the skyscrapers or skylines, being a small-town girl. That year I remember Mumbai, the invincible city was struck by its worst tragedy when the terrorist attacks took place. I remember how distraught and panic-stricken we all were. I was teaching at the Cathedral and John Connon school then and the most horrific news was from my class. I had lost a student who was living in a suite at the Taj with his family as his father was a Manager there and also the parents of another student from my class were mercilessly gunned down at the Oberoi Trident hotel. How devastated I was! Yet I had a firm conviction that time was a great restorer. Soon the scars would heal and recover. The verdant expanse of Chandigarh made me shut out the gloom of those bitter memories.

My walks were a flashback of memories that would propel me back into time. My childhood was spent in Allahabad, the city richly drenched with the legacy of the Nehru's. My mother who was a lecturer of English at a degree college once told me how the Nehru family once took up lodgings at our villa at Bank road since Anand Bhawan was under some construction. She knew I was always intrigued by ancient stories and how I had the knack of weaving some myself. Her passion for poetry, music and writing had rubbed off on me to a great extent. She was an overprotective mother ever since my two pattering feet and strawberry pink hands cradled her joys. A thyroid problem wasn't detected for many years and when it was diagnosed and medication given, she conceived me the very same month. So, when this little dumpling was birthed, she left no stone unturned in lavishing her motherly affection that bore rich dividends. She was certainly the best mother I could have asked for.

When I was four, my parents sent me to the most reputed convent school in Allahabad. As an adolescent, I realized that subjects like Mathematics and Science were not my cup of tea and I often daydreamed during these classes which were too drab for the poet in me to engross myself in. These lectures were barricades to my freedom, gripping me with frustration. I remember how my father, an eminent psychologist in his field, would motivate me to raise my own bar rather than compete with other classmates. But now that my parents weren't there anymore, I gradually weaned myself off my visits to Allahabad, my hometown after my mother's demise. Although, I am married to a doting husband and we have two grown up sons, the pangs of loneliness still persist in my languishing soul. My meanderings into time are so riveting that they often awaken a nostalgia of these bygone days.

Two years ago, while ambling towards the joggers' track in the Topiary park in Sector 35, I often noticed tawny squirrels frisking about, chasing each other on the velvety grass or nibbling hard, brown nuts thrown at them by some benevolent passers-by. Stray dogs marked their territory, mapping isolated corners to chew dry bones and left overs they would fish out from a garbage bin nearby. Birds would often roost there, cheeping merrily and creating a ruckus. Old couples would saunter blissfully in groups of two's and three's, gossiping and guffawing aloud at the recollections of a past occurrence. Young boys loitered around, vying for the attention of the opposite sex. They wore t-shirts with eye-catching captions. I recall one such fellow named Raj, a neighbour's overly pampered son with spiky hair whose t-shirt bore the most ludicrous captions like 'I'm Single and Ready to Mingle!' or 'I Love the Opposite Sex' splashed in bold crimson letters. Those were the days when the movie bug had bitten most youngsters who wanted to behave like the cool, hip and macho men, flaunting weird hairstyles and shades portrayed in the movies. Young girls on the other hand were a tad smarter. They would romp around in their t's and shorts, taking obnoxious selfies, while their roving eyes were rivetted in their direction. The only pre-requisite for a selfie was a pout or a victory sign and the company or ambience was of little consequence.

The sun often swallowed up these musings in a steaming cup of masala tea that I would purchase from a nearby tea vendor, Ranveer. He updated me on all the 'goings on' in the surreptitious lives of corrupt men and their agendas to gratify their insatiable thirst for wealth. I would ponder if life was only reduced to binaries of power versus money, love versus sex and religion versus secularism. But there were honest men like Ranveer who possessed a strong character and didn't surrender themselves to the vicious nexus of power-hungry wheeler dealers. Ranveer would sculpt me the weirdest interpretations and I had to keep nodding in approval or he'd forget an essential thread to link the plot that only got murkier each time. I firmly believed that every word spoken by him was God's truth, every grain of it.

On one particular visit to his tea-stall, I noticed a stocky gentleman, a dandy in a motley-coloured, outrageous attire. He alighted from his swanky black Rolls Royce car, wearing a fluorescent green turban, white trousers and a matching green psychedelic shirt. He flashed a smile at Ranveer who looked a bit intimidated by his belligerent demeanor. Later, when the man toddled off with his goons without paying for his tea, Ranveer apprised me that he was a local hip- hop singer who had tie-ups with the underworld. He even changed his cars every year. A car was a status symbol for the high society and Page three celebrities. Cars could enhance or tarnish their reputation, depending on their brands. Life was so complicated for tycoons and bureaucrats that I could scarcely bring myself to envy them. I preferred hailing from a middle- class family with minimal demands and expectations.

Talking about shady people, I met another one twenty years ago when I had recently relocated to Chandigarh. He happened to be a distant uncle who had amassed a lot of wealth and priceless acquisitions which I later discovered weren't his own but belonged to others. Uncle D would pick up things from shops on the pretext that he'd pay up later when he never really intended to settle bills in the first place. Within a few months, his wealth and assets escalated disproportionately to his real income compelling him to leave lock, stock and barrel from the city. I thanked the almighty for infusing us with wisdom that we did not fall into his sinister trap and lend him anything. Our relationship had soured already when he tried to dupe a close relative's family on one such occasion but he was unsuccessful.

There were other intriguing encounters that I can faintly recollect now. The walks in parks were quite stimulating and eventful back then. I recall meeting this elderly lady- J, an ardent birdwatcher, no 'negative connotations' please! Whenever she found me, she would latch on, giving me a well-documented history about the numerous species of birds she had encountered on visits to the bird sanctuaries. We would sit down on a bench and I'd give her a perfunctory nod occasionally, while she'd update me on their life span, food habits and even their mating. I wondered how such a plethora of knowledge had gone in vain. She should have become an Ornithologist, or at least transformed me into one. Within a few days, I decided to upgrade myself to a different park to vent my frustration and stretch my fertile imagination, being a poet. I sought recourse in another one close by, but before I could continue my musings in this new found paradise, I realized I was being stalked. A street dog had taken a queer fancy to me and he decided to follow me like 'Mary's little lamb'. If I happened to go to pick up groceries or get myself a relaxing hair spa, he would be parked outside faithfully with a Cheshire cat grin, waiting for me. Finally, we parted ways one day when he found himself an emaciated little pariah mate. That was the end of the stalking and I was glad he had found lady love at last.

My nature walks continue to enchant me to this very day and have given me a whole new perspective on life. Despite the fact that Covid-19 has confined us to our little microcosm, the walks have expanded into a repertoire of moments that would have otherwise been inconceivable. They rejuvenate me, dispelling negativity associated with the deadly virus. I still adhere to the norms of social distancing, especially with the 'bird watcher lady' in sector 35 and ensure I keep my mask, head phones and other protective gear on at all times to avert unnecessary intruders. But the irony is that we can't camouflage our souls behind those masks of indifference that distance us from the world.

The vicissitudes of life envelop me, yet I have learned to shrug them off and move ahead, shedding my inhibitions dauntlessly. From the pusillanimous child to a spirited woman, the journey has been long and gruelling, yet it constantly ignites within me a fire that will never get extinguished. My life has been a raw onion as I peel off its layers that sometimes sting my eyes or tug at my heartstrings unfolding a new facet of myself. At times I feel I am a mirror looking at a new face each day. The faces might be transitory and may intermingle or vanish, yet the memories will still remain etched to the soul that is overflowing like a river in spate.

Bio:
Vandita Dharni hails from an eminent family of educationists. She is a gold medalist in English from the University of Allahabadand also earned a Ph.D. degree in American Literature. Her articles, poems and short stories have been published in Criterion, Ruminations, GNOSIS, HellBound Publishing House and International magazines like Immagine and Poessia, Synchronised Chaos, Guido Gozzano, Sipay, Our Poetry Archive, Written Escapes, Primer Antologia De Poetas Del Proyecto De Unamos Al Mundo Con La Poesia- Mexico and Poleart, Albania.

The Body of Memories

Her poem, *The Endangered Tiger* was given an honourable mention in the Guido Gozzano. She has published three anthologies, *Quintessential Outpourings*, *The Oyster of Love* and *Rippling Overtures*. She has edited anthologies and has also reviewed several poems on poetry sites such as 'Poetry Review' on Facebook. She has been honoured with the Poetic Galaxy Award 2018 by the Literati Cosmos Society, the World Poetic Star award 2019 by the World Nation's Writers' Union, and the Rabindranath Tagore Award for Poetry in 2020 by the Arpita Foundation at Brindavan, Mathura.

MEMOIR EXCERPTS

BOOK EXCERPTS

The Body of Memories

Finally, She Showered: Novel Excerpt

Anita Nahal

[Excerpts from Anita Nahal's recently completed novel which is a combination of prose and onegin stanza. The passages below are not synchronous with as these appear in the novel. The novel is a single mother's journey from India to America with her young son in search of peace and a new place to call home. Trying to distance themselves from domestic abuse, Priya leaves all and everyone. Do they find peace? At what cost? Read some snippets below from the novel, partly fiction and partly a memoir. The novel covers a time frame of decades yet expressed in a couple of hours. Returning to her hotel room after her son's wedding, Priya wants to take a shower, but each time she thinks of doing so, her memory pulls her to some incident, event or emotion from the past or present that broke or made her. Finally, she showers, with the water being symbolic of release, acceptance, and resurgence.]

I.

Circa 2017 and back and forth, and back and forth

All morning it had been raining, except for the hour or so when the wedding procession danced towards the entrance of the hotel. Priya's son, Avijeet was getting married. It had been fifteen years since she had decided to leave India with her young son to create a peaceful life for themselves. She could feel her heart knocking as she placed her right hand on her chest trying to calm it, with the left adjusting her sari *pallu* making sure her midriff was not visible. Standing at the tall glass windows on the second floor of the hotel just before the procession began, Priya heaved a long sigh-- relief and apprehension amalgamated like an uncomfortable mixture of tea and coffee in the same cup. Pursing her lips, hugging herself, she swayed side to side like a swing in a gentle wind. It was still drizzling, lightly…very auspicious omen...the rain that is... at least that's what India's old wives' tales echoed, no matter if everyone got drenched with the bride's make up running and the groom's turban dripping!

Folks were running around everywhere trying to complete last-minute stuff and her texts were endless.

"Do all the men from our side have their turbans tied?"

"Has the second pundit for the wedding ceremony arrived? Did he get some tea and cookies?"

"Did you order an Uber for the pundit who came this morning for Avijeet's turban ceremony?"

"Did you pay the make-up women?"

"Mom, where are you? The photographers want all family members outside. Come quickly." The last text from her blessing, brought her out of here reverie, and she turned and hastened out, picking the pleats of her sari. Her gold pencil heels sparkled through glass reflections. This Cinderella may not have found her prince charming yet, but her son could be a shining one for someone.

II.

"Mahima, I think I'm going to sink." Priya said to her close friend sitting at a South Indian restaurant opposite her college. The year was probably 2000. These two had built a very strong bond since they did their Master's together and then a one-year French speaking course at the Alliance Française in New Delhi...almost twenty years ago.

The server arrived and Mahima asked Priya gently, "Okay...first tell me what you would like to eat?"

"What…" waking up from a reverie, Priya responded, "Maybe a plain *dosa* with lots of coconut *chutney* on the side, and a little bit of *sambhar*. What about you?"

"I'll have a *masala dosa* with lots of potatoes in it!"

"Shall we share a plate of *idly also*?"

"Sure."

As soon as the server walked away, Mahima looked at Priya, and she looked back almost chocking up. "What's going on, Priya?"

"Well, you know what's been going on …has been going on for so many years. We had a huge fight last night. He keeps abusing me on the smallest of things. And then he has the nerve to tell me that I can abuse him back if I wish. I am not trained to do that…but yesterday I let him have it…told him fuck you and fuck off…both together…can you believe that? He was shocked and of course shouted back at least ten times, "Fuck you, fuck you, fuck you, fuck you…" went on and on with his teeth gritting and face reddening. I thought he'd have a heart attack! I feel one day I am going to be sucked into a cauldron of some murky looking stuff. You know, the kind you might find upon mixing burnt caramel, dirt and oil." Mahima held her hand.

"And the mixture is moving fast, very fast like in a whirlpool, and I am flaying my hands, calling for help, but no one answers before I'm pulled in."

"What? How's that possible? Where was Avijeet?"

"Oh gosh, he'd be the first to jump in to help me. But I don't envision him in my yucky daydreams as I don't want him to be sucked in as well. I want him to remain safe after I am gone."

"No one is going anywhere," said Mahima softly. She tried to make Priya laugh, "And how do you know how yucky a

The Body of Memories

mixture of burnt caramel, dirt and oil is? Hunn? Have you made it? Tasted it?"

"It sounds yucky," Priya said, smiling a bit. "And, yes, I know, I know…I'm not going to sink, really, I know. I will fight it. We both… Avijeet and I… we are going to leave India."

"Good…" Mahima smiled in reassurance.

III.

Go Priya go
Run fast run
Take your son and go
To a place far away and then some
Can't be the moon or the once declared-non-gratis-poor planet Pluto
It's far out… too far out, a bit too
Much…don't you think? But maybe across the oceans
From where at least once they'd settled their emotions
They could fly back to see her dad
Come for a short while… not disturbing anyone
Foreign or home spun
A forced balanced cocktail Priya made, both happy and sad
That's what most folks want… no? A normalcy may come from their journeys?
In that effort they keep writing new, rehashed or retold stories.

We cook, we clean
We work, we sleep
We love, we have sex, we hate…the latter a word Priya likes to keep unseen
Our mean struggles we don't wanna forget, while desirous to reap
From all that's good and gone by

Like some decisions, some choices, some fleeting magical
fly-
byes, or times that'll never come back…
Like many, many milestones, some moved, some stuck…
Missed births, funerals and weddings…
The natural or adopted

Or situations to which one adapted…
Don't you think it's all semantics?
With some feelings thrown into the mix?
Will AI be unique or offer a different fix?

Her life, she thought and believed, was going by
Going, going, gone
No need to stay or pry
Going, going, gone like in Bob Dylan's song
She emphasized, "No need for me to pry too much into my
own thoughts
Might be there are too many droughts
Oh, don't you feel sorry for me
For I'll always will have gusto and oomph in me
Will not vegetate feeling lonely…
What lonely, lonely, lonely?! Got my dear ones
And near ones.
Everything is my son, friends, and my family
Those who sit heavy in plush velvet-tapestry-kind-a sofas
of the past
Might not have too many crying during their funeral
flower-less repast."

As she aged, alchemists tugged at her sleeve often
And gypsies gestured to her
Come join us in your years of autumn
With graying hair at your temples, hair
Graying all over
Including in the forest, which is normal, not rare
The aging
Hopefully maturing

The Body of Memories

Her restless travels
Her restless needs
Her desires and wants
Now quietly straddling the times
Time had not changed
Only the "times" had changed.

IV.

Priya looked at the neat handwriting on the note nestled among soft orange roses on one of the side tables in her hotel room. It is from her just married son, Avijeet. She pressed the note to her lips as her eyes filled up with an extremely contended-fulfilling kind of feeling. The wedding celebrations had gone extremely well. While gratefulness sat in her heart, a small part of her filled with inertia and malaise.

V.

Combing her hair strands all back, she took off her jewelry preparing to shower. Despite the air conditioning, she was sweating from the July heat. They had to do the wedding in the summer months as most of the relatives could get leave from work only at that time. Otherwise by Hindu traditions, weddings are generally not held between June and October.

"You think your Gods will be angry?" Rosella asked her when the wedding date was fixed.

"I hope not, and in our defense, we live in the US, so maybe the summer month rule does not apply here," she smiled.

She shook her clothes trying to fan herself and scratched her tattoo near her left armpit which tended to become slightly irritable in severe heat.

It was a warm August afternoon ten years before, in 2008, when Priya and four of her colleagues from Pavers

University reached U Street in Washington DC to find a good and clean tattoo artist for her. Gentrification had changed much of the U street corridor.

"We've got to find a tattoo studio that is neat and tidy with instruments all sanitized," said Perry, his expression one of grave concern. I hope she doesn't get an infection, he thought. She's so keen on getting a tattoo…very surprising for a woman from India…and at an older age. "What's your son going to say when he sees your tattoo? Or your parents when you go back to visit them?" he inquired a bit hesitatingly.

"Oh…my son already knows…and he doesn't mind. And my parents… well sadly mom has passed but I think she would have loved the tattoo, and my dad is not going to mind…I think he'll be okay…he's pretty cool about most things. Except that he never let me go out with boys and never let boys come home!"

VI.

The police jeeps drove off with the same fanfare as they came. It was becoming embarrassing for them all, and especially exhausting for Priya to prove emotional abuse which shows no scars.

"Why didn't you go to the police station and file a complaint as the inspector said?" her dad asked later.

"Papa, the inspector was stinking of alcohol. He seemed drunk. I didn't think it was wise to go the station at this time of the night to file a complaint. Only last week there was this news story about a woman…quite like me…mind you, it has nothing to do with money and education…just that you are a vulnerable woman… she was raped by two policemen when she went to lodge a complaint about something at her local police station."

The Body of Memories

"Oh…okay…You did the right thing then."

"Ya…I am so tried papa… maybe I'll go and visit the Crime Against Women Cell next week to see what recourse I have." These were departments within police stations manned by women officers. But they also recommended that till she lodged an official complaint, nothing could be done. Her visits to a renowned woman lawyer too were becoming repeatedly staid and weak.

"Are you going to file for divorce, Priya? When will you decide? How long will you take?"

"I know…I know…I'm just afraid that he'll do something."

"He might do something even if you don't." Priya knew she would never have the courage to get a divorce in India…she and her son had to leave the country…that was the only way out.

A year later, before Priya and Avijeet's next visit, her dad was killed in a road accident…right on their street. He was walking back from the local store in the ascending night. Some of the streetlights were not working and as he turned the corner to their house, a guy in an old dusty Fiat took a fast turn from behind him and hit him from the back. He passed on the way to the hospital.

VII.

As she lay down on half-raised pillows
And on the sheets cool and light
There was a knock at the misting windows
Might be the wind saying goodnight
Marriages are made in heaven they say
Not all last though in such a way

That can give that effervescent lift
From one old soul to another as a gift
See what some epics bade
Like in the Mahabharat, Draupadi's, settled in seconds of
ignorance
And by her mother-in-law Kunti's refusal to relent to her
own indifference
Or in the Ramayana Sita's, whose was surely said to be
made
We can learn a lot from epics
A great deal from culture and myths, and life's needs and
requirements.

To end this one marriage, mother and son went to a place
Much south of North Virginia
Where the lawyer had his office space
And the day they had to go for divorce in south of Northern
Virginia
A close friend of Priya
Was coincidently out of town. The lawyer fella
Not wanting to change already twice changed date
Said, "Rush to my office, be not late."
Twice she'd gone back on her decision
The lawyer was not amused
Not having many to guide, Priya was confused
And after much debate, her choice came with precision
Though papers had gone to India before
This time she wasn't afraid… let her marriage go sore.

"How old is your son, is he eighteen?
If, yes, ask him if he'll be your witness?"
"Yes, he is, he is nineteen."
Her own son was in her divorce, so fearless
After it was done, mom & son sat in the car
And Priya let go things held close, and far
From her roots. It all seemed so unreal
Not sure which of her lives… Indian or American were
surreal

Her tears came along with stomach sickness
Bringing also a pain deep in her chest
She wept for long, as emotions wouldn't rest
Then a tranquility followed, removing her pent-up
weakness
Opening the door of the car, she stepped out
A different air she breathed. Of hopes, new sprout.

Who would have known,
Her own blood, would bring her long- awaited freedom and
peace
Who would have known?
He'd bring her a new kind of lease
Without conditions or demands
Like relentless shells on unstable sands
Be her savior, again and again
Never to shift when things were in vain
Avijeet was a wise old soul
From early on in age
He'd been her broken soul's bandage
Sent to her from Heaven's bowl
Had it not been for him, Priya would
Long ago have died, on a wretched pyre of wood.

No more fake agendas written by some men
No more equality diminishing
No more pendulum shaking Zen
No more fake standards lowering or raising
Why some men slouch on recliners, beer in hands?
Why then they unbuckle their belt, zip open their pants?
Why such exhibitions don't come from women?
Are fertility eggs stronger than tasteless semen?
Is exhaustion an excuse from housework?
Even pretending not to be emasculated
Pretending to be in a fool's paradise elevated
Seems their power egos tend to over work
Men need to learn more about their tools

Before smearing those who learn to swim in the smallest of
pools.

Priya fell asleep
She knew not when
Holding Avijeet's note she went to sleep
Not counting proverbial sheep to ten
Not thinking too much
Next morning, she felt the soft touch
Of flowers that she had spread
At the doorway to receive the newlywed
A few diyas framed as a slight drizzle fell
And she placed idols and sweets on a thali
And tons of sheen from dried spilt milk, without too much
folly
Finally, she scooped some saved Ganga water to sprinkle
On her DIL and son. A new story begins
A new journey begins.

****

Glossary:

*Chutney: A sauce made from fruits, sugar, vinegar or lemon
juice, and some spices*
*Diya: A small cup-shaped (without handles) oil lamp made
of baked clay*
*Dosa: A pancake made of flour and lentils, typically part of
South Indian cuisine*
Draupadi: Heroine in the Hindu epic, Mahabharat
Ganga: The Indian name for the River Ganges
Idly: Pancakes made of steamed rice
Kunti: Mother-in-law of Draupadi in the epic, Mahabharata
Mahabharat: A Hindu epic
*Masala Dosa: Spicey potatoes and onion filled pancake
made of flour and lentils, typically a part of South Indian
cuisine*
Pallu: The end part of one side of a sari

The Body of Memories

Thali: A stainless steel plate
[This excerpt was previously published in, Lapis Lazuli, Spring 2020.]

Bio:
Anita Nahal, Ph.D., CDP is a poet, professor, short story writer, flash fictionist, and children's writer. She teaches at the University of the District of Columbia, Washington D.C. Besides academic publications, her creative books include, two volumes of poetry, a collection of flash fictions, four children's books, two edited anthologies of poetry (with Dr. Roopali Sircar Gaur) and one edited anthology of nursery rhymes (with Dr. Meenakshi Mohan). A third volume of poetry is scheduled for release in December 2021 by Kelsay Books. She has recently completed a novel. Nahal's poems and stories can be found in national and international journals and anthologies in the US, UK, Asia and Australia. Nahal's poems are also housed at Stanford University's Digital Humanities initiative, and she is also a columnist and guest contributing editor for New York based *aaduna* journal. Two books of Nahal's are prescribed on university syllabus at the University of Utrecht, The Netherlands. Nahal is the daughter of Indian novelist and professor, Late Dr. Chaman Nahal, and educationist mother, Late Dr. Sudarshna Nahal. Originally from New Delhi, India, Anita Nahal resides in the US. Her family include her son, daughter-in-law and their golden doodle. For more on Anita: https://anitanahal.wixsite.com/anitanahal

Till the River Runs Dry (Memoir Excerpt)

Bhaswati Ghosh

At six, I had already been discovered a prodigy. By my grandfather that is. One summer morning as Dadubhai dipped his Marie biscuit into the teacup, I jumped up to his lap. Even as he balanced the cup and saucer to save them from the sudden gymnastics of his granddaughter, my sight darted toward the bulky tome on the round table before us. I leant forward and picked it up in a mighty weight-lifting effort, before it plopped into my lap with a thud. It took me some effort to open the musty-scented edition of *Mahabharata*. Before long, I was reading out loud the text imprinted on its withering, yellowed pages. This was teeth-breaking, tongue-twisting Bengali, heavily loaded with Sanskrit. Dadubhai was stunned and called out to Titti, my grandmother, "*Ei je*, come here and see what Tutun *shona* is up to!"

Titti came out of the kitchen, wiping the sweat on her forehead with the end of her *sari*. As I ran my fingers through each letter, joining them up in my mind to form whole words before uttering them, Titti came closer and took a seat across Dadubhai and me. I looked up to her, collected her smiling nod, gave her a return smile, and got back to my play— locking the letters and half letters to pronounce the full words. This was my second year of learning the Bengali alphabet, and we were on to complex letters at school. When I saw my grandparents getting impressed with my diction-ability, I decided to read out one full paragraph. And read I did, notwithstanding the pronunciation road bumps occurring after every word or two.

"I always knew our Tutun was special. Is this a small thing, reading such tough passages? And that too from

The Body of Memories

Mahabharata!" Titti proclaimed with authoritative pride. She was, after all, the in-house language maestro. A writer with ability to match the best in the contemporary Bengali literary world, Titti had but limited credentials because of her distanced existence from the publishing circuit based in West Bengal. Even so, this enduring optimist insisted her granddaughter be enrolled into a school that taught Bengali, our mother tongue.

Indeed, Titti had reason to be happy that sultry May morning—when she stopped her cooking midway and came out, her *sari* stained with turmeric and her hands greasy—to hear me reading out those jawbreakers from the great Indian epic.

That year, a book of rhymes, part of my second-grade syllabus, ran out of stock in the only two Bengali bookstores in the capital. But our teacher would have none of that. Bashful that I was, facing the snarling lady at school daily was an ordeal I could do without. When I had spent about a week in bookless misery, our postman brought us a package. This was the first time I had seen a real parcel. I ran inside the house and called Titti to come and receive it because that's what the postman asked me to do. As she took the package in her hands, she held my chin gently and sent a smiling flying kiss my way. I knew I had done the right thing—brought her to hold a packet that meant something special for her.

"Here," she said, handing me the parcel. "Do you want to open it?" I had just lost a couple of milk teeth that year. Toothful or not, the grin on my face stretched like elastic the moment I opened the neatly-taped package. Three new books came out of it—my rhyme book, *Ramayana for Children* and *Mahabharata for Children*. When I looked at Titti gaping with disbelief, she said, "I wrote to Renu Titti to send these books from Calcutta. Does my Tutun *shona* like them?" "I do!" I said, hugging her quickly and hopped my way to the other room to show Ma *my* parcel.

Titti and Ma were the only two bread earners in our family back then. The two ladies were shouldering a challenge no one would envy—feeding a family of six, which included two school-going children; paying the rent; and keeping pace with spiraling household costs—all with their modest salaries. Yet, there was no concern over money when it came to introducing me and Dada, my brother, to the joy of books. Titti would shell out money freely to make us both members of the Delhi Public Library, using her membership subsidy—a perk of her government job. Going to the library with Titti was a weekly jaunt Dada and I wouldn't miss for anything—rain, fever, or exams. As the people, demons, and beasts from regional folktales, Buddhist Jataka tales, and Hindi comic books burst into our world, its territory swelled at an excited pace.

Titti's personal space had never been as expansive, though. A memoir she wrote a few months before her death tells me how, all through her life, she had negotiated life inside concrete matchboxes. She never experienced the luxury of a small quiet corner to write in, let alone possess a desk and a chair. For as long as I can remember, I found her squatting on the living room floor with her ruled register and ball-point pen, wiggling out every scrap moment from her million chores—day job, paying electricity and water bills, cooking, feeding us, going to the bank, post office, ration shop (to pick up groceries for the month), gas station (to book cooking gas)—to scribble her soul out on the paper. Even as I nurtured dreams of becoming either an engineer or a journalist upon growing up, I saw the manifestation of the much romanticized "struggling writer" before me. Only, writing was not a struggle for my grandmother; it was her daily quota of oxygen. Disregarding the demands of her fatigued body and stressed mind, she would write every single day, fighting drowsy eyes and bleak prospects.

Recognition was shy of making friends with Titti. Her six-decade-long writing career saw four published books with little marketing support; scores of published articles and some short stories with paltry compensations.

She did have a few good friends though, who had it in them to appreciate the depth of her writing. Social activist Pannalal Dasgupta, who had served as an armed revolutionary in India's freedom movement and founded Tagore Society for Rural Development, one of the oldest and largest civil society organizations in eastern India engaged in rural development, was one of them. The editor of *Compass*, a newsletter highlighting issues of rural importance, he was like a family member to us. His other glorious attribute was that he belonged to Faridpur, the neighboring district of Barisal, Titti's birthplace. All through my growing years, I saw this strange affection among Bengalis of East Pakistan for fellow land-lost compatriots. Every time Mr. Dasgupta visited us, Titti, him and Dadubhai would have avid nostalgia sessions over endless cups of *cha* or homebred milk-sugar tea. From rivers to village fairs and community festivals like *nabanna* and *rashjatra*, the reminiscences always beat the hours to chat. And each time they remembered their village life, they took me on a surreal trip to the green vistas of rural Bengal I am yet to see with my eyes.

Although I didn't understand Titti's pain fully while she was around, I felt its intensity all the same. By middle school, I had become her confidant. She would share with me the frustrations of being unable to have regular contact with Bengal-based publishers, the agony of getting estranged from her very supportive parental family and landing into her in-law's house at fifteen. "When, after a twelve to fourteen-hour day of tending to household chores, I couldn't find a book or even a newspaper in the house, I would read flaps of spice packets. At least it was some printed matter."

She used to hide a small notebook and a pen inside her blouse. The minute other female members left the kitchen, she would scrawl away furiously. Having seen her despondency, would I have chosen to be a writer? You bet not.

Like most writers who eat and breathe their craft, Titti perhaps dreamt of being a full-time writer. Yet, she had to take up one job after the other to keep the kitchen embers burning.

Did I *choose* to be a writer? No. But then neither did Titti. A bird doesn't choose to sing. The song chooses its birds. And then the bird has no choice but to sing, with or without food in its beak.

Bio:
Bhaswati Ghosh writes and translates fiction, non-fiction and poetry. ***Victory Colony, 1950*** is her first book of fiction. Her website is bhaswatighosh.com

Banana Lane: A Childhood Memoir

[A Portrait of one Grandmother's home]

Kavita Ezekiel Mendonca

Introduction

Grandfather's book

My grandfather's book travelled with me a long way, from India to my adopted home overseas. His name, Principal Moses Ezekiel (J. & J College of Science, NADIAD B.B. & C.I.RY). Its title, 'History and Culture of the Bene-Israel in India'. The book documents the history of the Jewish community into which I was born. The slim volume was published on October 4th 1948, on Rosh Hashanah, the Jewish New Year. My copy is very old and the first page is torn. I think the back page, or pages, are also missing. My grandfather has dedicated it to his sister, Sarah, and in the preface (where he makes several confessions) he says that 'this book is merely a labor of love.' I am struck by the simplicity of his writing and the personal touch he gives to his account of the story of our small, but significant community. The humility with which he writes the Preface strikes me each time I return to reading it.

This memoir is a portrait of the home of my paternal grandmother and about the Bene-Israel community of Jews, to which I belong, and in which I grew up in the city of Bombay, now Mumbai. Sometimes, being the only Jewish student in my school and college, made me a kind of curiosity. I felt like little Nell in the Old Curiosity Shop, the novel by Charles Dickens. Besides, though not an orphan in the strictest sense of the word, living without my mother, for complicated family reasons, while she was still alive, often made me feel like one. I was nick-named 'Shylock', when we studied Shakespeare's Merchant of Venice in school, and accused of killing Christ, even though I protested I was not there when his Crucifixion happened. And almost always, the question I asked my father was, 'Are we Jewish Indian, or Indian Jewish.' My father would reply that we were both! And overseas, in my adopted home, hardly anyone has heard of an Indian Jew, and people express much surprise at my identity.

Chapter 1

Banana Lane and Penny Lane

[One lane separated the two houses where my parents lived. Destiny walked that short distance, bringing them into that union, humans call marriage.]

I loved the Beatles and I loved the song "Penny Lane". It has remained one of my favourites. My father had gifted me a book of their song lyrics which he had purchased on one of his trips to New York, with an inscription on the first page, 'To Kavita, with faith in her potential'. It is taking me a lifetime to try and fulfill that potential, and the book has been lost in transition between the many homes and places I have moved to, over the years. If anyone discovers its whereabouts, I would be willing to offer a small reward!

My father, with whom I lived in my paternal grandmother's home, was a unique man; kind, generous to a fault, *'unpractical'* and totally unworldly. He was an intellectual, totally dedicated to his craft—a true poet at heart, writer, teacher, and dreamer, always calm, cool and collected. I rarely saw him angry, but when he lost his temper, he pronounced my name by biting his lower lip, *Kavitam*, not *Kavita*. Then you stood at a distance, and timidly asked what crime you had committed. You trembled to think what the consequences could be, but usually it was some kind of gentle admonition with a touch of philosophical advice.

At 'The Retreat', my paternal grandmother's house, was a magical place with old-world charm, a creaking wooden staircase, gleaming brass pots to store water in, Jewish cooking at its very deliciousness, and warm, larger-than-life personalities, the dozens of pigeons in the high rafters that made their nests and raised their young. Sometimes, an egg fell to the floor beneath with a young dead chick, lifeless and still. At such times, I wept not just for the chick, but for its mother. My grandfather said it was nothing to worry about, as the cycle of life includes such small setbacks, but to a young child, the sight of the lifeless little bird was devastating.

It was here at 'The Retreat' that I was raised by my grandmother, my aunt Hannah, her kind and loving husband, who passed away too early, and whom we called 'Brother,' and my father. I spent most of my childhood and youth there. They were religious and observed all the Jewish customs and traditions. My grandfather was present for some of the time too, but he was mostly away, being the Principal of a college in Nadiad, in Gujarat, a state in Western India. Friends, neighbors, aunts, uncles and cousins gave me their time and companionship throughout this difficult phase of my life. I went to live at 'The Retreat', when I had turned just eleven.

Perhaps, 'The Retreat' contained a kind of symbolism as the name for my grandmother's home, which would be inextricably woven into my life story.

I would look forward to Sundays. My mother spent the day with me, bringing some treats to be stored in the fridge for the coming week. The pigeons were my constant companions. Their cooing was a backdrop to my daily life. Sometimes, bats flew through the open windows and got so confused, they didn't know whether to call this place home, or fly to a different spot. We had a saying that if a bat flies in, a baby would follow. I did not have a baby till many years later in life, but the saying stuck in my mind, as did many other of my grandmother's words and sayings. A white kitten even managed to stray in through the front door, but my grandfather (*"papa"*) would not let me keep it because he said cat hair was not good for health. I have never had a home without cats after marriage! Sorry papa! I could have titled my memoir 'My family and other Animals', but that title has already been taken and I don't want to be accused of plagiarism!

The small trip down *Banana Lane,* as I nick-named the street between the two grandmothers' homes, was a balancing act. From one grandmother's house to another's, it was a ten-minute walk on broken sidewalks filled with hawkers, beggars, taxis and a never-ending sea of humanity. This was a veritable Banana Lane. My mother hoisted up her saree to her ankles, held our little hands tightly as she made her brisk, determined visits each Sunday to both grandmothers' houses, with my younger sister and I. She had decided to kill two birds with one stone. We tried to struggle free so we could skip along, as little girls are wont to do. However, since the lane was crowded with men in *lungis (a kind of sarong)* loading green and yellow bananas in various shapes and sizes, bound for the local markets, the street often became slippery with banana peels in varying states of decay. I remember vividly the big, stone warehouse, stacked with bananas from floor to ceiling, and the half-clad men tossing bunches of bananas onto the trucks, calling out loudly to each other in the local language. We were tempted to eat the bananas too, but were denied by my strict mother, saying that it was important for us to reach our destination quickly, and return home quickly by a bus we could not miss. "Another bus will take a long time to come". That was a repeated chant whenever we ventured out from our own home. The image of the men balancing themselves on top of the mountains of bananas on the banana truck, is still clear to this day. If I were an artist, I could sketch that picture.

Now back to 'The Retreat'...

The Body of Memories

The paternal grandmother's house was where my parents took me directly from the hospital when I was born. It was my first home. The hospital was called New Hospital for Women, or as I mistakenly called it, Hospital for New Women. Looking back now, I am quite confident that my mother was transformed into a new woman after I was born. Some family secrets must be kept, so I will not elaborate on the significance of my statement. She always said that I was daddy's girl, had his curly hair and unworldly traits, much to her chagrin. That left her to be the only practical person in the household. I have inherited my father's unworldliness and share some of his *'unpractical'* nature.

My parents shared a partitioned room with my father's brother, his wife and his young son. My grand-mother was a very kind, compassionate, and gentle woman, soft spoken and with gray-green eyes. We called her *Aai*, which means mother in Marathi, a language we spoke at home, the language of the Bene-Israel of Bombay. *Aai* was calm and collected, and founded and ran her own school for poor and disadvantaged children, in a very poor neighborhood of Bombay called Dongri. The school was called Vijay Vidyalaya. My aunt, Hannah, who lived with us at 'The Retreat', also taught at the school.

My grandmother loved every one of her grandchildren equally, and believed in eating the "First Fruits of the Season", because "the Torah said so". The cost was a consideration, but not of great significance, and the famed Alphonso mangoes were especially sweet! She believed in comforting a crying woman whose alcoholic husband had thrown her out of the house in a drunken rage. Often, it was midnight when the front-door bell rang, but she put a pot of tea on, and counselled her gently in the large stone kitchen, sitting with her at the square Formica-topped dining table, till the crying woman calmed down and returned to her home, relieved of her burden, at least temporarily. It was never too late, or too early, for her to help someone in need whether she was exhausted from a day's work or fast asleep at midnight. When she died, there were forty buses hired to ferry the crowds of people who loved her and wanted to attend her funeral. There was no room on the street she lived on, so the drivers had to park on other streets as close to the house as they could. I watched from the window as people boarded the buses in a sort of silent procession.

It seems I was destined to watch life's events from windows.

Every evening my grandmother, my aunt Hannah and myself would take three chairs from the house, place them on the verandah, and sit and watch the world go by. Both my grandmother and my aunt would dress immaculately in their sarees with their jewellery adorning their necks and ears, and smelling of the fresh flowered *gajras* (jasmine garlands) in their hair. Both believed in dressing for the occasion, as if they were about to go out to a fancy event for the evening. We all sat there until it turned dark. During the evening both aunt and grandma expressed their hopes about my meeting a 'nice young man' to marry. They kept repeating the fact that I should not be sitting with two 'old ladies,' but insisted the man must be educated so my grandma would have educated grandchildren. Later, I was to fulfill her wish, but she did not live long enough to see either the husband or the grandchildren. My aunt did meet my little son, if ever so briefly. She had left to make *Aliyah* to Israel and had come to India with her sister-in-law for a brief visit.

My grandmother's house was aptly named 'The Retreat'! I did not know then, that from the age of eleven, I would spend the remainder of my youth, retreating from the tragedies of life, until a man would come and sweep me off my feet! She and my aunt had constantly prayed for a good husband for me. The definition of 'good' was that he should care for me, and give me educated and beautiful children, as I have mentioned earlier. 'The Retreat' was a metaphor for my childhood that only those who were a part of it, will understand. 'The Retreat' was where we all congregated on special occasions or simply to visit our amazing

The Body of Memories

grandmother and another aunt and uncle. Aunts, uncles, cousins and even our friends would eat "red" or "green" mutton or chicken curry with coconut rice, made according to Jewish culinary tradition, and large potato-covered patties with a ground meat filling. It was bewildering how the kerosene stove could cook for so many people, balancing the large pots on the glowing flame. Later we cooked with bottled gas on a cooking range with two burners. During mango season, my grandmother would purchase *kayris* (raw mangoes) and make sweet mango pickle, we called *Muramba*. The pickle would be stored in large earthenware jars, and each family was given one jar to take home and enjoy.

We celebrated *Malida,* a kind of Thanksgiving ceremony for special occasions such as the birth of a baby, or before a wedding or a housewarming. When I moved into my new home overseas, my Jewish friends came to the house, and we prepared *Malida (*sweetened *Poha* -- flattened rice - with jaggery and slivers of almond and ground cardamom, and fruit*)* together, and they recited the prayers in Hebrew. Passover was a very important festival. Its significance was well known to me, and we ate the specially unleavened bread with treacle at this time. Hanukkah (the festival of lights) and Rosh Hashanah (Jewish New Year), were festivals I particularly loved as a child. The silver Menorah in my mother's home had pride of place in the same corner of the living room shelf for all of my childhood and youth. On Fridays and Saturdays, before sundown, we lit the Sabbath lamp and gathered around while a prayer was recited. At the end of the prayer, it is customary to put both your hands towards the flame and then bring it to your lips in a kiss. This is called *Hathboshi,* which literally means 'hand kiss'.

Everything that was significant, happened at the Retreat. Lots of music from cousins who had their own rock bands, to poetry readings from my father, and lectures on nutrition from my grandfather, who was ahead of his time in the field of health and nutrition. He ate garlic raw and took long, brisk walks. My father did that too, despite the pot-holed and crowded streets, including a large horse stable across the street from the house. When there was a fire, the horses would run wildly down the street, neighing and whinnying frantically. A fleeing horse, or two, would enter the compound of 'The Retreat', and I watched the majestic creature from the window. At night, a man would be mercilessly beating his escort, a prostitute that made him angry or disappointed, or simply dissatisfied. My father would immediately want to venture out onto the dark street in the middle of the night to stop this 'inhumanity', as he called it. The largest red-light district in the city, was on the street parallel to my grandmother's house. Perhaps also, this was why it was called 'The Retreat'. Built in the days of the British, it was a collection of seven one-storey bungalows with a large wrought-iron gate and a mud compound running through it, where we took our walks with friends each night at 10 p.m., and where a boyfriend walked his dog on rainy nights, throwing love notes at a special silhouette appearing at the window. We had to wash our feet before getting into bed, they were so muddy! The space between the roof of our house and the neighbor's was open to the sky and the stars that peeped through at night were especially beautiful.

'The Retreat' adjoined a girl's school on one side, another girl's school in front, and a large mosque next door. Down the lane, past the bakery and turning right was the synagogue, where another very sweet aunt lived across the street. She made the best *Ghasacha halva* (a dessert made from China Grass) in the world. It was a kind of a sweet Indian dessert. My poem 'China Grass Halwa,' is a tribute to her love and her culinary skills.

Some nights though, I would climb into my aunt's bed at 'The Retreat' as the ghostly apparition of a man, dressed in white, would appear to me. Although the door was tightly latched, he managed to come in and stand beside my bed. To this day, I do not know who he was. Perhaps he was the prophet Elijah, come to protect and watch over me. I later wrote that experience into a poem called, 'The Man in White'.

I learned most of the Jewish customs and traditions from my sweet and loving Hannabai Aunty. She was actually my father's cousin. She loved me unconditionally, prepared 'Batate Pohe,' a sort of savory Indian cereal potato snack whenever I was hungry or not, and diligently read all one hundred and fifty psalms every Saturday. Her husband, whom we called 'Brother', loved me too and allowed me into their room at any time of night or day, when I was a very little girl living at 'The Retreat', much to my mother's dismay. Hannabai enlisted my help in squeezing the grapes for the grape juice for the Sabbath prayers and taught me how to pray 'The Shema.' During an earthquake in 1991, in the mountain town where I lived and worked, I recited The Shema a "million" times, and was convinced that it stopped the ground from shaking. Faith is a wonderful thing. I can even sing 'The Shema' to this day and love the faith it gives birth to in me. Again, I later wrote that experience into a poem. It was called, *I Still Sing 'The Shema'*. The poem is awaiting publication. Hannabai Aunty had very long hair which she coiled into a tight bun at the top of her head. She said that her father would not allow her to leave it loose, and that girls in those days were not to be seen or heard when visitors came to the house. She told me that on several occasions, she was challenged by doubting Thomases, to uncoil the bun and prove how long her hair really was. My mother too, had very long hair and wore it in two braids. Hannabai aunty rubbed oil into my long curly hair each Friday night, and on Saturdays she sat on a low stool and helped me wash my hair with Shikakhai (Shikakhai soap pods had been previously soaked and made into a frothy shampoo). Hannabai Aunty self-studied English and Hebrew, and immigrated to Israel in her early sixties.

It was her dream to make *Aliyah,* but it was my loss to be left behind. I silently mourned her leaving, and was informed that she had settled happily in the Promised Land. What a woman! I felt she had nerves of steel, along with her heart of gold…

Bio:

Kavita Ezekiel Mendonca was born and raised in a Jewish family in Mumbai. She was educated at the Queen Mary School, Mumbai, received her BA in English and French, an MA from the University of Bombay in English and American Literature, and a Master's in Education from Oxford Brookes University, England. She has taught English, French and Spanish in various colleges and schools in India and overseas, in a teaching career spanning over four decades. Her first book, *Family Sunday and Other Poems* was published in 1989, with a second edition in 1990. She has read her poems for the All India Radio in Mumbai, and her poem 'Family Sunday' was featured in an Anthology of Women's Writing. Her poems have also appeared in *Destiny Poets,* U.K, *Poetry India, SETU, Café Dissensus,* among others. She writes Poetry and Short Fiction. Kavita is the daughter of the late poet, Nissim Ezekiel. She manages her Poetry page at https://www.facebook.com/kemendoncapoetry/

Porridge & I: A Post-Colonial Story
Roopali Sircar Gaur

[Excerpt from *Porridge & I: A Post-Colonial Story* (unpublished memoir of my childhood with my sister Parijat who was renamed Porridge by our governess Doris who refused to pronounce Indian names. The story begins in Wellington in the Nilgiris where my father was posted in his Regiment, the 2nd Madras. It captures a period long gone. Since the narrator is a child, the spellings and expressions may not pertain to expected standards of the adult world.]

25ᵗʰ April, 1958

The Cook House Built in 1856

A long open verandah with pillars runs from the dining hall, straight into the Cook House built in 1856. Its roof slopes but the red chimney sits straight on it without rolling off. The kitchen is very old and has yellow walls. Stuck inside the wall is a big oven which also has big iron doors Made in England by Smith &Sons 1854. It is right next to a *choolha* which is also stuck in the wall but it doesn't say where it is made.

Cook's black tree fingers cook English *khana*. "Baby, I making Pot rost, spinech soofley, sheperd pie and lamb stoo".

Somedays in the afternoon when Doris is sleeping. Porridge and I slip inside the Cook House and watch Cook pluck a plump white goose of all its soft white feathers, making the goose's skin full of goose pimples. He holds it up by its long, twisted neck and hums like a bumble bee as he dip-dip dips the dead duck into a drum of boiling hot water. This way Porridge and I get to seeing what a goose looks like from inside its soft feathers. Cook also boxes and pinches and punches flour into breads and buns. All that flour on his black face makes him look like a white English ghost. Cook steams caramel custard pudding in a tin box tied with a string and then decorates it with cream and sugar paste which he puts inside a brown paper cone and squeezes it to let the cream come out in wavy shapes. Another pudding he calls 'blackmanj' is pink in colour and has wavy cream and sugar roses on it. Cook bakes plum cakes with raisin just before Xmas.

One day the Dhobi man who stops to chat with Cook and sips hot tea from a tin mug lifted his dirty brown and blue lungi and held out a sausage in his hand and asked us, "What is this baby?"
Just then Cook had turned around and the checked lungi had fallen like a curtain over his hairy dhobi legs hiding the sausage. We couldn't answer Dhobi man's question and never answered because we have not got another chance to inspect the sausage.
Porridge says, "let us go and ask him to show it again", but he just goes away with the bundle of clothes. Cook doesn't give him any tea anymore. We are worried about Dhobi man because the sausage has stuck inside our head forever and forever. What was it? What is it ? WHAT WAS IT? What had he done with it? Porridge never again took me to the Cook House built in 1856.
"I am so happy," Doris said, "You girls are learning to be obedient. You girls should not talk to the servants."
"But why? But why?"
"Because they are servants, that's why."

The peach tree which grows on the land behind the Cook House built in 1856 has turned pink and white. A squash creeper has crept up its back and green squashes hang with their heads down like pears with soft white hair on it. Ramulu who is Cook's helper washes the black pots and pans and grows squash cabbage, carrot and beet in the

The Body of Memories

kitchen garden. Mother is very proud of Ramulus green fingers. Porridge and I have been searching for his green fingers. Even in the day, all his fingers look as black as his face. May be his blood is green. Poryphyro, the fat red rooster who wakes us all up in the night when we are all dead sleeping because he can see the sun rise in England, does green potty. Every day Cook dumps Ramulu's green garden vegetables   into boiling   hot   water   and stirs it till it thickens into   a disgusting purple and   green soup. Dad reads us a story by a man called Shakespeare who knows a green-eyed monster. Porridge says he keeps it in his bed.

Doris eats her dinner with Mother and Dad, but some days she eats alone in her room. Porridge and I eat our supper in the dining room with two girls who wear half saris because Chinamma, Papa sweepers aunt from his mother's side says they are not married and are not allowed to wear full saris.

"These girls, *chinna junglees*". Cook pointed to Irti and Sarukai. "They living in forest with father and second mother before Kuddappa contractor bringing them here for building road. I seen them sitting on footpath crying because Kuddappa not paying them. Poor chinna papas, they very very hungry".
Cook looked at the two "junglees" with a twinkle star inside his black eyes. "Is Doris our second Mother?" Porridge asked. Cook covered his mouth with a small kitchen towel and went away touching his ears with both hands, saying, "*Aiyo Ramachandra Ramachandra*! Like this words not speaking. Madam hearing madam getting very very angry. I telling you baby log." He wagged his finger at us.

"Why should Madam get angry?" Miss Doris laughed. Her green silky skirt is so tight that I can see her white panty. Her gold hair is tied in a pony tail. "I look after these two girls all day and many times at night. Don't I darlings? I teach them their lessons and I take them out to play. I am not off to parties and dance halls. I do much more than Madam Mother dear does." Cook nodded.

Sometimes he says "oh yus yus Doris missy." Whenever Miss Doris speaks to him Cook loses his voice. But his small black eyes move up and down, up and down her dress. *Dhobi* man also looks at her panty. He likes looking at clothes. Whatever Miss Doris says Cook says is "just like words of Goddess Swetamvati."

Chinamma, Papa sweeper's aunt from his mother's side spits every time Cook talks like this... "White mem making Cook head silly". Irti and Sarukai stand straight and quiet behind us. For supper Dakshnamurthy Bearer brings trays of smoke coming out, food from the Cook House built in 1856 and puts it with a clitter clatter noise on the big, high old wooden table which makes Porridge and Me into Snow Whites dwarfs.!
Every day we ask him: "What has Cook cooked today?" And every day he says, "I not knowing... You plis asking Cookswamy." Cook comes in behind him wiping his hand on a red and white towel and says, "today I making Lamb cutless, debill yeggs, garlic bread and cabbage bitroot soup". And then he makes a cat like face and asks, "You liking to yeat debills eggs Miss Doris no?"

Every day he makes the same things and makes it look new. He even gives them new names so that we think we are eating new things. Miss Doris likes the Devils eggs. Cook boils eggs and then covers it with meat which he crushes in a grinding stone and then fries it in oil. Porridge and I like it too. Why they are called Devils eggs she doesn't know. We pass small bits into Irti and Sarukkai's hidden, hungry hands who then put it quickly into their small, greedy mouths which go plonk into their empty stomachs.
Whenever Cook makes his sad face and says, "Poor hungry chinappas. They very poor," Miss Doris puts her hand up.

The Body of Memories

"That's enough, *khansama*! We don't want to hear anything more about these junglee girls". Cook shakes his sad head from side to side. Doris says Indian cooks are called *khansama* in English.

Did I tell you Doris is an English governess? Aunty Leeta Bosey was asking Mother, "Where is that *gora* English governess of yours?" Cook says Miss Doris's husband was Governor of Madras who went back to England. But Chinamma, Papa sweeper's aunt from his mother's side says Gandhiji must have beaten him with his stick and thrown him out of India. Miss Doris hates lazy gossiping people who don't do their work. she says she is English and the English are not *Kaam Chors* like these lazy Indians who always cheat on work. All this talk makes Porridge sulk like a puffed-up frog with goose bump skin. Cook, Bearer, Maggie, Maggie's Mother, Papa the Sweeper Boy, and Chinamma, Papa's aunt from his mother's side and even *Dhobi* man whom we hate because of his sausage, work so very hard. My dearie's, of course they cheat and lie and are lazy. Why do you think they are so poor? Doris doesn't want to know because she says she knows.

Today I asked Mother if Cook, Bearer, Papa, Maggie, Maggie's mother, the sweeper boy and Chinamma are lazy and she snapped at me like a crab, and said if they are then they have learnt to be lazy from Doris. All day she does nothing except show off her white skin.
I asked Dad why we are all so poor and he thought a bit and said, "There are so many reasons. We will talk about it later. And anyway, since when have you started counting yourselves among the poor? And by the way poor girls don't eat Kit Kat chocolates all day or have an English Governess for a companion!"

Cook, we are sure will know why he is poor. When I asked him, he pushed a matchstick into his left ear which is full of hair and twisted his thick lips and made a ball of his fingers with the big thumb sticking out and shook it up and down in front of his face, "You want to know? You want to know why I so poor? God giving my country bad *kismet*, babee. I am suffering for that reason wonly. If wonly English Sahibs not going away, I am becoming rich. India becoming rich."

How can India become rich? Mother says the English made us all poor. They stole all our things and became rich themselves. Chinamma Papa, the sweeper's aunt from his mother's side stopped sweeping and looked at Cook with one closed eye and said, "*Aiyo aiyo*!! See who talking and then she spat into the dirt she has gathered with her broom. Chinamma who is very poor feels she is poor because she is a woman and of low caste.

Next *janama* I am asking Periyar for making me man. Brahmin man. Then I eating sweet *tayeer sadam* every day, putting ash bottooo on my head and having fatty ladies pressing my white butter thighs. Cook hates Chinamma's sharp laughter and calls her a mad low- caste wuman.

When she smiles, Doris's teeth shine like pearls. When she heard how Cook lost his chance to become rich, she also snapped like a crab and said, "Oh yes, certainly. Why not? He could have sold sugar and rice and raisins from the English Sahib's kitchen. How else? Indians ---always steal." Porridge becomes very angry when Doris speaks like this and says she will tell Mother.

Doris quickly hugs her and says: "Daaarling! You are like us. I am only speaking about these poor dirty Indians. If they were not lazy and wicked, would they have become slaves. Now would they? Sometimes Mother also says such things. Only she doesn't ever never says 'dirty Indians'.

The Body of Memories

Doris scolds us every day for letting the purple beet and cabbage soup go cold. "Don't you want rosy red cheeks?" She asks us. "Yes Doris, and no, please." We groan, holding our stomachs with our hands. This makes Doris worry for us. Oh you poor dears. Khan- s- a -m -a! she yells at Cook, "Throw this rubbish soup out. Baby log will fall sick."

Irti and Sarukai hate the thick purple beet and cabbage soup. Cook threw the soup out but we know he is ready to throw away anything, even his life, like the hero in Tamil films. Maggie's Mother and Cook talk all the time about English Ladies and Indian Men.

30th April 1958

The Blue Mountains slope into gardens of tea trees and the meadows roll down all green and soft, all the way down to a place called Coonoor. Women who look a little like Maggie's Mother carry baskets on their head to the market place. Inside the baskets, there are potatoes, cabbages, red pimentos and green rhubarb which turn red when boiled and hard green thorny rose looking artichokes. The sides of the blue hills are patchy with red strawberries waiting to be eaten with sugar and cream. Cook stews green and pink peaches and bakes toffee apples. Lemon grass and tea smell everywhere.... Ohhhh!!These English people must have loved this Little England of theirs, "Leeta Bosey aunty let out a big peppermint smelling breath. Theirs? They grew all their favourite things here. They brought seeds and plants from England and changed everything here. Even grass! Just imagine. Now we are enjoying all this. Ohhh, they made a heaven here.

Porridge wanted to know what happened to the seeds and plants that grew here before they brought their seeds and plants from England. Oh! Those *junglee* plants? Native stuff. Only fit for forest dwellers. The local madrasis put tamarind and curry leaves into every dish. See... thanks to the

English, you can have olives, strawberries, thyme, asparagus, artichokes, avocado, pimento, rhubarb, lamb chops-- everything you get in London just sitting here in your own Nilgiris.!! She replied. But Maggie and Chinamma have never eaten artichokes. Even Cook doesn't eat roast lamb or strawberries. He loves sambar and rice and mulugtanni made out of tamarind and pepper. Porridge didn't sound polite. Darling Aunty Leeta Bosey explained, "Cooks and ayahs don't matter. Don't bother your head about them. They can chew curry leaves and suck tamarind and live happily ever after. "But Leeta, do you really think that is fair? Think about it. What if we grow all our trees, vegetables and pulses in England? What will the English eat?" Mother asked.

"Thank God we can't grow Indian vegetables in England! After all we are not their rulers". Leeta Bosey aunty replied. "You see, only when you rule a country you can change everything. Language, landscape, food, culture etc. We Indians are incapable of ruling others. We are good at *jee huzoor, jee huzoor.* Anyway, why are we complaining about all these wonderful English fruits, flowers and vegetables? Oh! I can't imagine life without strawberries and cream. Ahhh!"

Porridge waited for Leeta Bosey aunty to finish the dream bowl of strawberries and cream... "But what about Cook and Chinamma? How can they live without curry patta and tamarind?" "Oh, now this is too much. What's got into you girls? Worrying about the servants and their food habits? I think that Doris is leaving your girls to roam about the servant quarters while she makes eyes at your handsome husband." Mother laughed, "Now Leeta, stop this foolish talk". Porridge didn't speak to anybody all day. Not even to Papa the sweeper.

Aunty Leeta Bosey took a deep breath and looked at mother in a worried way. "You better be careful I say, of that Doris

The Body of Memories

woman. All this roses and creamy white colour hides a black heart". Her experience of English girls, she says, has taught her that one must never allow an outsider to take away what is rightfully yours. "We must protect what is sacred to us. We must never give up, no matter what the trials and troubles. Love wins everything". Leeta Bosey sounded just like Gandhi Ji. Mother reads out from books to us what Gandhi Ji had taught Indians and all the people in the world. He taught us that this land is our Mother and very sacred and we must love and protect it and not let others take it away from us. This land is ours. Like Jesus, he said we too must love our enemy. Exactly what Leeta Aunty had done. She had driven away the English woman who was kidnapping her husband Mr. Bosey and then she lived in England and even named her daughter Rani Victoria after Queen Victoria who was an English woman and also had no morals because all English women have no morals. She had forgiven her enemy. Like Gandhiji and Aunty Leeta, Porridge too wants to feed all the poor. I don't think the poor will like Cook's beet and cabbage soup or his caramel custard. Irti and Sarukai hate it. And they are very poor.

On Sundays when Dad goes riding, Mother drinks tea with her friends in the Gymkhana Club and we walk with Miss Doris on the green lawn holding her soft white hands which are soft like mother's black velvet blouse. She looks so beautiful, just like THE ONE found on the Isle of Capri. Many times, we can hear Dad singing in the bathroom. His voice passes through the hot water running out of the tap marked HOT. In the song, he has found her on the Isle of Capri tied to an old walnut tree. So now we know Dad is the one who has rescued Miss Doris. That is why she calls him "My Hero!" "I love this wine", she laughs with her golden hair thrown back. When Doris drinks the red shiny juice from a glass with a long thin handle, her eyes glitter red and green and stars sparkle on her teeth and roses dipped in cream fall out of her cheeks. Sometimes she calls him "Captain". In the morning she calls him Sir.

Aunty Leeta Bosey doesn't like all this one bit. She is quite sure she says that English women have no morals. Which means they are not good. "This and this alone is the reason that English men, who are all so good are forced to go to brothels."

Porridge says it must be awful to eat broth every day.

"Why don't you go out and play?" Mother very sweetly asked Porridge.

You see, Porridge made herself very comfy opposite Aunty Leeta. Her mouth open, her legs spread apart. Aunty Leeta wore a sari the colour of the ash which gets heaped inside the fire place every winter after midnight. Thin gold lines run in and out of it, picking up the lines of sunlight which fell on it straight through the big glass window on her right side, and set it on fire. I saw the golden flash of one gold tooth in her mouth.

"You look tired, my dear," Dad took the cup of tea from Mother. "Oh, I had a busy day. Leeta was here and she spent all day long talking about the seven years she lived in England with her husband Mr. Robin Christopher Bosey when he had gone to study anthropology at Oxford University and where he was given a considerable amount of money to write a book on the subject of "Why Non-White Races Become Slaves So Easily."

"You see, His father's father Mr. Nepal Chondro Bose had on his grandson's birth given him the beautiful Hindu name Nobin Chondro. N.C. Bose. In cold England, far away from his young wife and aged parents, he suffered severe loneliness. That is when this English barmaid daughter of his beef-eating landlady seduced him and he went to church and became Mr. Robin Christopher Bosey. Her in-laws who were "pure" Hindus died of a broken heart soon after.

The Body of Memories

At once Leeta decided to leave for England to fall at the Queen's feet and tell her, "Look you are a woman, I am a woman. Can any woman bear to have her husband snatched away? What if your husband is lured away by another woman, will you tolerate it? You must help me. We women must stand together." And when I asked her, "Which queen are you talking about?" Guess what she answered? "Victoria, of course!"

Queen Victoria is dead. I kindly reminded her. "Oh, all right, the King then. But then all these men are the same. Kings or slaves. The moment they see a woman, they go mad. Especially if they see a *gora* white skin." She had sold all her gold which her father had given her on her marriage, and what a grand marriage it had been with three hundred guests and hundreds of kilos of Hilsa and Rohu fish cooked in mustard oil fresh from her maternal uncle Subroto Sorcar's oil press and one thousand pieces of the finest *roshogollas* dipped in saffron coloured sugar syrup. There was English food too, Mulligatawny soup, Shepherd's Pie, Chicken Stew and Blancmange, and Snow Ball Pudding and Smoked Hilsa, because the Governor Sir Timothy Clare was also invited, but he couldn't come due to prior appointment as he had to meet the Queen in the Buckingham Palace, which he couldn't possibly refuse, because no one can refuse to meet the Queen.

Isn't the Queen dead? Porridge had asked. I was in the story too. "That is okay." She waved her hand impatiently. "The English don't let them die. Long live the Queen...Oh! I mean King. The English food had to be given away to the poor." I had sunk with Mother into the big big sofa-chair and its cosiness made me glad I wasn't poor.

"Did the poor like it?" I asked. "Like what?" Leeta aunty had stared at me through her gold rimmed spectacles. She looked irritated. I sucked my thumb.

"Aunty Leeta is asking you something. Why don't you speak?" Putting my thumb behind my back, I asked Aunty Leeta who was now giving me those "Take your time. I am a very patient woman and I love children" look.
"Did the poor like the English food?" My voice came out like a squeak. Aunty Leeta looked happy at my question. "They liked it? Of course darling, they loved it. They love English food". And then she looked carefully at me. "Why else would I give it to them?"

Dad lit his pipe and looked at Mother who was saying, "With the gold that her father had given her on her marriage, Leeta bought herself a first-class ticket on The Queen Elizabeth I and sailed for England. So many Indian and Englishmen fell in love with her on the ship, but like a true *pativrata* Indian woman, she remained faithful to her lord and master Mr. Nobin Chondro Bose. After all, hadn't Savithri snatched her husband Satyavan from the hands of Yama, the god of death? What is an English girl, that too, the bar maid daughter of a beef-eating hotel *walli* compared to Yama the GOD OF DEATH? The moment the bar maid saw Leeta, a true Indian wife who had crossed the turbulent sea alone to get her husband back, she left the *maidaan* and fled, to prey on some other lonely married Indian man away from his wife in India. Leeta is convinced about this."

Mother stopped and smiled. "Leeta Bosey's life story is amazing. It is, she says, just like what happened to Vyjanthimala in that what's it's name film where she goes in search of her husband in Tokyo. Her daughter Mallvika was born nine months later. In England. They call her Vikky, after the Great Queen Victoria".

This time Dad bent his head back like Miss Doris and laughed loud and clear. "Poor NC."

"The story hasn't ended yet! Leeta made a discovery. Because of his English name, Robin Christopher Bosey, her

The Body of Memories

husband was quickly promoted, which meant more money. When he returned to India, all doors opened to him. When they went to England again, nobody shut the door on their face.

"The English are really great people. It is only these white-skinned women..." She said... Now she is happy with his new name. "After all, we must allow a person to keep his name."

When Mother returned after seeing Aunty Leeta off, Porridge was still sitting on the tall stool, her feet dangling high above the ground. She looked like the ugly gnome in our story book.

"Do you think Dad will change his name?" She asked Mother in a worried voice. "Now don't be silly. Stop swinging your feet and get off that stool. You shouldn't be listening to grown-ups talk. I have told you so many times". Mother was angry. Porridge was worried. "How will I recognise Dad?" Mother thought for a moment. "It is not we who have to recognise him." She said. "Then who?" Mother didn't reply. "Then who?" Porridge pestered. Then Who? I thought.

Bio:
Dr Roopali Sircar Gaur, Ph.D. former Associate Professor Dept of English Delhi University is a poet-performer, writer, ecologist and social justice activist. A widely published columnist and writer, she has served on academic conference panels worldwide. She has taught Creative Writing at the Indira Gandhi National Open University. Her book *The Twice Colonised: Women in African Literature* is a seminal text on gender studies and post-colonial literature. She has co-edited two poetry anthologies *In All the Spaces-Diverse Voices in Global Women's Poetry* (2020) and *Earth, Fire, Water, Wind* (2021) together with Dr Anita Nahal, both during the pandemic. She is founder-editor with Aabha Rosy Vatsa of "*Saraswati*" an on online literary and art journal in English and Hindi. Roopali is featured in several

publications worldwide, including *The Kali Project: Invoking the Goddess Within / Indian Women's Voices,* and her poems are also housed at Stanford University's Digital Humanities initiative, *Life in Quarantine: Witnessing Global Pandemic,* and in the University of Bath's *UK Transnational* project. She is curating two more anthologies by members of the Armed Forces and the other on food memories.Roopali is the Founder-President of YUVATI, and Mera Kitab Ghar a non-profit organization in India, working for women and children from marginalized communities. A PhD from Jawaharlal Nehru University (JNU), New Delhi she graduated from Mount Carmel College, Bangalore, with an M.A. and B.Ed. from Osmania University, Hyderabad.

She may be contacted at roopalisircar@gmail.com

The Ocean and I: Memoir Excerpt from Gypsy Wanderings Part 2

Sunil Kaushal

The pandemic has bestowed the word 'corona' with a deathly notoriety. The dictionary gives its synonyms as aureole, crown, circle, light, wreath, rosary, tiara; a part of the human skull between the two parietal bones is also called corona as is a long cigar and also a circular chandelier hanging from a church ceiling.

As a rule, I do not listen to the news, for I can do nothing to stop calamities or check a pandemic in its march of reaping lives. All I can do is be responsible in taking as many precautions and safety measures as possible, to protect myself and those around me. The news imprints my brain with images of calamities and disaster, violence and crime, injustice and suffering, hunger and deprivation besides a million other images of humanity wallowing in wretched misery. I derive no vicarious pleasure of suffering by proxy. But since the word keeps popping up more frequently than one blinks in a day, my mind also ruminates around it at times. For me it has a special significance, connected to an adventure in the past.

In 2006, August 1st, I was living in Chennai, India. There was to be a total solar eclipse that morning, over which scientists globally were agog with excitement for its great scientific import. It was of great astrological significance also. People were acquiring black glass plates or x-ray sheets through which to look at the eclipse.

My niece lived in Thiruvanmiyur, less than half a kilometer from the Breezy Beach, as it was called. I decided to spend the night at her place and go early in the morning to the beach where I could see the eclipse fully, having equipped myself with an old x-ray film.

On the way we met a family of three generations taking turns gazing at the eclipse through a black glass plate mounted on a stand. As we looked at them with curiosity, the older gentleman invited us to take a peek too.

It was a spectacular marvel not to be missed. There was a corona of wonderful oranges and reds all around, the clouds lit up, some dark in silhouette, some golden, glowing yellowy-orange in the distance. You could see the shadow approaching against the clouds and then rushing away.

Wanting to view nature's wonders unhindered by buildings or other manmade distractions, we walked on towards the beach which lay ahead spread in all its glory.

Chennai is extremely warm and humid in August, but gusts of refreshing sea breezes kept cooling the sweat that rolled in droplets from our bodies. Normally, the beach is flat with the waves almost dying out at the waterline. However, during the monsoon months, roughly August to October, the tides rise higher eroding the sand on the beach, forming a sand pit. That day the sea was almost seven or eight feet lower than the sand bank on top, almost like cliffs, but gradually sloping downwards. The water rose in small

The Body of Memories

waves, reaching the edge of the sand below, where it became flat.

Because of the beliefs of harmful radiations from a solar eclipse, the beach was deserted, except for three pundits in white dhotis and topknots with a long white cotton scarf flung over their glistening, naked chests, except for the sacred thread. They sat on the sand bank getting some paraphernalia ready for a puja, perhaps for some astrological or spiritual benefits or to appease the elements.

Two other men stood at a distance of about a hundred metres, studying the eclipse through a telescope like thing. There were no boats visible up to the horizon. The darkness at eight in the morning reflected on the huge expanse of the ocean, gave it a surreal effect. I was mesmerized. My niece had her morning chores to attend to, so I told her to go home.

A few drops of water occasionally sprayed me when a wave rose a little higher as I sat down to meditate. It was a welcome respite from the humidity. Usually my chakra cleansing meditation takes about twenty minutes. I opened my eyes to find the sea appear a little sinister and mightier in that impregnable, secretive darkness which had grown denser.

The three pundits and two men had left. I could see the back of a man, probably a fisherman, walking below at the waterline, at some distance. Seeing him, it occurred to me that I had not dipped my feet in the ocean that day.

I usually spent some time walking, feeling one with nature, collecting some interesting looking shells while I jumped around, trying to escape stepping on small red baby crabs burrowing up from the sand, with the waves lapping at my feet. Climbing down was almost like tumbling down, for the slope was steep.

I strolled around a little bit and turned to climb up, calling it a day. The waves seemed to be coming a little faster. I was halfway up the slope when a large wave came from behind lashing at my body, throwing me face down on the sloping sand bank. I tried straightening, but the wet sand kept slipping under my feet and my body sinking in the wet sand.

As the wave receded, I struggled upright, discovering I had lost one slipper and started groping in the sand to find it. After a while I gave up, realizing the futility of it. Struggling and clawing, slipping and sinking into the wet sand, I somehow reached the top. As soon as I tried to straighten up with my upper body and thighs on top of the sand bank, my lower legs and feet still hanging down, another wave, much more ferocious and higher flung me down again.

Stunned but not beaten by the unexpected second onslaught, I stood up, dusting the sand off my clothes. My bottle of water lay where I had left it. Washing my face, I started for home. Then I realized I was still holding the single slipper in my hand. Not wanting to litter the ocean or the beach I had clung on to it, so inbuilt are certain habits. Seeing a dustbin, I chuckled to myself as I threw the slipper into it, telling myself that being meticulous beyond a point is no great virtue.

Walking back barefoot on the freshly laid melted tar in the torrid heat was a grueling punishment in itself and the dirt and stones on the side of the road made it difficult to walk there too. On reaching home, when I narrated the whole incidence, my niece was horrified and said, "Since nobody was around when this happened, we would never have even known what happened to you, had the waves swept you away. Expert swimmers and fishermen have been swept away."

That night a few thoughts about what had happened started nibbling at my brain, but I slept deeply after taking a pain killer. My body felt thrashed by the beating it had taken. Next morning my niece said, "Auntie, do you know there were mini-tsunamis rising in the ocean yesterday because of

The Body of Memories

the increased electro-magnetic pull, because the sun, moon and earth were in one straight line?"

It was then that the fear of being swept away and swallowed by the ocean started raising its head. A puny sixty-year-old woman pitted against the monstrous ocean which held the collective power of all the oceans in this world, as its might. I felt like an unarmed soldier come out victorious after a combat with a heavily armed enemy!

Bio:
Dr. Sunil Kaushal, gynaecologist, trilingual writer from India, published globally has won many awards. Her poems have been translated into French, German and Greek also. She has been conferred with multiple awards for literature, writing and her other accomplishments, including The Enchanting Muse Award (International), The Women Achiever's Award 2019 (hosted by Literoma), Best Lioness President, Asia, among others. Her poems have been featured in the Limca Book of Records as part of the Amravati Poetic Prism2018. Recently the Gujarat Sahitya Akademi recognised her as one of the 150 outstanding poets of India.

Her book of memoirs 'Gypsy Wanderings &Random Reflections' has recently been awarded The Nissim Award by The Significant League (International) for its 'Exquisite prose'. Besides writing she is fond of Sufi music, fine embroidery, sketching, baking and globetrotting.

A Daughter's Journey into her Father's Memoir

Silent Life: Memoirs of a Writer by Chaman Nahal

Review: Anita Nahal

Physical journeys, emotional, metaphorical, philosophical and of self-exploration to the point of self-depreciation, journeys that reflect upon the nature of life and humans are spilled over the 286 pages of my father's gripping memoir, *Silent Life*. Published in 2005 by Roli Books, the memoir stops when he turns seventy. By his own choosing. He says on page 273, "I was seventy in 1997 and that's where I want to end... one has to stop somewhere..." We would joke with him that his life had been anything but silent. Over time I comprehended why he selected that title, or that blurry, shadowy image for the cover page. Despite how much we might say, sometimes loudly, or even writing about it strongly, yet at the end of it all, we come and go alone... silently most of the times, even when in physical pain. And then when we are alive, we still seek silence on numerous occasions for varied reasons. It's the juxtaposition of the universe with humans that confronts us deeply and when we are confused or shocked or numbed, silence takes over. As a writer, our life can be especially alone and silent when searching excruciatingly or embarrassingly for answers to colossal metaphysical questions of 'Who are we?' 'Where did we come from?' 'Where will we go after this life?' 'How do we behave so we don't hurt others?' My father's humanism is what shines through like a golden star in his memoir trying to find solutions, mostly withdrawing humbly, in silence! The reality of human limitations, human compulsions, needs and desires, sometimes to our detriment is a recurrent theme in my father's memoir. However, the return to basics of family, surviving and thriving is also deeply embedded in the book.

I found fascinating how my father weaves daily living with mammoth philosophies and constantly checks himself throughout life, trying to improve upon himself. He would have liked to improve others instead, like we all do, yet he also accepted its impossibility, like we all grudgingly do too! Talking about injustice…individual or collective, promoting fairness, equality and equilibrium in what he saw as wrong and unhinged, plus the duality within himself and most humans also is a constant theme in the memoir. My father travelled extensively in India, the US and to the UK, Italy, Australia, New Zealand, Sri Lanka, Hong Kong, Japan, and Fiji to name a few countries, and his objectivity in speaking about the positives and negatives in different places is refreshingly unrelenting.

The occasion, inspired a poem.

'Buddha's Tooth'

We come to you, reverenced sir
To seek your protection,
Our faith is often a pretence
For your love and affection.

You carved a path for us
We took the easier way,
Sullied by pride and want
We ever remained astray.

The seas you crossed, the lands you traversed
Your canopied Kandy shrine,
We kneel before them
To heal, to rise, and to shine.

My father was a prolific writer with 27 books, and numerous, numerous articles. He would wake up early in the morning, stay up late and find every possible time and opportunity to write down the words jostling to burst out. His most well-known work was his novel, *Azadi,* on the partition of India. Originally written in English, with the title in Urdu (why that is so is another story!), it was translated into numerous Indian and foreign languages, and became part of many syllabuses in India and abroad. He was awarded the prestigious Sahitya Akademi award for it in 1977 plus other awards later on.

[my father's pic]

He called himself a novelist, yet at a plethora of places in the memoir, it reads like a prose poem. His words are lyrical and enchanting. He would often tell me, "I wish I could write poetry like you do." I would be quick to say, "Oh, you can write anything, you are so good!" And we know as a fact that he had written a long poem on India titled, *Bharat, Bharat, Hum Is Ki Santan (India, India, we are its children)* for Doordarshan, Delhi which was created into a song by Doordarshan. Sung by Udit Narayan and Vani Jayaram with music composed by Bhajan Sopori, it ran for many years before the evening news. Sadly, the song is not given in the book and I can't find a copy. There are a couple of poems strewn around my father's memoir though. I had forgotten that was the case, and I smiled because my just completed novel is a combination of prose and poetry.

My recollections of my father and his remarkable teachings have always remained clear and fresh in my mind. And this honestly written, very readable memoir reminds me that many of my traits, philosophies, mannerisms, and words, and much more comes from him…and my mother. I feel my memoir, whenever I write it, if I do, would have many similarities!

Bio:

Anita Nahal, Ph.D., CDP is a poet, professor, short story writer, flash fictionist, children's books author, and D&I consultant. Currently she teaches at the University of the District of Columbia, Washington DC. Besides academic publications, her creative books include, two volumes of poetry, Hey... Spilt milk is spilt, nothing else (2018) and Initiations (1988), a collection of flash fictions, Life on the go-Flash fictions from New Delhi to America (2018), and three children's books: I love Mummy and other new nursery rhymes, When I Grow Up and other new nursery rhymes and The Greedy Green Parrot and Other Stories (1993-1995). Her poems and stories can be found in national and international journals including, Aberration Labyrinth, Better Than Starbucks, Aaduna, River Poets Journal, Colere, Setu, Poetryspective, and in a number of Medium publications in the US, Confluence in the UK, Lapis Lazuli in Asia and The Burrow in Australia. Nahal received an honorable mention in the 2017 Concrete

Wolf Chapbook competition. Nahal is co-editor (with Roopali Sircar Gaur) of the anthology, In All The Spaces-Diverse Voices In Global Women's Poetry (2020). She is also a guest contributing editor for aaduna journal and is co-host of the monthly online creative series, Tan Doori Gup Shup. Nahal is the daughter of Indian novelist and professor, Late Dr. Chaman Nahal, and her mother, Late Dr. Sudarshna Nahal was an educationist, author and principal of a K-12 school. Originally from New Delhi, India, Anita Nahal resides in the US. Her family include her son, daughter-in-law and their golden doodle. For more on Anita: https://anitanahal.wixsite.com/anitanahal

----